To

Margaret and
Norman,

With love,
Janine x

Security Issues in the Post-Cold War World

Security Issues in the Post-Cold War World

Edited by

M. Jane Davis

Department of International Politics, University of Aberystwyth, UK

Edward Elgar
Cheltenham, UK • Brookfield, US

Published by
Edward Elgar Publishing Limited
8 Lansdown Place
Cheltenham
Glos GL50 2HU
UK

Edward Elgar Publishing Company
Old Post Road
Brookfield
Vermont 05036
US

British Library Cataloguing in Publication Data
Security Issues in the Post-cold War World
    I. Davis, M. Jane
    327.116

Library of Congress Cataloguing in Publication Data
Security issues in the post-cold war world / edited by M. Jane Davis.
    Includes bibliographical references and index.
    1. Security, International.   2. World politics—1989–   I. Davis,
    M. Jane
    JX1952.S42   1996
    327.1'72'09048—dc20   95–39638
                                                                        CIP

ISBN 1 85898 334 7

Typeset by Manton Typesetters, 5–7 Eastfield Road, Louth, Lincolnshire LN11 7AJ, UK.

Printed in Great Britain at the University Press, Cambridge

Contents

Contributors

Amitav Acharya is Associate Professor in the Department of Political Science, York University, Toronto, Canada.

Alan Collins is a doctoral candidate in the Department of International Politics, University of Wales, Aberystwyth, UK.

Simon J. Davies is a doctoral candidate in the Department of International Politics, University of Wales, Aberystwyth, UK.

John C. Garnett is Woodrow Wilson Professor of International Politics, and Head of the Department of International Politics, University of Wales, Aberystwyth, UK.

Clive Jones is Lecturer at the Institute for International Studies, University of Leeds, UK.

Alan Macmillan is a doctoral candidate in the Department of International Politics, University of Wales, Aberystwyth, UK.

Rowland T. Maddock is Senior Lecturer in the Department of International Politics, University of Wales, Aberystwyth, UK.

Jennifer G. Mathers is Lecturer in the Department of International Politics, University of Wales, Aberystwyth, UK.

Justin Morris is Lecturer in the Department of Politics, University of Hull, UK.

Richard Stubbs is Professor in the Department of Political Science, McMaster University, Hamilton, Ontario, Canada.

Nicholas J. Wheeler is Lecturer in the Department of International Politics, University of Wales, Aberystwyth, UK.

Richard Wyn Jones is Lecturer in the Department of International Politics, University of Wales, Aberystwyth, UK.

Abbreviations

ASEAN	Association of Southeast Asian Nations
ASEANFTA	Association of Southeast Asian Nations Free Trade Association
ASEANRF	Association of Southeast Asian Nations Regional Forum
CDLR	Committee for the Defence of Legitimate Rights
CFE	Conventional Forces in Europe (agreement)
CIS	Commonwealth of Independent States
CSCE	Conference on Security and Cooperation in Europe
CTBT	Comprehensive Test Ban Treaty
EU	European Union
GATT	General Agreement on Tariffs and Trade
GCC	Gulf Cooperation Council
IAEA	International Atomic Energy Agency
ILO	International Labour Organization
IMF	International Monetary Fund
INF	Intermediate Nuclear Forces (agreement)
LAP	Least ambitious programme
MAD	Mutual assured destruction
MIRV	Multiple independently targetable re-entry vehicle
NACC	North Atlantic Cooperation Council
NAM	Non-aligned Movement
NATO	North Atlantic Treaty Organization
NIE	Newly industrializing economy
NPT	Non-Proliferation Treaty
NWFZ	Nuclear weapon-free zones
OAS	Organization of American States
OAU	Organization of African Unity
OSCE	Organization for Security and Cooperation in Europe
PLO	Palestinian Liberation Organization
PNE	Peaceful nuclear explosion
START	Strategic Arms Reduction Talks
UAE	United Arab Emirates

UNAMIR	United Nations Assistance Mission for Rwanda
UNCED	United Nations Conference on the Environment and Development
UNEP	United Nations Environment Programme
UNSC	United Nations Security Council
WEU	Western European Union

Acknowledgement

The editor wishes to acknowledge the invaluable assistance of Dr M. Wright who, tirelessly and uncomplainingly, attempted to induce at least a modicum of computer literacy in her distinctly unreceptive brain.

Introduction: conflict and security in the 'new world order'

John C. Garnett

During the Cold War many people believed that all that stood in the way of a harmonious and peaceful world was a hostile Soviet Union committed to a militant ideology which was anathema to the West. Richard Nixon expressed this popular opinion as follows: '... but for Russian intransigence the world would now be enjoying the pursuits of peace. Mankind today is sick with anxiety and torn by fear of another world war, solely because Russia wants it that way' (Waltz 1959, p. 157). And it was this thought which, when the Cold War crumbled in the late 1980s, led to a sudden surge of hope. The 'evil empire' had collapsed and, as Francis Fukuyama pointed out, the ideological struggle had ended in an outright victory for capitalist values (Fukuyama 1989, pp. 3–18). In East–West relations the nuclear threat evaporated, the arms race wound down, the Iron Curtain was dismantled. If Richard Nixon had been right in his analysis, *nothing* now stood in the way of a new Golden Age. President Bush proclaimed the dawn of a 'new world order', and this phrase captured the spirit of optimism which fired the imagination of so many people. Even the United Nations, incapacitated for so long by Cold War rivalry, began to take on a new lease of life.

But, of course, Richard Nixon was not right. Soviet intransigence may have fuelled the Cold War and preoccupied the thoughts of Western statesmen for over 40 years, but to believe that international politics would somehow be miraculously transformed by the removal of the Soviet threat was naïve in the extreme. It neglected the fact that most of the world's problems – particularly those in the Third World – were hardly affected at all by East–West hostility and would not be much affected by its removal. It also reflected a singularly unhistorical and obsessive perspective on the Cold War. Even a cursory look at the world *before* the Soviet threat emerged in the late 1940s should have alerted everyone to the probability that all would not be plain sailing *after* the threat had disappeared. The events of 1989 may have signalled a shift in the balance of power, but there was never any possibility that they would bring about a transformation in international politics. The last decade of the century is, in essentials, no different from any of the decades which preceded it. We still live in an ungoverned world of states which recognize no authority above themselves and whose conduct is minimally constrained by considerations of law and morality. We still live in a world in which most people are condemned to live their lives in abject poverty and misery. The endless and frequently violent human struggle for scarce resources shows no sign of diminishing, and international relations remains an arena of endemic conflict.

At this fundamental level of analysis, the end of the Cold War was a relatively unimportant event, no more significant than any of the other major shifts in the balance of power which have occurred since the rise of the Westphalia system. Certainly there was nothing in it to justify the high hopes which it engendered, and it is very surprising to find a historian of Michael Howard's eminence falling victim to the euphoria of the early 1990s: '... the structure of world politics has been changed, and changed irrevocably ... 1989 is likely to be seen as a historic turning point, one ending the catastrophic era that began in 1914. It has been an annus mirabilis; a truly wonderful year' (Howard 1990, p. 32).

Our argument is that, five years on, we ought not to be surprised that the world does not seem to have improved very much. Ordinary people, in both the developed and developing world, have not experienced a quantum improvement in their conditions of life, and there are few signs that they are likely to do so in the foreseeable future. The problems which face the world – overpopulation, poverty, environmental degradation, resource depletion, and so on – are as serious as ever, and although the agenda of political issues confronting statesmen has changed, the list seems as intractable as before.

Of course, in terms of current affairs, it would be foolish to underestimate the significance of the demise of the Cold War. It has revolutionized East–West relations, destroyed the bipolar system, and rendered obsolete habits of thought which coloured the perceptions of an entire generation. John Garnett, in Chapter 1, examines the impact of these changes on European security, and Jennifer Mathers, in Chapter 2, looks at the way Russia is adjusting to a radically different domestic and international environment and the loss of its superpower status. But the novelties in the present situation ought not to blind us to some old issues which have hardly been touched by the end of the Cold War. The problem of horizontal nuclear proliferation, for example, remains as worrying as ever. Nicholas Wheeler and Simon Davies, in Chapter 7, reflect on the historical record of the global nuclear non-proliferation regime, and discuss ways in which we might make progress in the years ahead. In Southeast Asia, the end of bipolarity has highlighted the complexity of the linkages between economic change and regional security, at the same time reviving territorial disputes in the South China Sea. In Chapter 5, Amitav Acharya and Richard Stubbs explore the implications of these linkages, and assess the prospects for regional economic growth and stability among the states which comprise the Association of Southeast Asian Nations (ASEAN).

The 1990s have taught us, if we needed to learn the lesson, that international politics, like life, is one damn thing after another. No sooner has one conflict evaporated than our attention is focused on new sources of tension – in Eastern Europe, the former Soviet Union, the Balkans, the Middle East and parts of the Third World too numerous to mention. These conflicts do not threaten us with Armageddon in quite the same way that superpower nuclear rivalry did, but they raise the prospect of a permanently violent future over which we may have very little control.

One of the most interesting features of the conflicts which now confront us is that many of them do not fit the traditional pattern of inter-state war which has hitherto dominated international politics. War *between* sovereign states remains a possibility, but we are witnessing an upsurge in *intra*-state conflict where the main actors are ethnic groups, sometimes supported by state governments. 'Ethnicity' is at the heart of political life in countries as diverse as Burma, Fiji, Rwanda and Sri Lanka and, of course, the former Soviet Union and Yugoslavia. As Donald Horowitz has pointed out, 'Ethnic conflict is a world wide phenomenon' (Horowitz 1985, p. 3), and when he wrote *Ethnic Groups in Conflict* in 1985 he estimated ethnic violence had claimed more than ten million lives since the end of the Second World War (Horowitz 1985, p. xi). Today, in 1996, the figure would be much higher.

A number of contributors to this book touch on the subject of ethnic violence. Both John Garnett and Jennifer Mathers say something about ethnic violence in Europe and the former Soviet Union. Neither offers much in the way of solutions, but the seriousness of the problem is emphasized in both chapters. While recognizing the positive aspects of democratization within ASEAN, Amitav Acharya and Richard Stubbs identify the potential for ethnic strife as marginalized minorities, excluded from economic benefits, attempt to achieve political autonomy in the hope of prising a fairer distribution of wealth and political power from the dominant majority community.

The meaning of both 'ethnic group' and 'ethnic violence' probably needs some clarification. An 'ethnic group' is sociologically peculiar. It is neither a 'race' nor a 'nation', but since it contains elements of both, a little analysis of those terms may be helpful. 'Race', if it means anything, refers to a *physical* bond between people. Those who are of the same race are of the same physical type. They share the same physique, the same skin colour, the same facial characteristics, and so on. When Hitler talked about 'thinking with the blood' he was referring to race – to shared hereditary characteristics which cannot be altered – and hence, if the term 'race' has any place at all in our politically correct world, it fits into the biological sciences. By way of contrast, the term 'nation' belongs to social science because it refers not to any physical bonds between people, but to a shared *mental* outlook arising out of common perceptions about history, religion, language, culture and political aspirations. Putting it crudely, 'races' are genetically determined whereas 'nations' are culturally determined. Now an 'ethnic group' or '*ethnie*', as the French would call it, is welded together by both the biological and social characteristics of its members. It must be identified by both its racial and cultural cohesiveness.

Ethnic violence is violence perpetrated by one ethnic group against another ethnic group simply because of the racial and cultural differences between them. What is so horrifying about pure ethnic violence is that in it innocent people are tortured and brutalized and killed, not because of anything they have done, not even because of their politics, but simply because of *who they are*. That is what is so terrible about the persecution of the Jews in Germany, the Tutsis in Rwanda, the Tamils in Sri Lanka, the Kurds in Iraq, and the Muslims in Bosnia.

It may be worth contrasting ethnic violence with normal political violence. In the political arena most violence is Clausewitzian in the sense that it is motivated by political purpose. For example, acts of terrorism are politically motivated; indeed, it is the political motive behind terrorist activity which distinguishes it from criminal violence. At a higher level, inter-state war is also politically motivated. The belligerents disagree about something and seek to resolve their disagreement by the use of force. Again it is the sense of purpose which gives war a degree of dignity and rationality. And it is worth adding that wars are, for the most part, conducted according to the rules, both moral and legal, which operate in international society. It may be going too far to describe war as a *civilized* activity, but there is a grain of sense in that thought.

Ethnic violence is quite different. It is not about the pursuit of interests; it is about *malevolence*, and it is not restrained by any rules, either legal or moral. In ethnic violence anything goes, and that is why ethnic conflicts are so brutal and savage. There is something primitive, barbaric and emotional about ethnic violence which makes ordinary warfare look reasonable in comparison.

Ethnic violence is a fact of life, and phrases like 'ethnic cleansing' (surely one of the most sinister terms to enter our vocabulary) have alerted us to its horrors. But we need to remind ourselves that it is not a new phenomenon. The history of the Indians in North America, the Incas in South America, the Aborigines in Australia, and the Maoris in New Zealand is a testament to ethnic violence. Indeed, there is a traditional pattern here – colonization or conquest followed by oppression or extermination – which bodes ill for the future. It seems that when governments practise ethnic violence they often do so with great ruthlessness, using the entire apparatus of state power.

But it would be a mistake to think that government involvement in ethnic violence is invariably malevolent. Far from exacerbating ethnic violence, governments often act to control and limit it by trying to hold the ring between hostile ethnic groups. That is what Marshal Tito did so successfully in Yugoslavia, and Stalin and his successors did in the Soviet Union and Eastern Europe. Unfortunately, when governments lose their grip – and that basically is what has happened in the Soviet Union and Yugoslavia – then they can no longer hold the ring. Age-old tensions which have simmered away beneath the political surface suddenly burst into life. This is the pattern in the Balkans and the former Soviet Union, and it may happen in other parts of Europe as well (see Chapter 1). But perhaps the best example of what can go wrong when governments lose control is the case of India when British rule came to an end in 1947. Without anyone to hold the ring between them, Muslim and Hindu communities fell upon each other, and, in consequence, more than a million people were slaughtered.

Governments sometimes practise ethnic violence by taking sides in ethnic conflict, but they can play a very positive role in controlling ethnic conflicts, particularly those which occur within their boundaries, but also those which cross state frontiers and threaten international stability. Some governments seem able to meet the challenge of ethnic violence, but others fail miserably. Democratic governments have a particular problem because the 'tyranny of the majority' is built into the democratic process, and this can easily lead to ethnic hostility. It will be interesting to see whether the new democratic government of South Africa is up to the task of moderating Xhosa–Zulu violence and Black–White tensions. The totalitarian governments of the Soviet Union and Eastern Europe were rather good at keeping the lid on ethnic conflict, and so too were the European colonial powers in Africa and Asia, but their democratic and not so democratic successors seem much less surefooted.

When we think about ethnic conflict we need to rid ourselves of three comfortable assumptions: first, that it couldn't happen here; that civilized people are somehow immune from this kind of barbarism. Ethnic cleansing in Bosnia is surely close enough to shake our complacency in that respect. Second, we need to rid ourselves of the notion that people can be educated out of ethnic violence. In the 1930s and 1940s Germany was one of the most educated and culturally advanced countries in the world, and yet the nation which produced some of the world's finest music and philosophy also engineered the Holocaust. Education scarcely touches those raw emotions, buried deep in the human psyche, which lie behind ethnic violence. Third, we need to reject the popular assumption that ethnic violence is a pathological, abnormal phenomenon. Anyone who reflects on the long history of ethnic conflict and its prevalence in every continent of the world is driven to the conclusion that this kind of behaviour is depressingly normal. The Dark Ages are closer to the surface of contemporary politics than most of us care to admit, and it is dangerous to believe that current manifestations of ethnic violence are no more than monstrous aberrations.

This rather gloomy analysis is compatible with, and not very different from, that of Samuel P. Huntington who, in a provocative and influential article in *Foreign Affairs* in 1993, predicted that the fundamental source of conflict in the years ahead will be cultural. 'Nation states will remain the most powerful actors in world affairs, but the principal conflicts of global politics will occur between nations and groups of different civilizations ... . The fault lines between civilizations will be the battle lines of the future.' Europe provides a good example of Huntington's theory. As the ideological division into communist and capitalist camps disappeared, the age-old cultural division between Western Christianity on the one hand and Orthodox Christianity and Islam, on the other, re-emerged. 'The most significant dividing line in Europe ... may well be the eastern boundary of Western Christianity in the year 1500' (Huntington 1993a).[1] This cultural fault weaves its way from the Balkans to the Mediterranean, and conflict along it has been going for 1300 years. Now it has to be said the cultural conflict predicted by Huntington is much wider than the localized ethnic conflicts of the sort we have been discussing. Nevertheless, there is a degree of overlap, and it is not a coincidence that a good deal of ethnic conflict is concentrated around cultural fault lines. The current violence in Bosnia is a case in point. And in terms of intractability there is a clear similarity between 'ethnic' and 'civilizational' conflicts which arises out of the fact that neither ethnic makeup nor cultural membership can easily be fudged. An individual may change his politics and ideology by an act of will, but he cannot change his racial characteristics or his cultural heritage. Animosity which arises out of these things cannot be easily eradicated. Alan Macmillan, in Chapter 3, examines the ideas of Huntington, and speculates about their persuasiveness in the post-Cold War world.

Our interest in the 'clash of civilizations' should not blind us to the more mundane conflicts of interest which lie at the heart of international politics. Conflicts about territory, resources, prestige, security and influence are endemic, and, in dealing with them, politicians are permanently preoccupied with the defence of their state's national interests. The question of 'who gets what, when and how' continues to dominate the behaviour of states which are in unceasing competition for more than a fair share of scarce resources, some of which are tangible, like wealth and oil, others of which are intangible, like prestige and security.

While Amitav Acharya and Richard Stubbs identify the phenomenal economic and security advances among the ASEAN states, they also caution that the potential for inter-state and intra-state conflict certainly exists, despite the best efforts of institutional mechanisms such as the ASEAN Regional Forum to ameliorate regional tensions. Clive Jones's chapter on the Arab Gulf States (Chapter 4) also examines security problems in a traditionally conflict-ridden area. The thrust of his argument is directed towards revealing the complex interplay between domestic and international politics in this part of the world. He shows how social, religious, ethnic and economic tensions within Arab societies now present as big a challenge to their governments as threats from the outside. And he suggests that continuing dependence on the West for military help fuels this internal opposition, particularly when it comes from Islamic militants.

If 'conflict' is a ubiquitous and inescapable phenomenon, then so too is its corollary, 'insecurity', that feeling of danger which comes from uncertainty and instability. No one likes living with insecurity. It is psychologically unpalatable to almost everyone, and most human beings take whatever steps they can to minimize it. At the 'personal' level this is done by seeking permanent employment, saving, taking out insurance, making provision for pensions, and so on. At the 'state' level it is done by adopting stabilizing constitutional arrangements, by buying security through defence expenditure, by pursuing the national interest and by fostering a peaceful world in which states can pursue their objectives without recourse to violence. The concept of 'security' lies at the heart of this book and most of the contributors have something to say about it. The first part of John Garnett's chapter examines some of the ways in which the concept has evolved. Richard Wyn Jones (Chapter 10) examines it from the perspective of critical theory. Acknowledging the unpredictable, uncertain and conflict-prone nature of the new international era, he provides a revised theoretical explanation intended to serve as a signpost in the unfamiliar security environment of the post-Cold War world. In Chapter 2 Jennifer Mathers examines current security issues from a Russian point of view. Rowland Maddock looks at the problem of 'environmental security' and explains the inadequacies of a 'state-centred' approach to managing the environment. He makes the point that the problem of environmental security is inherent in the process of modernization and development. Justin Morris examines the problems faced by a revitalized United Nations attempting to grapple with the security demands of the post-bipolar World. He contends that the UN's recent interventionary activity is not necessarily indicative of a return to the ideals and hopes of the authors of the Charter, and warns that while the original objectives of the Security Council seem more achievable than at any time since 1945, any expansion of the UN's collective security role to include the protection of human and political rights threatens to jeopardize the fragile consensus which has evolved since the ending of the Cold War.

All the authors recognize that the search for security can be self-defeating because there is a sense in which it is a 'zero sum game'. The process by which a state seeks to enhance its own security, perhaps by rearmament or alliance, may have the unintended effect of diminishing the security of other states who invariably react by increasing their own military strength. This in turn promotes a reaction from the initiating state, and, before we know where we are, an 'action–reaction' process of competitive rearmament is underway. At the end of the day neither side is more secure but both are a good deal poorer and more paranoic. This 'security dilemma', as it is fashionably called, has attracted a good deal of scholarly attention, particularly by those who have sought ways of escaping it or at least mitigating its consequences. In Chapter 9 by Alan Collins, the logic of the 'security dilemma' is examined. The analysis emphasizes an element of tragedy in the human predicament. Fearful of their neighbours, statesmen are inexorably pushed towards self-defeating policies which, in the long run, exacerbate the very problem they are trying to solve.

And in the critical area of economic security – which is a key to so many other security problems – we can again hear echoes of the 'zero-sum game' which is at the heart of the 'security dilemma'. The fruits of the earth, though not necessarily finite, are certainly limited. Unfortunately, human greed is infinite, and it follows from this that the avarice of some can only be satisfied at the expense of others. Wealth, like military security and privilege generally, is always at somebody's expense. In much the same way that the military security of the strong is paid for by the military security of the weak, so the economic security of the haves is provided by the economic insecurity of the have-nots. Understandably, the rich are reluctant to relinquish their privileged status, and they have the power to perpetuate their advantage. This does not augur well for the future security of the dispossessed.

This book clearly emphasizes the multidimensional nature of security, and the need to recognize that in many parts of the world 'security' is not seen primarily in military terms. In the Third World in particular, people are threatened by poverty, ill health, starvation and persecution rather than external aggression. And it is worth pointing out that the predicament of these people is to some extent neither of their own making nor a result of malevolence on the part of anyone else. In terms of their economic deprivation, for example, they are the victims of a world structure which unintentionally condemns them to permanent insecurity. The world monetary system, created by Bretton Woods in 1944, established the International Monetary Fund (IMF) with the prime purpose of promoting free trade.

Given the experiences of the inter-war depression and the self-defeating protectionist policies which were pursued, there were good reasons for believing that capitalist countries could only prosper in a world where exchange depreciations, import controls and all barriers to trade were minimized. The IMF was supposed to iron out balance of payment imbalances whenever they occurred by providing advice and money to states in difficulties. Though it has performed this technical function satisfactorily, its effect has been to sacrifice the economic interests of poor primary producer countries to the smooth operation of a market mechanism which favours the interests of developed Western states. Third World governments are encouraged to accept IMF loans, but the conditions which are applied to them often have devastating effects on their countries' economies. In effect, Third World states are involuntary members of a system which they did not design, in which they have little influence, and which in practice (though not in theory) works against their interests.

Similar arguments can be levelled against the post-war international trade regime created by the General Agreement on Tariffs and Trade (GATT). Again, the system is non-discriminating in the sense that its rules are applied equally to all members, but its effect has been to seriously disadvantage Third World states whose economic weakness requires a degree of 'reverse discrimination' in their favour. The tariff system which emerged favoured the developed world and paid scant attention to the needs of primary producers who suffered the consequences of unstable commodity prices as well as protectionist policies around markets in the Northern hemisphere. Despite concessions which have been made round its edges, the current trading regime remains biased towards Western interests, and, as with the monetary system, it is difficult to avoid the conclusion that Third World countries are trapped in a structure which they neither devised nor approved of. For Third World countries the world's economic framework is a 'security dilemma' which is as intractable as the military 'security dilemma' (Thomas 1987, chaps 3 and 4).[2]

The thrust of this book is to suggest that, despite the ending of the Cold War, 'security', whether defined narrowly or widely, is a scarce commodity. There is not much of it around, and in many parts of the world it is a luxury beyond the wildest dreams of ordinary people. Of course, no one can blame governments for trying to maximize their share of this scarce commodity, but at the end of the day, all of us must consent to incur some risk.

NOTES

1. This point has been made by William Wallace and is quoted in Huntington (1993a) on p. 20.
2. An excellent discussion of Third World security problems is to be found in Thomas (1987). See, in particular, Chapters 3 and 4 for a persuasive analysis of the way in which the monetary and trading systems structurally disadvantage poor countries.

1. European security after the Cold War

John C. Garnett

SECURITY – THE PROBLEM OF DEFINITION

Professor C.E.M. Joad, a regular panelist on the BBC's 'Brains Trust' during the 1940s, used to infuriate listeners by beginning his response to every question with the words, 'it all depends on what you mean by …'. He was surely right to point out that many words, if not quite as malleable as Humpty Dumpty believed, are subject to a variety of interpretations and that in the interests of clear thinking some precision is desirable.

'Security' is the sort of word that Professor Joad would have enjoyed playing with. In the 1950s Arnold Wolfers drew our attention to its 'ambiguity'. Goodness knows what he would make of it today, now that its meaning has become almost infinitely elastic. If as B. Buzan has complained, 'security' used to be an underdeveloped concept (Buzan 1983, pp. 3–12), it is surely now becoming overdeveloped, so wide in its scope that it is in danger of being emptied of meaning. If a term is stretched to mean everything it risks meaning nothing.

An examination of the question 'security against what and for who?' reveals what a multifaceted concept it has become. After the Second World War, the term 'national security' had purely military and defence connotations. It was intimately linked to the 'realist' tradition of thinking about international relations, and the military flavour of the concept neatly complemented ideas of power and interest and the rather tough-minded approach to foreign policy which seemed appropriate for the Cold War years. Walter Lippman argued that a state 'is secure to the extent that it is not in danger of having to sacrifice core values if it wishes to avoid war, and is able, if challenged, to maintain them by victory in such a war' (Lippman 1943, p. 51). Arnold Wolfers reached a similar conclusion. 'Security, in an objective sense, measures the absence of threats to acquired values, in a subjective sense, the absence of fear that such values will be attacked' (Wolfers 1962, p. 150).

Of course, the *feeling* of security is not an objective fact but a subjective sentiment, a feeling of confidence that the disasters of war and the vagaries of international life can be avoided or absorbed, either by ultimate victory or good management, so that the state, its institutions and its way of life can continue to exist in a fundamentally unimpaired fashion. Clearly, national security is a complex notion, the consequence of a subjective evaluation that a number of vital interests – the physical survival of the state and its people together with their independence and economic well-being – are not likely to be thwarted in the foreseeable future. 'Security' is obviously connected with 'peace', but the two concepts should not be confused. It is perfectly possible for states to feel secure even when they are at war, and highly insecure when they are at peace. At the time of Yalta the Allied powers felt secure because the outcome of the Second World War was assured. At the time of Munich they felt insecure despite the condition of peace (Garnett 1970, p. 33). Because the feeling of safety which we associate with security is subjective, there are many instances of states feeling secure when, objectively, they ought not to. The United States before Pearl Harbor is a case in point. Equally, the reverse may be the case. Britain, during the nineteenth century often experienced bouts of insecurity despite its virtually unassailable position and power.

Whatever it means, it seems clear that no state has ever been able to feel confident of security. The fact that each exists in an anarchical society alongside other states means that every state must learn to live with an element of insecurity. If insecurity is inherent in international society, then it may be that the problem facing modern states is not how to improve their security but how to live with the increasing degree of insecurity which they face. This was hinted as nearly 150 years ago when Sir Robert Peel commented, 'I believe that, in time of peace, we must by our retrenchment, consent to incur some risk. I venture to say that, if you choose to have all the garrisons of all your colonial possessions in a complete state, and to have all your fortifications secure against attack, no amount of annual expenditure will be sufficient to accomplish your object' (Cobden 1862, p. 145).

If this was true in Peel's day it is even more true today, when states are threatened by weaponry unimaginable in the nineteenth century and a whole host of other threats which have nothing to do with armed forces or military power. Today, environmental damage, drugs, economic deprivation, population growth and migration, global warming and resource depletion all threaten the security of states in ways which would have been quite beyond the comprehension of our grandfathers. It may not be psychologically comfortable either to accept a level of risk which our forefathers found intolerable, or to strive for a level of security which they would have regarded as hopelessly inadequate, but lower expectations may be the only way out of our problems. We should not assume that all security problems can be solved any more than that all diseases can be cured. One does not have to be a 'structural determinist' to believe, first, that the way the world is organized makes it very difficult to solve some of the problems which we face, and second, that changing the way the world is organized is well nigh impossible.

The recent trend towards expanding our notion of security probably began in the 1960s when Robert McNamara suggested that security implied the freedom of a state to develop and improve its position in the future. 'Security is development and without development there can be no security ... development means economic, social and political progress. It means a reasonable standard of living, and reasonable in this context requires continual redefinition; what is reasonable in an earlier stage of development will become unreasonable at a later stage' (McNamara 1968, pp. 149–50).

More recently, the security agenda has been further widened to cover the whole gamut of economic, social, ecological and demographic issues which now face us. It is persuasively argued that, particularly since the end of the Cold War, it is very misleading to confine security analysis to traditional military threats to the territorial integrity of states. It is not that these traditional threats have disappeared – though the threat of planned major nuclear war has surely receded – but that other threats now seem more pressing. Alongside this expansion of the security agenda has developed a feeling that 'security' can no longer be conceived of simply as 'the absence of insecurity', any more than 'peace' can be regarded as 'the absence of war'. 'Security' should be considered more positively, as requiring the building of a more just and humane world in which human beings are better able to realize their aspirations and potential.

Many years ago Salvadore de Madariaga described 'insecurity' as 'the feeling of danger that arises out of the feeling that the order of things in which we live is unstable' (de Madariaga 1936, p. 134). It is a good starting point for a discussion of European security because it leaves open the question of *who* or *what* is experiencing these feelings. Are we talking about the insecurity of *individual Europeans*, those millions of citizens who live in European states? If we are, then, in combating insecurity, we may be led to explore a range of immediate problems as varied as state oppression and injustice, unemployment, poverty, inadequate health care and pensions, and a breakdown in law and order. More remotely, we may be led to examine such problems as environmental pollution, population growth, global warming, etc. since all these developments will eventually impact on the quality of life of individual Europeans. Ken Booth has identified 'security' with 'emancipation', the freeing of humans from those constraints which stop them from carrying out what they would freely choose to do (Booth 1991b, p. 319); such a goal implies the lifting of unacceptable legal, social, economic, moral and physical constraints (Booth 1991b, pp. 313–26).[1] One feels that, for him, security at this level is almost synonymous with happiness.

Are we talking about the insecurity of European *states*, the political collectives in which individuals live? If we are, then this will enable us to shift the level of analysis by largely ignoring the immediate welfare worries of those who live within states, and concentrate on problems relating to subversion, ethnic violence, external aggression, the erosion of sovereignty, balances of power, etc. However, at this higher 'state' level the security agenda would still have to include the same environmental, population and resource problems which worry individuals within states. The old obsessions with rearmament and alliance are simply not sufficient to deal with the new security dilemmas of a complex, interdependent world. The sensible approach to state security under current political, military and economic conditions must start by recognizing that even potential enemies have common interests and that 'security interdependence' is now a fact of life. 'Common security' assumes that security is not a 'zero-sum game', and that even enemies can enhance their security by collaborative arrangements (Booth 1991a, pp. 344–54).

Are we talking about the insecurity of a *collectivity* of states, an alliance grouping like the North Atlantic Treaty Organization (NATO), a security grouping like the Organization for Security and Cooperation in Europe (OSCE) – formerly known as the Conference on Security and Cooperation in Europe (CSCE) – or an economic–political grouping like the European Union (EU)? If we are, then our concerns will be different again, focusing perhaps on 'pan-European' relations, new 'security architecture', collective defence and security, European relations with the USA and the wider world.

Are we talking about *international insecurity*, the insecurity of international society as a whole? If we are, then our attention may focus on problems of international stability, development, peacekeeping, international organizations and new structures for promoting order and peace and justice. We would, to quote A. Buchan, be trying to bring about 'a state of affairs in which the inhibitions and disincentives to waging war are stronger than the incentives … a state of affairs in which the alternatives to a forceful solution of any conflict are as numerous, as sparing of national pride, as readily available, as human wit can devise, whether they be political, diplomatic or judicial' (Buchan 1963, p. 3).

Where does this ground-clearing exercise leave us? It leaves us in no doubt that a comprehensive discussion of European security in all aspects and at all levels is beyond the scope of a single essay or even a single book. Such a venture would require a massive multidisciplinary study which brought together expertise from political science, international relations, history, sociology, law, psychology, demography, environmental studies – to name but a few. The flavour of this essay is less eclectic and more traditional. It is state-centred, even West European state-centred, and defence-oriented, but written with an awareness that this rather narrow approach needs to be connected both to other levels of analysis and other areas of concern.

It is state-centred because when it comes to the management of European security, governments are still the key players; and it has a military–defence orientation because most of those governments still see security issues primarily in those terms. In a sense, much of the current academic debate about security is concerned with elaborating how decisionmakers *ought* to look at security issues; but this essay is more about how they *do* look at them. And it has to be said that in foreign offices and ministries of defence official discussions of European security still typically revolve around such matters as border disputes, ethnic violence, terrorism, military threats, instability, balances of power, arms control, alliances and other security architecture.

Of course, the current ferment of ideas about security which has been generated in the academic community has not gone unnoticed in official circles, and, in so far as it has penetrated the intellectual milieu in which officials operate, it has affected their thinking. So far, however, its impact has been felt round the edges of the subject rather than at its centre. I have tried, therefore, to be sensitive to the myriad of ideas now associated with 'security', to put narrow defence issues into a wider context, and to encourage an awareness of risks and problems which may fall between the cracks in official thinking.

TWO CONTRASTING COLD WAR VIEWS

In the context of European security the two most significant events since 1945 are, first, the emergence of the Cold War in the late 1940s, and, second, the demise of the Cold War 40 years later. More than anything else it is our attitude towards the Cold War and its termination which colours our perspective on the security problems facing Europe in the run-up to the millennium.

The parameters of the debate are set by two sharply contrasted views about the Cold War and the post-Cold War world into which we have now moved. Both interpretations are caricatures of reality – gross oversimplifications of complex events – but they are pedagogically useful in that most analysts, even if they cannot wholeheartedly accept either view, generally lean towards one or the other.

One view is that the Cold War was a terrible and dangerous period in European history, and that ending it has enormously improved the prospects for European security. This interpretation reflects the common-sense perspective of the man in the street who remembers all too well the tensions and miseries associated with East–West crises and an unending arms race. The second view, equally crude but at the opposite end of the spectrum, is that the Cold War was good for European security and that ending it has opened a Pandora's box of new dangers. This is a less popular perspective but one that enjoys a certain credibility among defence specialists (Mearsheimer 1990, pp. 5–56).[2]

Each of these extreme perspectives deserves further elaboration. Those who are persuaded by the first view can point to a number of very unpleasant features associated with the Cold War years. First, the nuclear sword of Damocles that hung over East–West relations throughout the 1950s, 1960s and 1970s. Nuclear war seemed distinctly possible, if not likely, and Europe was the place where most people thought it would be fought. Few people were unaffected by the nuclear dread which permeated popular opinion on both sides of the Iron Curtain.

Second, the various international crises which sporadically erupted in East–West relations and which raised the spectre of transforming the

Cold War into a 'hot' war. From the Berlin airlift in 1949 to Soviet interference in Poland in 1981, the surface of East–West politics was periodically ruffled by incidents which seemed to have the potential for escalation built into them. The building of the Berlin Wall in 1961, the invasion of Hungary in 1956, the Cuban missile crisis in 1962 and the Czech crisis of 1968 were all spectacular developments which raised the temperature of East–West relations to danger levels.

Third, the artificial division of Europe into two armed camps divided by what Winston Churchill described as an 'Iron Curtain', a physical barrier which split families and peoples and cut Germany in half. The Cold War meant that Europe was frozen – for almost half a century – in an unnatural posture set by the meeting of Allied armies in Germany at the end of the Second World War and by two sharply delineated spheres of influence. The formation of two powerful alliance blocs facing each other institutionalized this division of Europe, and it is probably fair to say that the strategic doctrines of each side did little to reassure the other about the peaceful 'defensive' intentions of its enemy. Neither Soviet *Blitzkrieg* tactics nor NATO 'first-use' doctrines were particularly comforting.

Fourth, the arms race which led to a massive build-up of arms in the European theatre. Throughout the Cold War, Europe was the most heavily armed piece of real-estate in the world, and for many people this represented a gross waste of resources as well as a major source of East–West tension. High levels of military expenditure hindered economic development in both Western and Eastern Europe, but their effect on living standards in Eastern Europe was particularly devastating.

Fifth, the ideological conflict between communist and capitalist systems which exacerbated East–West relations. Some observers saw the Cold War in largely ideological terms – a clash of mutually exclusive ideologies each determined to build the world in its own image. Propaganda machines on both sides of the Iron Curtain were engaged in a constant war of words which did little to encourage good relations.

Sixth, the misery of Eastern Europe, governed by totalitarian regimes, drained of resources by the Soviet Union, and condemned throughout the period to poverty brought about by an unworkable economic system. For the millions of people who were denied basic freedoms and human rights, and compelled to endure low standards of living and the rigours of a police state, the Cold War had very little to recommend it.

All these depressing characteristics of the Cold War make it clear that the postwar years ushered in a dark and depressing period of European history which is accurately symbolized by the Berlin Wall, miles of barbed wire and hundreds of border control towers. Naturally, those who saw the Cold War in this way joyously welcomed its demise. How much of the credit for those momentous events of 1989 should be given to Mr Gorbachev who, with his ideas of *glasnost* and *perestroika*, brought a breath of fresh air to East–West relations, and how much should go to President Reagan for his tough stance on arms control and human rights, is difficult to determine. But the transformation which occurred in East–West relations when the Berlin Wall came tumbling down is not in doubt.

Tension virtually evaporated overnight. Nuclear war became no more than a remote possibility. People began to move freely between East and West for the first time in nearly 50 years. Economic connections began to grow at an enormous rate as communist regimes were toppled from power all over Eastern Europe. Democracy began to take hold in countries with little or no experience of democracy, and market econo-mies began to replace the command economies of communism. The ideological war disappeared, and with it the propaganda and censorship which had distorted perceptions on both sides of the European divide. The arms race, always a barometer of East–West tension, began to wind down – at the strategic level in the Strategic Arms Reduction Talks (START), at the theatre level in the implementation of the intermediate Nuclear Forces (INF) agreement, and at the conventional level in the implementation of the Conventional Forces in Europe (CFE) agree-ment. Politicians began to talk about a 'peace dividend', and levels of military alert were stepped down. The Warsaw Treaty Organization was disbanded, and tough questions began to be asked about the rationale for NATO in a world in which the Soviet threat had disappeared. In the heart of Europe the two Germanys were reunited.

And, of course, it was not just Europe that was affected by the end of the Cold War. Over the years the relationship between the two super-powers had fluctuated between one of outright hostility to the more muted 'limited adversary' relationship implied by 'détente'. Without going so far as to suggest that 'détente' was being transformed into 'entente', the United States and the Soviet Union, in the early 1990s, began to develop a much more positive 'business-dealing' relationship. The possibility of collaboration instead of confrontation seemed on the cards, and evidence of this was to be found in their accord in the

Security Council of the United Nations. For the first time since its creation in 1945, it began to look as if the UN might at last be able to undertake the role for which it was originally designed. A 'new world order' seemed to be possible, if not imminent.

Those who shared this vision of a brighter, more secure future for Europe bolstered their analysis with a number of arguments. First, they pointed out that the historical record suggests that democratic states do not wage wars against other democratic states. Hence, as Russia and the states of Central and Eastern Europe adopted democratic constitutions their aggressive impulses would disappear and they would become *status quo* powers in a peaceful Europe (Doyle 1983; Sorensen 1992; Weede 1984). Second, they reminded us that the economic pay-off from aggression against post-industrial societies such as those which exist in Western Europe is much less than it used to be. The shift towards knowledge-based forms of production in advanced industrial economies has reduced the ability of aggressors to exploit captured territory. Old-fashioned 'smokestack' economies can be exploited much more easily than modern economies (van Evera 1990–91, pp. 14–16). Third, the optimists took note of the fact that new security architecture is being built to replace the old balance of power system of alliances. An interlocking network of organizations – the European Union (EU), the Western European Union (WEU), NATO and the OSCE (formerly the CSCE) could form the basis of a new collective security system able to identify, condemn and defeat aggression in the European theatre (Zelikow 1992, pp. 12–30).

Given this analysis it is easy to see why the end of the Cold War sparked such optimism. For the first time in nearly half a century Europe was on the move again, and a degree of normality was restored to European affairs. It was not the normality of the nineteenth century or the interwar years, when Europe was characterized by nationalism, deep rivalries and balance of power politics, but a normality which took account of the many changes, particularly in the field of communications, international institutions and interdependent economies, which have transformed the European scene since 1945.

And there are two other senses in which post-Cold War Europe became more 'normal'. First, it was freed from the burden of superpower rivalry, and could no longer be regarded as a flashpoint for the Third World War. Second, European politics became *parochial* politics, regional politics with little impact upon the rest of the world. Today, new centres of power have quite eclipsed the old European capitals, and Europe may benefit enormously from being sidelined in this way.

Unfortunately, there is a more gloomy interpretation of the changes which have taken place, and the views of those who fear the ending of the Cold War must now be examined. Those who look back on the Cold War with a degree of nostalgia have identified a number of virtues in it. They point out, with some justification, that the last 45 years have been the most stable in the whole of European history. If we compare the first 45 years of the twentieth century with the second 45 years we can see what they mean. In the first 45 years we suffered the two most destructive wars the world has ever seen, the growth of fascism and communism, the rise of the dictators, and large-scale genocide in Europe. Over 50 million people died violently in those years. However, by way of contrast, during the 45 years since the Second World War Europe has enjoyed prolonged peace and perfect stability. Less than 15 000 people have died violently (Mearsheimer 1990, p. 10).

This relatively happy state of affairs has been brought about, so the argument goes, by the nuclear stalemate which successfully deterred aggression, and by the existence of two alliance blocs which, by dividing Europe so clearly and precisely, imposed a stable order on what has traditionally been a highly volatile part of the world. Through NATO, the United States dominated and managed the military arrangements of Western Europe, and through NATO West German aspirations for unification were controlled. The Western alliance promoted peace and security in Europe partly through its deterrent and defensive roles, but it is worth mentioning that it also encouraged stability by promoting détente with the East and solidarity in Western defence planning.

On the other side of the Iron Curtain, order and stability were imposed by the Soviet Union acting through the Warsaw Pact, which, for the Soviets, was a vehicle for legitimizing their presence in Eastern Europe. As a result of Soviet domination, all the countries of Eastern and Central Europe were prevented from pursuing domestic or foreign policies likely to threaten the peace of Europe. Admittedly, there was a hint of trouble in Hungary in 1956 and in Czechoslovakia in 1968, but it was quickly stamped on and contained by the Russians. It is possible to imagine these uprisings in Eastern Europe 'spilling over' into the West, but on the whole they did not pose a threat to European security. They were internal Warsaw Pact problems and so long as NATO regarded Eastern Europe as a Soviet sphere of influence in which it would not interfere, very few dangers emanated from Warsaw Pact countries revolting against Soviet domination. The preponderance of Soviet power and the tacit superpower understanding about spheres of influence meant, in effect, that the whole of Eastern and Central Europe was taken out of the arena of international politics for nearly 45 years.

Given the troublesome history of that part of the world, many West Europeans breathed a sigh of relief, and were quietly grateful for the way in which the Soviet Union kept the lid on the myriad of political tensions which simmered beneath the surface of Warsaw Pact unity. Taking the argument to its logical conclusion, we can see that NATO countries might reasonably have bolstered rather than undermined the Warsaw Pact Organization as a vehicle for controlling and managing the affairs of Eastern and Central Europe. And in a similar vein, the Warsaw Treaty countries should perhaps have supported NATO as an organization for managing change in Western Europe.

Fundamentally, so the argument runs, postwar peace rested on four basic facts. First, the existence of a bipolar world in which two major players, the superpowers, managed events through a relationship which has sometimes been described as an 'adverse partnership'. A bipolar world, it is claimed, is inherently more stable than a multipolar world in which decisionmaking is in the hands of dozens of independent players. Second, the existence of 'mutual deterrence' which inhibited aggression on both sides through the fear of unacceptable retaliatory punishment. No gains that could accrue from adventures in Europe could possibly outweigh the losses implicit in nuclear war. Third, the absence of expansionary nationalism in Europe (Mearsheimer 1990, pp. 11–29). The excesses of German nationalism in the 1930s and 1940s cured most West Europeans of this particular disease, and, in Eastern Europe, the iron fist of Soviet power kept nationalism at bay. Fourth, the steadily growing prosperity of Western Europe meant that many Europeans had too much to lose by aggressive behaviour.

For those who think along these lines, the Cold War represented a 'golden age' in the troubled history of Europe – a period of unprecedented peace and stability in which the likelihood of wars was no more than a prevalent illusion. Even at the height of the Cold War, when East–West tensions seemed particularly tense, there was never any serious risk of war breaking out since neither Russia nor the United States was likely to risk Armageddon for the sake of anything in Europe. They might have postured a bit over Berlin or made political capital out of the latest 'crisis', but, despite popular fears, a shooting war was never more than a remote possibility.

Now that the Cold War is over, everything is different, but those who lament its passing believe that the prospects for peace and security in Europe have deteriorated rather than improved. Their pessimistic vision of the future runs something like this: the old order has crumbled; with the collapse of the Soviet Union bipolarity has broken down, and, with the winding up of the Warsaw Pact, the European alliance system has also broken down. Both American and Russian influence in Europe has diminished as both superpowers have become increasingly obsessed by domestic problems. The Clinton administration is increasingly introspective, and has no clear policy towards Europe. Boris Yeltsin is equally preoccupied with 'domestic' problems, some connected with the creation of a market economy, others with controlling organized crime and holding together what is left of the Russian Empire.

The possibilities of both inter-state and civil violence in Eastern Europe and the former Soviet Union are greater than at any time since 1945. We need to remember that most of the states of Eastern Europe are twentieth-century creations with disputed borders, diverse ethnic populations, and troublesome minorities (Zielonka 1992; Larrabee 1990–91).[3] Few have a good track record in democracy, and in all of them ethnic violence is never far beneath the surface of political life. Deepseated animosities, suppressed by Moscow since the end of the Second World War, are now back on the political agenda. If the transition from command to market economies proves too painful the area may become a source of instability and tension. In short, according to the pessimists, when the Cold War ended, Europe exchanged stable peace for unstable peace, 'macro' nuclear threats for 'micro' conventional threats, order for disorder, certainty for uncertainty. Pierre Hassner made the point rather neatly. 'If the description of the Cold War was "neither peace nor war", that of the post-Cold War period is "both peace and war"' (Hassner 1993, p. 4).

Now it might be thought that this rather gloomy view of European security in the 1990s would automatically lead those who hold it to look back on the Cold War with some affection. But this does not necessarily follow. It is perfectly possible to regard current dangers and uncertainties as an acceptable price to be paid for the demise of a brutal system which oppressed millions of people. Even if the Cold War was 'good for European security' and its demise a source of new dangers, the change may be welcomed on the grounds that although 'security' is an important value, it is not so important that all other values must be sacrificed to it. In other words, the argument here is that the price – in terms of sacrificing other values – that had to be paid for safeguarding the security of Europe during the Cold War was too high. Arguably, it may be better to incur new risks if this allows hitherto downtrodden people to enjoy a better quality of life in which such values as freedom, justice and prosperity are respected.

Of course, in an ideal world there would be no conflict between the pursuit of security and the pursuit of all the other values which contribute to the sum total of human happiness. But in the flawed reality of politics it is often necessary to make choices which trade one value against another. In democratic societies, for example, people may have to choose between tolerating terrorist activity or losing democratic rights. Or they may have to accept higher taxes (greater poverty) or suffer inadequate defences (less security). In the territory of the former Yugoslavia citizens longing for independence and peace and democracy may, at the end of the day, have to settle for independence *or* peace *or* democracy.

In other words, colloquially speaking, nothing is for free and you cannot have your cake and eat it. Security is a scare commodity, and, like all scarce commodities, it has to be paid for by sacrificing other values. This analysis suggests that the debate about European security during and after the Cold War may resolve itself into a difference of opinion about values – a difference between those who think that the security of the state is so important that any sacrifice is worth making to secure it, and those who think that there is a price beyond which it is not worth the candle. Strategists and soldiers tend to fall into the first camp; politicians and ordinary taxpayers into the second.

FOUR CRITICAL QUESTIONS

Is there any Danger of Europe being Dominated by a Hegemonic Power?

This, as Edward Mortimer has pointed out, has been a traditional concern of European statesmen since the Renaissance, and it is not irrelevant today (Mortimer 1992, p. 7). Two possible candidates are worth considering – Russia and Germany. Clearly, the Soviet threat – whether real or imagined – which dominated NATO attention throughout the Cold War years has disappeared. The likelihood of Russian troops making *blitzkrieg* strikes across the North German Plain is close to zero. Nevertheless, Russia remains a military heavyweight in both nuclear and conventional terms, and even if it is not quite the super-power it once was, it wields more than enough military power to cause Europeans to worry about its future intentions. At the moment the Russian leadership has too many other things on its mind to contemplate aggression, and, arguably, has not yet articulated a clear foreign policy even to itself, let alone to the rest of the world. It is difficult to imagine any plausible political scenario in which Western Europe would figure on a Russian hit list. And even if it did, the practical difficulties of carrying out an attack would be formidable. Apart from the considerable constraints which have been imposed on Russian military power by the CFE agreement, Russia is now separated from Western Europe by the 'buffer' states of Poland, Belarus and the Ukraine.

And yet, though it is quite foolish to talk about the possibility of a 'New Cold War', it is possible to discern worrying developments in Russian society. There is no doubt that many Russians are disenchanted with the West. They are unhappy with the level of economic assistance they have received; they resent their country's diminished status as an '*ex*-superpower'; they object to Western criticism of the way they handled the Chechnya problem. All these feelings have fuelled the resurgence of popular nationalism, which, in its extreme form, finds expression in the ramblings of Mr Zhirinovskiy (Zhirinovskiy in Morrison 1994),[4] but which, in a more modest vein, is reflected in a somewhat more assertive Russian foreign policy. There is already abundant evidence of Russian willingness to use force to secure its interests when this seems necessary. There are even hints that some Kremlin 'hard-liners' would like to revive a version of the Brzezhnev doctrine of 'limited sovereignty' to justify intervention in the 'near abroad' or even further afield in ex-Warsaw Pact countries. This time, intervention would be justified not if socialism were threatened, but if Russian security were compromised. As befits a major regional, if not world, power, Russia is likely to want neutrality from its former Warsaw Pact allies, access to the Baltic ports, international recognition of a legitimate sphere of influence, a monopoly of military intervention rights in all former states of the Soviet Union, and full participation in 'pan-European' security organizations. It is far too early to say whether the Russian bear is on the prowl again, but if it is, it seems likely to confine its wanderings to its own backyard, i.e. the territory of the former Soviet Union.

It is difficult to know what to make of all this. The reality of Russian power is unquestioned. As General Colin Powell has reminded us,

Russia remains, both in terms of manpower and weapons, by far the largest military power in Europe, and is capable 'of destroying the United States in less than thirty minutes' (Mortimer 1992, p. 8). And yet, here and now, there are no signs that Russia poses a threat to Western Europe or is deliberately pursuing confrontational or imperialist policies. In practical terms the question facing Western defence planners today is 'How much effort should we invest to insure ourselves against an admittedly dangerous but very unlikely contingency? And the probable answer is 'Not much'.

The possibility of German hegemony in Europe rouses strong feelings if only because German aggressions have already threatened European security twice this century. The French statesman Clemenceau put his finger on the problem when he complained that Germany was simply too big for Europe. Between 1945 and 1990 that particular problem was solved by the division of the German nation into two independent sovereign states. But now Germany is reunited and already much more economically powerful than any of her European partners. Even in military terms the new Germany is the strongest conventional power in Western Europe. These simple facts, combined with a whiff of right-wing German nationalism, have stirred old memories and fears of a resurgent Germany.

It seems reasonable to believe that Germany may very well end up dominating Europe by virtue of sheer size and economic clout. But it would be a legitimate and quite different kind of hegemony from that which is evoked by recollections of the Hitler period. It would be hegemony based on economic preponderance rather than military force, and if only for that reason, it would be an acceptable though unpopular state of affairs.

There is, of course, a possibility that an economically powerful Germany might one day wish to turn itself into a militarily powerful hegemon. Those who worry about this possibility should perhaps be reminded of two facts. First, since 1945 German foreign policy has been uniformly virtuous, and at present there are no signs that it is about to change direction. Second, although Germany is an independent sovereign state, it is now enmeshed in a network of institutions – of which NATO and the EU are the most important – which constrain its independence and tie it firmly into Western policy. The containment of Germany has been a priority for most West European states since the Second World War, and, perhaps wisely, the Germans have not resisted it. Of course, within the parameters of Western policy it is only reasonable to expect Germany to seek diplomatic and political influence commensurate with her economic strength. In that sense a more 'independent' Germany is probably inevitable.

The only scenario in which an old-fashioned hegemonic Germany has any degree of plausibility is one in which the overlapping economic and security structures which have been so carefully constructed over the last 50 years have collapsed. If Europe fell apart, then it would revert to a loose society of states in which the age-old game of power politics was the only game in town. There would be no 'security community', and 'defence', to use current jargon, would have been 're-nationalized'. In such an environment as this, Germany would, as Mortimer has hinted, 'sooner or later re-emerge as the continent's most formidable military power' (Mortimer 1992, p. 10). This is not a very plausible scenario because there are no pressures in Europe to dismantle or unravel the sophisticated network of institutions which has been built. Indeed, the pressure is to extend and develop them.

Could Local Violence beyond Europe's Borders Threaten West European Security?

Now that the restraining hand of autocratic government has been removed, traditional nationalist and ethnic tensions have returned to plague the states of Eastern Europe, the former Soviet Union and the Balkans. There are potential border disputes between almost all the states in the area – between Romania and Russia, Romania and Hungary, Poland and Germany, Poland and Lithuania, Poland and the Ukraine, Poland and Slovakia, Poland and Belarus, Greece and Albania, Greece and Turkey, the Czech Republic and Germany. Pockets of ethnic minorities live uneasily in most countries in the region (Zielonka 1992, pp. 10–32). There are 25 million Russians living outside Russia and 3 million Hungarians living beyond the borders of Hungary. Sizeable Hungarian minorities exist in Romania, the Ukraine, Slovakia and Serbia. There are Poles in Lithuania, the Ukraine and Belarus. There are Germans in Poland and Romanians in Bessarabia. In the former Soviet Union nationalities are even more intermingled. The 1979 Soviet census estimated a Soviet population of 262 million people divided into 104 nationalities living in 15 Soviet republics (Evera 1990–91, p. 49). Now that the Soviet Union has been dismantled, border disputes and ethnic tensions have become endemic (van Ham 1994, p. 30).[5]

The principle of self-determination has a virtuous ring about it, even to the point of being enshrined in the UN Charter, but in many ways it is a source of disorder rather than order in international relations. When one considers the patchwork of nationalities in Eastern Europe and beyond, it is a principle with popular appeal but little practical relevance. Indeed, that is the tragedy of 'self-determination' in this part of the world: it can neither be ignored nor implemented. We are faced with a complicated pattern of ethnic and nationalist diversity which cannot be matched to any conceivable pattern of sovereign states. Hence the inevitability of ethnic strife no matter what marginal territorial adjustments are made, *and no matter what agreements are reached by governments.*

This last point is an important one because there is a tendency to believe that when governments reach agreement problems are solved. In the case of border disputes complicated by ethnic and nationalist issues, this is a dangerous assumption because what happens round borders depends more on people than on governments. It is all very well for Germany to guarantee the German–Polish border, but what really matters is what Germans living in Silesia think about it. In a similar vein we need to recognize that when Poland and the Ukraine renounce territorial claims against each other, nothing is solved without the acquiescence of 300 000 Ukrainians living in Poland and 500 000 Poles living in the Ukraine. And when Hungary denies any revisionist claims against its neighbours we need to be aware of how little that may mean to the people on the ground.

Ethnic violence has already surfaced in the former Soviet Union (where over 160 border disputes have been identified) and the Balkans, and no one could rule it out in Central and Eastern Europe. And yet we should not regard it as inevitable. A good deal of ethnic and nationalist violence is fuelled by political and economic discrimination. If countries can, in a reasonable time scale, move, however uneasily, towards just and fair societies in which there is a modicum of economic growth, then the chances of avoiding serious conflict may be good. But if things go wrong the future of many of these countries is bleak. There is something peculiarly nasty about the sort of ethnic–nationalist violence we are contemplating. Unlike normal political violence which can be accommodated within a Clausewitzian philosophy and which is geared to the pursuit of *interests*, ethnic violence is about *hatred*. It is primordial, barbaric and beyond reason (Goldstein 1994, p. 158).[6]

In Western Europe it is widely believed that if this sort of violence breaks out in Eastern Europe and beyond, it will cause such turmoil that Western European countries are bound to be affected. Before we acquiesce in this view it is worth asking ourselves why we believe it. Why do we accept the theory of 'spillover'? One reason may be to do with vague memories of the First World War, and a feeling that the Allied powers were dragged into it by events in Sarajevo. Or perhaps we may have more recent memories of finding ourselves at war with Germany because of events in Poland. Either way, it seems that what happens in fairly remote places has the power to trigger our involvement. But there is a big difference between the Europe which existed before both World Wars and the Europe of today. Before both wars Europe was an arena for great power rivalry in which local tensions were exploited in a much bigger game. Today, with the Cold War part of history, that is no longer the case. Local violence, even large-scale local violence, is unlikely to trigger anything, and this is particularly so since there are no entangling alliances (apart from NATO) to swing into operation.

A second reason for accepting the 'spillover' theory is that there are two or three conduits which connect Western Europe to Eastern Europe and the Balkans. These conduits form vectors through which turmoil may spread (Mortimer 1992, pp. 13–18; Shehadi 1993, p. 54; Binnendijk and Simon 1994, p. 2).[7] One conduit takes the form of the pan-European security architecture which is currently being developed. If they mean anything, the connections which are being forged *via* 'Partnership for Peace', the OSCE (formerly the CSCE), the EU and the WEU, must signify a Western interest in the security affairs of states in Eastern Europe and beyond. None of this architecture implies anything so firm as a security guarantee on the NATO model, but it hints at the possibility of involvement. Even NATO can be seen as a vector through which local violence can spread and involve many Western powers. One official has speculated that if the war in Yugoslavia spread, 'this would set Greece against Turkey, bringing crisis to NATO; it would put Russia and the United States in opposite camps, calling into question their new relationship; and it would aggravate the differences between Community states. The Muslim aspect of the conflict would also have repercussions in France and for Spain's relations with the Maghreb' (Zaldivar 1993, p. 29). In a sense, all pan-European organizations are structural escalators to involvement in the domestic problems of Eastern Europe, and what is more, they confer legitimacy on such involvement.

A second conduit for 'spillover' is the minority nationalities whose rights are supported by Western states. No West European country is likely to turn a blind eye to persecution wherever it occurs in Eastern Europe or beyond, and for some countries the temptation to intervene, either unilaterally or under UN auspices, may be irresistible. It seems inconceivable, for example, that if Germans living in Poland were being seriously oppressed, and heading for the German border, Germany would not become involved. And German involvement would have implications for NATO and all the other organizations to which Germany belongs.

A third channel through which violence in the East could affect Western Europe arises out of the widespread acceptance by Western states of the philosophy of 'intervention'. It is now generally accepted that where there is large-scale human suffering, where internationally accepted norms of behaviour are violated, and where there are dangers of disorder spreading, then intervention, preferably under the UN umbrella, is justified (Freedman 1993, p. 39).[8] The likelihood of West European involvement in Eastern Europe and beyond has been further enhanced by a growing tendency to think of Europe as a *whole* and European security as indivisible.

Everyone is now aware of the importance of non-governmental relations in international politics. We have already seen how investment and trade can influence policy, but Pierre Hassner has made the point that the interpenetration of societies (in particular from a demographic and cultural point of view) is now becoming important. It is, as Hassner says, a diffuse and uncontrollable phenomenon – dependent on the movement of people and ideas – but in an important sense it is, like economic links, a vector for cross-border involvement which makes it increasingly difficult to isolate conflicts. The fact that over 5 million North Africans live in Europe, particularly in France, means that the Maghreb is automatically on the agenda of French and European politics.

Despite the possibility of Western involvement, we need to be clear that conflicts in Eastern Europe, the former Soviet Union and the Balkans are not, of themselves, a threat to Western Europe, and there is nothing inevitable about their spread. Indeed, recent experience of the violence in Yugoslavia demonstrates the possibility of containment providing the will is there. It should also be clear that 'spillover' is not an automatic process. It can be resisted by states which want to resist it. The problem is that some Western states may not want to resist it.

How Important is the Transatlantic Link to European Security?

When, in 1949, the United States entered into a legal commitment to defend Western Europe, this represented a reversal of traditional American foreign policy and a major diplomatic *coup* for European statesmen anxious to counter the power of the Soviet Union. It was widely realized that Western Europe, devastated and weakened by war, could not match the growing power of the Eastern bloc without American help. The US commitment, in the form of a promise enshrined in Article V of the North Atlantic Treaty, and a military presence on European soil, has been the linchpin of European security for over 40 years. During the whole of that period the United States has dominated NATO affairs, and while some Europeans (particularly the French), have been irritated by this security dependence, most have accepted it as an inevitable price to be paid for the massive security subsidy (worth about 90 billion dollars per annum) which the United States has provided.

The collapse of the Soviet Union has undermined NATO's mission and removed the basic rationale for US involvement. Inevitably this has sparked a debate on both sides of the Atlantic about the future role of the United States in Europe. Arguably, Europe now figures much less prominently in US security calculations. Although isolationist sentiments are never very far beneath the surface of US domestic politics, there are no signs that the United States is contemplating a 'fortress America' policy. It could, however, respond to the 'bring the troops home' syndrome by reverting to the more traditional policy of holding aloof from European affairs until the balance of power was so threatened that it became necessary for the United States to use its weight to restore the balance. Essentially this was the policy pursued by the United States in the first half of this century. Curiously enough, it is not far removed from current French thinking. The French would like the United States to become an 'ally of last resort', that is to say, a friend who could be relied upon to bail Europe out if the going got rough, but who, for the rest of the time, would be content to remain benevolently on the sidelines (Mahncke 1993).[9] To date, American politicians have not expressed much interest in this role, and it is difficult to see what would be in it for them.

The Clinton administration has not articulated a clear European policy, but official thinking seems to favour a positive, ongoing engagement in the affairs of Europe, perhaps with the objectives of managing the balance of power, preventing the 'renationalization' of European defence, promoting US economic interests, retaining leverage and influence over European affairs, countering a residual Russian threat, pacifying and stabilizing intra-European relations etc. Europe is one of the wealthiest bits of real-estate in the world, accounting for about a quarter of the world's economy, and, if the federal aspirations of the EU are realized, a new superpower in the making. The United States, despite its growing Pacific interests, would surely not want to be excluded from influence in this major sector of the world economy.

Most European states also favour continuing US involvement, particularly in a period of flux and uncertainty about events in Russia and Eastern Europe. Given the many imponderables, the American guarantee looks like a useful insurance policy for which the European premiums are not outrageously high. Most Europeans also recognize that for the foreseeable future NATO is the only organization in Europe with enough military clout to count for anything, and they recognize that without the American contribution to that clout the alliance would be emasculated. Malcolm Rifkind has made the point: 'No European country, or group of countries, could supply the intelligence, lift or sophisticated firepower that America supplies. Nor can there be a European substitute for the additional political authority or the deterrent capacity of the United States' (Rifkind 1993).

Of course, none of this implies that the American commitment will remain at its historic level. There is general agreement, on both sides of the Atlantic, that the European pillar of the alliance must be strengthened, and current ideas about developing the WEU reflect that feeling. If and when a European defence identity emerges it is possible to envisage further reductions in US forces in Europe. However, although there is nothing sacrosanct about 100 000 men, numbers are not totally irrelevant; below a certain figure – and it is difficult to know what the figure is – the psychology of commitment begins to look questionable. It is also possible to envisage, in the years ahead, a reduction in American influence over alliance decisions and a reduction of American staff in key positions. But the consensus for some kind of continuing US involvement remains a strong one – and one which is shared by Eastern European countries who are particularly conscious of the importance of military power in countering whatever threat may emanate from Russia (Snider 1992–93, pp. 24–39; Powell 1992; Schwarz 1994; Nelson 1994; Garnham 1994).

Do European States Face Military Threats from Beyond Europe?

With the serious exception of threats posed by the proliferation of nuclear weapons and other weapons of mass destruction, the answer to this question is probably 'No'. Europe is, of course, confronted by political instability in the Middle East and North Africa. Various writers have identified a new 'arc of crisis' stretching from the Maghreb, through the Eastern Mediterranean, to the Balkans and the Persian Gulf, where the probability of revolution or war is relatively high (Joffe 1991–92; Gasteyger 1991–92). But instability is not of itself a threat – though it may give rise to threats. The states of the Middle East, North Africa and the Balkans are more likely to direct their wrath against each other than against Western Europe, and, even if they had Europe in their sights, it is difficult to see what they could do, militarily speaking. Arguably, from a purely military perspective Europe now exists in a more benign environment than at any time in the last 50 years. Of course, it is always possible to imagine bizarre 'worst-case' scenarios in which new hegemonic powers in Asia threaten Western Europe, but in any reasonable time frame these scenarios are pretty far-fetched. European states will undoubtedly face difficulties in dealing with the outside world, but they are unlikely to face the prospect of a mortal blow being struck against them. What is much more likely is that they will be faced with a multitude of domestic conflicts threatening political stability in surrounding areas, or local inter-state wars in which Western interests are threatened.

Two areas of particular concern are the Middle East and the Maghreb, and both of them are threatened by Islamic fundamentalism. Now Islam does not enjoy a favourable press in the West. Ordinary people connect it with fanaticism, religious intolerance, the suppression of human rights, crusading zeal, ethnic violence and terrorist activity. There is a widespread feeling that conservative Islamic states are sources of political instability because of their undemocratic regimes, and fundamentalist states represent revolutionary forces in international society and are likely to show scant respect for international order and the accepted norms of civilized behaviour. These latter feelings are understandable because at one level there is an incompatibility between Islamic ideas of universalism and the idea of a state system, and at another level Muslim activism in the form of terrorist activity has done nothing to improve the image of Islam in the West.

But we need to remember that Islam is not a monolithic ideology: it comes in as many varieties as Christianity and most of those varieties are quite at home with the idea of participating in international society (Piscatori 1992, pp. 310–33). The Islamic world is disunited, bereft of serious military power and ruled by an ideology which has no appeal whatsoever for Western societies. Although some Muslim states are anti-Western and harbour international terrorists, they cannot be regarded as posing a serious military threat to Europe. Even Libya, with intermediate-range missiles capable of striking into Western Europe, seems an improbable enemy. Fundamentalism may wreak havoc in the Muslim world, and indirectly this may adversely affect Western interests, but as a *direct* threat to European security it is more of a bogeyman than a real menace. We should also remember that to a large extent Islamic fundamentalism is a symptom rather than a cause of instability, both domestic and international. Underneath the rise of fundamentalist Islam lie more familiar problems – a search for identity in a hostile world, poverty, unemployment, population growth, dissatisfaction with corrupt authoritarian governments. Islam has served as a catalyst for popular protest rather than being a prime cause of it.

More worrying to Europe than the vague threat of Islamic fundamentalism is the more plausible possibility that Middle Eastern oil supplies may be disrupted as a result of regional instability. Despite its own offshore reserves, Europe is heavily dependent on Middle Eastern oil. European states currently import about 25 per cent of their oil requirement from the Middle East, and this level of dependence is unlikely to diminish in the years ahead. Coupled with the fact that 60 per cent of the world's known reserves of oil are in the Gulf, this dependence suggests that Europe will continue to have an abiding interest in promoting sufficient stability in the Middle East to permit an uninterrupted flow of oil. At the moment there is no threat from the oil suppliers to 'turn off the tap' or even to jack up the price unreasonably. The 'threat' of disrupted supplies is an indirect one – a side-effect of instability in the region rather than malevolence on the part of any Arab country. In this kind of situation it probably makes more sense to speak of 'coping with crises' rather than 'responding to threats'.

Much the same point can be made about the Maghreb where the side-effects of instability are also likely to impinge on Western Europe. The states of the Maghreb share a number of common problems. First, rapid population growth which, on current demographic trends, will result in a doubling of the population in about 30 years. Second, massive unemployment which cannot be dented by any plausible economic growth. (The International Labour Organization (ILO) has calculated that half a million new jobs would have to be created annually just to prevent the situation worsening.) Third, economic stagnation and international debt which manifests itself in widespread poverty and unrest. Fourth, political instability in which corrupt and authoritarian governments struggle for legitimacy with Muslim fundamentalist parties representing a tide of protest, particularly from the young (Spencer 1993).[10]

However, as already argued, 'problems' are not 'threats'. There is no serious military threat from the Maghreb although at least two states – Libya and Algeria – possess missiles capable of reaching Europe. Nevertheless, European countries, particularly those in the EU, are right to be concerned about the possibility of massive migration from North Africa. Pulled by the economic magnet of relative prosperity in Europe, and pushed by oppression and poverty back home, uncontrolled migration could make the Maghreb the 'Mexico' of Europe. The Mediterranean is a somewhat better natural barrier than the US–Mexican border, but in an age of cheap and easy travel it is too flimsy to withstand the pressure of desperate people seeking work in Europe. The problem of migration is not a security problem in the accepted sense of the word, but large numbers of disaffected immigrants who are not integrated into the society which employs them can easily become a major source of social unrest, and, as was pointed out on pp. 29–30, a vector for entanglement in the affairs of their home countries.

CONCLUSION

Western Europe is virtually surrounded by areas of potential instability – Eastern Europe, the former Soviet Union, the Balkans, the Middle East and the Maghreb. The consequences of this instability are not immediately life-threatening to the citizens of Western Europe, but they are imponderable and on most calculations detrimental to Western interests. The 64 000 dollar question is what, if anything, should the states of Western Europe do about the problems which beset their neighbours? One response to this question is to admit that virtually nothing can be done, to acknowledge that West European states have neither the inclination nor the resources to make a significant impact on any of the problems we have identified. Those who think this way might be tempted to pull up the drawbridge, reinforce the walls and widen the moat. In effect they would recommend a policy of isolationism backed by defensive military power. Europe would become a prickly hedgehog, not much interested in what went on beyond its territory, but capable of giving any aggressor a bloody nose. It is a psychologically attractive posture for a prosperous, introspective part of the world surrounded by troubles of one sort or another.

But it is not a viable option. Western Europe is not an autarchic regional system able to prosper without reference to the wider world. In an interdependent world there are too many connections between states to contemplate isolation. Whether Europe likes it or not it cannot wash its hands of problems which lie beyond its borders, and it is not in its interests to try. All European states have an interest in promoting a stable world order in which they can go about their lawful business without fear of serious disruption. European involvement cannot guarantee stability, but by supporting the processes of democratization and modernization, and by encouraging economic growth and development, Western European states can move the world, albeit only marginally, in the direction of order and stability and peace.

Unfortunately, West European states have no coordinated philosophy of intervention, and public opinion within them is divided. Vague and laudable feelings that Europe must do what it can to help and cannot stand idly by in the face of widespread suffering in adjacent territories, are counterbalanced by the 'Vietnam syndrome' – a fear of becoming inextricably involved in expensive conflicts which cannot be 'won', and from which the participants cannot easily extricate themselves. When confronted with the question of whether to intervene beyond the Atlantic area, each Western European state will evaluate the situation in the light of its own interests, calculated on the basis of likely costs, gains and risks.

Intervention will be a favoured strategy in those situations where vital national interests seem threatened – as they were deemed to be threatened by Saddam Hussein's invasion of Kuwait. In other situations, where interests are not so clearly jeopardized, intervention will be more problematic. There is perhaps more plausibility about intervention in Eastern Europe than in the Maghreb, if only because Eastern Europe is regarded as European, sharing Western culture, traditions and values, whereas the Maghreb is seen as being part of Africa and culturally quite distinct from Europe. But even in Eastern Europe there could be no certainty about West European involvement. European reluctance in these matters is well illustrated by nervousness about serious involvement in Bosnia.

Generally speaking, intervening without clear, achievable objectives, a finite time scale, and an escape route, is unlikely to appeal to democratic governments with an eye on the next election and a public expenditure problem.[11] Against this background of a nervous public, worried about open-ended commitments and 'quagmire' situations which sap resources and cost lives, governments are understandably cautious. The only exception to this is likely to occur where there are gross violations of human rights, and when public opinion has been roused by media attention to atrocities and human suffering on a large scale in locations which are not too far from home. Even in these circumstances only multilateral intervention (probably under UN auspices) has any degree of reliability, and this is likely to be undertaken reluctantly and as a last resort.

Not everyone in Western Europe is nervous about pursuing policies of intervention and involvement beyond its borders – particularly its borders with Eastern Europe. Already there is an impressive network of security organizations linking East and West, and there are many who would like to see the connections strengthened. The main argument of those who favour this policy is that it offers the best opportunity for influencing developments in Eastern Europe and Russia. The more these states become enmeshed in Western-oriented security organizations, the more likely they are to accept our values and the less likely they are to oppose us. It is an attractive idea and it explains much of the enthusiasm for expanding NATO through the 'Partnership for Peace' agreement (Bell 1994, pp. 27–41; Brzezinski 1994, pp. 67–82; Simon 1993, pp. 21–35; Clarke 1994, pp. 42–60).

The most important question facing NATO today is whether to go further than this by admitting to full membership either the states of Eastern Europe alone, or those states plus Russia. To opt for the first of these policies might be very dangerous because it could confirm all Russia's suspicions of encirclement and isolation. The second option, i.e. including Russia in the expansion of NATO, is strongly favoured by those who see the extension of the alliance as a way of influencing and containing it within a wider framework – in much the same way that, since 1954, Germany has been contained within NATO.

Unfortunately this option is not without risk. First, because it may involve present NATO members in conflicts far removed from the North Atlantic area. Some of them may need reminding that they joined NATO to avoid trouble, not to seek it out. Second, because there is a big difference between swallowing a defeated, docile, weak, guilt-ridden Germany, and trying to digest an assertive, unstable ex-super-power with the power to wreck the entire enterprise. When Germany joined NATO it shared a clear common interest with its allies. No comparable shared interest links Russia to NATO, and, by admitting it, NATO states may discover that they have bitten off more than they can chew. The other danger implicit in Russian membership is that it would diminish the attractiveness of the alliance to all those East European states whose prime motive in joining was to safeguard themselves against Russia. Those states are bound to ask themselves how much protection is afforded by an alliance which contains their most feared potential enemy, and which was never designed to protect its members from each other.

NATO members need to acknowledge that in present circumstances expanding NATO is not a simple matter of extending its membership (as it was in the past when Turkey, Greece, West Germany and Spain joined). It is about changing the nature of the organization from a fairly narrow collective defence structure to something else – precisely what has not yet been articulated, but it has all the hallmarks of a nebulous half-baked collective security organization (Claude 1962, pp. 94–190; Kupchan and Kupchan 1991, p. 160; Joffe 1992, pp. 36–50).[12] It is also about taking on new problems at present imperfectly understood in the West. Psychologically speaking, neither the United States nor Western Europe may be quite ready for all this.

NOTES

1. While Buzan's book, *People, States and Fear*, makes the best case for broadening the concept of security, not everyone is enthusiastic about expanding the concept of security. P. Morgan has made an effective defence of the traditional, narrow military definition. He says, 'Security studies should be focussed on international war, the threat of war, and the prevention of war'. See Morgan (1992).
2. The argument that the end of the Cold War is likely to increase prospects for crisis and war in Europe has been persuasively articulated by Mearsheimer (1990).
3. For a review of the potential troublespots of Central Europe see Zielonka (1992). For a review of potential instabilities in the Balkans see Larrabee (1990–91).
4. The views of Vladimir Zhirinovskiy and some selected quotations from his writings and speeches are to be found in Morrison (1994).
5. Peace in the territories of the former Soviet Union depends critically on how Russia responds to its minorities in the 'near abroad'. There are clear indications that President Yeltsin is not prepared to abandon Russian minorities just because they happen to live beyond the boundaries of Russia. In his 1993 New Year's Message on Russian television Yeltsin commented '... we shall remember the fact that millions, tens of millions of our compatriots reside in these states [the states of the CIS, the Baltic Republic and Georgia]. It is the right and duty of Russia and Russia's leadership to protect their interests'. Quoted by van Ham (1994).
6. The point is well made by Goldstein (1994) when he comments: 'Ethnic conflicts

are hard to resolve because they are not about "who gets what" but about "I don't like you"', p. 158.

7. Some vectors of insecurity are discussed by Mortimer (1992). Kamal S. Shehadi has coined the phrase 'contagion' to describe some of the mechanisms by which conflicts spread. He speculates that 'if the Serbs and Albanians of Macedonia are armed in anticipation of a Serb–Albanian conflict in the Kosovo region of Serbia, this could transmit the war to Macedonia'. See Shehadi (1993, p. 54). Others have speculated along similar lines. If ethnic violence broke out in Kosovo, 'the Serbs would likely move into northern Macedonia to destroy renegade Kosovars, and the Greeks would likely enter southern Macedonia to keep Kosovar refugees out of Greece. Since Macedonia has no ability to resist, Bulgaria might intervene to protect Macedonians whom they regard as ethnically close, and Albania might send volunteers and weapons to assist Albanians in Macedonia. As soon as Greece entered Macedonia, Turkey would likely respond by taking action against Greece in Macedonia or in the Aegean Islands. Two NATO allies could again be at war'. See Binnendijk and Simon (1994, p. 2).

8. But acceptance of the principle of intervention is hedged with reservations. In the words of Freedman (1993, p. 39), 'Britain, France and the United States are all reluctant intervenors, fearful of "quagmires", and are becoming consumed by a sense of historic gloom over the long-term prospects for much of post-communist Europe. So long as these countries do not feel directly threatened by developments in Eastern Europe they are likely to wish to continue to limit their liabilities. Even when, as in former Yugoslavia, humanitarian pressures oblige them to intervene, they set strict limits on both the scope and purposes of this intervention'.

9. An interesting and persuasive discussion of the role of the United States in Europe is to be found in Mahncke (1993). The minimum role advocated by the French is discussed on pp. 26–7.

10. An excellent discussion of the problems of the Maghreb and their likely impact on Europe is to be found in Spencer (1993).

11. The policy of the British government towards the conflict in Bosnia typifies the reluctance of many European states to involve themselves in any serious way which goes beyond minimal 'peacekeeping' operations and measures of humanitarian intervention. The then British Foreign Secretary, Douglas Hurd, made the point in his Chatham House speech on 27 January 1993: 'My own belief is that there is a British interest, shared with our allies, European partners and many others, in a safer and more decent world, but that the resulting effort needs to be rigorously disciplined and constrained .... Obviously we cannot be everywhere and we cannot do everything.'

12. The best and most thorough analysis of the weaknesses inherent in the idea of 'collective security' is to be found in Claude, Jr (1962, pp. 94–190). Despite being discredited by its historical record of failure, the idea of collective security refuses to die. Kupchan and Kupchan (1991), have recently argued that 'collective security can best preserve peace in post-Cold War Europe' (p. 160). A recent well-timed attack on the subject is by Joffe (1992), who makes the point (p. 46) that 'the nuclear age has added an existential risk that reduces any collective security system to a grandiose nothing'.

2. Russian national security policy after the Cold War

Jennifer G. Mathers

The end of the Cold War and the collapse of the Soviet Union left policymakers in Moscow facing profound challenges. Russia's leaders had the task of establishing new political and economic institutions, while at the same time determining Russia's national security interests and identifying threats to those interests. But while their counterparts in Washington, Bonn and London had the task of rethinking NATO, the Russians had lost the military and political alliance which they had led during most of the postwar period. Moscow could no longer count on the support of the countries of Central and Eastern Europe which had been its allies, albeit unwilling ones, while Russia was surrounded by fourteen newly independent states which had once been part of the Soviet Union and whose foreign policy orientations were initially unknown.

The first few years of an independent, post-Soviet Russia have seen its leaders engaged in a search for friends and allies in the international arena. During this time the emphasis in Russian national security policy has shifted from the initial almost exclusive concentration on cooperation with Western countries and the whole-hearted embrace of international and supranational organizations, to a more independent stance on some issues of special concern to Russia and the re-establishment of links with countries in the Third World which enjoyed good relations with the USSR. At the same time, instability closer to home has focused Moscow's attention both on its relations with the other former Soviet states (the 'near abroad'), and on threats to the territorial integrity of the Russian Federation itself.

TRENDS IN RUSSIAN NATIONAL SECURITY POLICY

Although its leaders declared the Russian Federation a sovereign state in June 1990 and attempted to influence the Soviet Union's relations with other countries, it is only possible to date the beginning of a truly Russian national security policy from 25 December 1991, when Mikhail Gorbachev formally resigned as Soviet president and control of the Soviet nuclear arsenal was handed over to the President of the Russian Federation, Boris Yeltsin.

Initially Moscow identified its national security interests very closely with those of the West, especially the United States. This is not at all surprising, given the mood and expectations which were prevalent in Moscow during much of 1992. Yeltsin and Russia's other leaders were still experiencing the exhilaration of their victory over reactionary, communist forces during the August 1991 *coup* attempt. There was a widespread enthusiasm among Russia's ruling élite, as well as among many of the country's people, for all manner of Western forms and institutions, and an intense desire to see Russia take its place beside the United States and the countries of Western Europe as an accepted member of the democratic nations of the world. The Yeltsin government contained a high proportion of young people, many with backgrounds as academics, who favoured a rapid transition to a full market economy and the creation and strengthening of democratic structures. The Russian Minister of Foreign Affairs, Andrei Kozyrev, fits this profile precisely. Kozyrev had previously been an analyst in one of the prestigious Academy of Sciences' research institutes specializing in international affairs. He was one of the most consistent and articulate supporters of the tenets of Gorbachev's New Political Thinking, which had stressed the values of international cooperation and the importance of reducing the threat which the Soviet Union posed to other countries, particularly to those in North America and Western Europe. Kozyrev viewed any lingering Russian concern about the possible hostile intentions of Western countries as outdated and groundless, arguing that the subordination of Western governments to the rule of law virtually eliminated the possibility that they would pursue aggressive foreign policies, asserting that 'in the system of Western states ... the problem of war has essentially been removed' (Marantz 1994, p. 727).

Furthermore, and not least importantly, the new regime in Moscow was very conscious that Russia could be rewarded handsomely in terms of aid, loans and investment from the developed countries of Western

Europe and North America if Russia's leaders demonstrated an appropriate spirit of cooperation with the major economic and political powers of the post-Cold War world. Just a few months after the collapse of Soviet power Yeltsin himself identified the entry of Russia into the civilized world community and the securing of as much support as possible from the outside world for the transformation of Russia as the two principal tasks of Russian foreign policy (Bluth 1993, p. 48).

During 1992 and the beginning of 1993, therefore, Boris Yeltsin's Russian government continued, and even went beyond, Gorbachev's policy of pursuing good relations with the Western countries. The main theme in Russian national security policy during this early period was distancing the new Russia from the old Soviet Union in every way possible, especially by reducing the threat which other countries perceived from Russia. To accomplish this goal, Yeltsin's government embarked on a series of measures designed to reassure the leaders of Western countries and demonstrate that Russia was worthy of their trust.

Russia's control over the nuclear weapons of the former Soviet Union and its commitment to strategic arms control were the areas about which the Western powers required the most reassurance, and Russia's government lost no time in providing it. As early as December 1991 all four Soviet republics with nuclear weapons stationed on their territory (Russia, Ukraine, Belarus and Kazakhstan) pledged to abide by the Strategic Arms Reduction Treaty (START) signed by Presidents Bush and Gorbachev in July 1991. Similarly, Russia joined the other former Soviet states in January 1992 in agreeing to the OSCE (formerly CSCE) framework. Boris Yeltsin reiterated the absence of any hostile intent towards the West with his statement in a January 1992 interview on US television, in which he declared that Russia would no longer target American cities with its strategic nuclear missiles, although no similar assurance was forthcoming from the United States. In the course of this same visit to the United States the Russian president also called for joint American–Russian work on a 'Star Wars'-type project to provide a defence against nuclear missile attack for both countries. Russia further demonstrated its willingness to behave responsibly as a nuclear weapons state by agreeing to participate in a programme jointly sponsored by the Americans and the Germans to employ former Soviet nuclear weapons scientists in peacetime projects.

In June 1992 Presidents Bush and Yeltsin agreed the terms of an 'American–Russian Charter', which asserted that the two countries no longer regarded each other as adversaries. The meeting between the American and Russian presidents produced a plan for further steep reductions in both countries' strategic nuclear weapons arsenals, which was the basis for the second START agreement, signed by Bush and Yeltsin in January 1993 (Bluth 1993, p. 49). While START I marked a significant new step in strategic nuclear arms control by providing for cuts in the number of warheads deployed by each side, START II represented another qualitative change in US–Russian arms control by providing for the elimination of all land-based missiles equipped with multiple independently targetable re-entry vehicles, or MIRVS. The fact that START II banned land-based MIRVed missiles (the largest component of Moscow's strategic triad) but not multiple warheads on sea-based missiles (the traditional strength of the American side), indicates that the Russians were still pursuing Gorbachev's strategy of placing good relations with the West and the achievement of arms control agreements at, or close to, the top of the Kremlin's list of national security policy priorities.

During 1992 and the beginning of the following year the Russian leadership also demonstrated its willingness to cooperate with the West and to make amends for past (Soviet) mistakes outside the arena of nuclear weapons and arms control. Concrete examples of this spirit of cooperation range from the chiefly symbolic such as the January 1992 Russo–Finnish agreement nullifying the postwar pact which committed Finland to neutrality, to active support of Western sponsored proposals in the United Nations. Russia's support in the United Nations Security Council in May 1992 for economic sanctions against the Yugoslav Federation enabled the leaders of Western Europe and the United States to pursue their policy of international isolation of the Serbian leaders. In general the Russian government demonstrated a great deal of enthusiasm during this period for the United Nations as a post-Cold War coordinating body for regional, multilateral security structures (El-Doufani 1993, p. 107). Russia continued to demonstrate through its actions that the old days of Moscow's obstruction of Western policies and unilateral use of the military as a tool of its national security policy were at an end. The troops of the former Soviet army were steadily withdrawn from Eastern Germany, Central Europe and the newly independent Baltic states of Latvia, Lithuania and Estonia. In fact in December 1992 Yeltsin agreed to speed up the withdrawal of Russian forces from Germany by four months to meet a new deadline of 31 August 1994. At the same time, Russia pursued the strategy begun by

Gorbachev of reducing Moscow's commitments to former client states in the Third World such as Libya, Iraq and Angola, and embracing former enemies in the international arena. When Moscow hosted a round of the Arab–Israeli peace talks in January 1992 the Russians demonstrated a noticeably critical attitude towards the Palestinian position and a commensurate tolerance for the Israeli point of view. Similarly, Yeltsin was quick to invite the then President of South Africa, F.W. de Klerk, to Moscow, evidently to make amends for generations of Soviet opposition to that country's apartheid regime (El-Doufani 1993, p. 107).

During this period of intense cooperation with the West, the Russian government even indicated its intention of addressing the long-standing and bitter territorial dispute which had soured Moscow's relations with postwar Japan: the ownership of the Kurile Islands. The Soviet Union occupied the islands of Etorofu, Kunashiri, Shikotan and Habomai when Moscow entered the war against Japan in August 1945, and subsequently consistently refused to discuss Japan's claims for the return of the islands. Following the collapse of the USSR, Tokyo made it clear that the lack of a settlement in the Kurile Islands dispute was the chief obstacle to significant Japanese investment and financial support for Russia's transition to a market economy. The signals which the Russian government sent regarding the Kurile Islands were somewhat contradictory. On the one hand, Yeltsin, clearly playing to his audience during a tour of Russian provinces, declared that the islands would remain under Russian control. On the other hand, Russian Deputy Prime Minister Mikhail Poltoranin indicated during a visit to Japan in August 1992 that the Russian government was prepared to find a solution to the dispute which was acceptable to Tokyo, and that Yeltsin himself would put forward a proposal during his visit to the country the following month (Buszynski 1993, pp. 51–2).

But the 'diplomacy of smiles', as critics termed the pro-Western, conciliatory tendency in Russian foreign and national security policy, quickly came under fire at home. The abrupt reversal of Russia's apparent intention to return the Kurile Islands to Japan was one of the first indications of an imminent change in policy. Boris Yeltsin's planned visit to Japan and South Korea was cancelled only days before it was due to take place, with Russian officials citing 'domestic problems' as the reason for the cancellation. By the middle of 1993, Russian national security policy was undergoing a noticeable shift, as Moscow began moving away from enthusiasm for Western concepts and institutions and attempted instead to assert a more independent line on national security policy issues.

This shift in Russia's national security policy orientation can be attributed to two main factors. The first is the influence of domestic politics and, more importantly, the increase in the power and influence of more conservative factions and institutions in Russia since late 1992. Rapid inflation, a fall in production and general dislocation and uncertainty, which have been the results of Russia's transition to a market economy, created a conservative backlash on many fronts, including that of foreign and national security policy. The desire to return to the perceived economic stability of the Soviet era has been most prevalent among the older generation and others not well-equipped to prosper in the new, less forgiving environment. But even many of those who have benefited from the post-Soviet economic freedoms have been known to express nostalgia for the days when they were citizens of a superpower, which pursued its own independent policies in the international arena. With increasing popular support for political parties and groupings advocating more overtly pro-Russian, nationalist and assertive policies – demonstrated in part by the strong showing of Vladimir Zhirinovsk[i]y's Liberal Democratic Party in the December 1993 parliamentary elections – it is not surprising that the Yeltsin government has adopted some of its critics' positions on national security issues in order to deflect criticism at home. As Russian Foreign Minister Andrei Kozyrev explained, 'Russian foreign policy inevitably has to be of an independent and assertive nature. If Russian democrats fail to achieve it, they will be swept away by a wave of aggressive nationalism, which is now exploiting the need for national and state self-assertion' (Griffiths 1994, p. 713).

Kozyrev's belief in the danger posed to Russia's future by the 'red–brown coalition', a right-wing group of neocommunists and extreme nationalists, was dramatically illustrated at a meeting of the CSCE (subsequently known as OSCE) in Stockholm in December 1992. The Russian Foreign Minister, well known for his willingness to cooperate with Western policies, sent shock waves through the assembled foreign ministers by denouncing Western interference in the Baltic states, expressing Russia's intention to exercise hegemony over the other parts of the former Soviet Union, and pledging military support for the Serbian position in the conflict in the former Yugoslavia before storming out of the room. To the intense relief of his audience, Kozyrev soon returned to explain that he had been demonstrating the sort of line that Russia would be likely to take in its relations with other countries if the opposition to Yeltsin succeeded in gaining power (Adomeit 1995, p. 45).

The second main reason for the shift in Russia's national security policy stance is the failure of a cooperative, pro-Western position to bring tangible benefits in terms of aid, trade and investment. Russian disappointment in the slow and limited response of Western governments and companies is, to a large extent, a function of Moscow's unrealistically high expectations in late 1991 and early 1992. The major economic powers in North America and Western Europe were unlikely to provide large-scale economic aid to Russia in the early 1990s, suffering as they were from recessions and finding themselves in the process of implementing policies of economic stringency at home. In fairness to the Russians, however, it is important to remember the enthusiasm with which Western leaders greeted the collapse of communism in Eastern Europe, and their tendency to make rash promises about the material assistance they would provide to a democratic Russia. Western leaders promised $2.5 billion, then $24 billion in aid, but much of the foreign aid was linked to Russia's implementation of specific policies or was earmarked for purchasing goods from Western countries (de Nevers 1994, p. 12). But regardless of how the blame is apportioned, the result was growing Russian disillusion with the prospects of substantial help from the West, and a perception that Russia's acquiescence to the foreign policy priorities of Western countries was often taken for granted. These perceptions helped to weaken the position of those in the Russian government, such as Kozyrev, who favoured a pro-Western line.

As a result, in order to quieten critics at home and to ensure that the world's leaders once again heard Russia's voice, Moscow began to take steps to establish a more independent and a distinctly Russian stance on a number of issues. One of Russia's new policies in the area of national security which the leaders of the United States and Western Europe found most disturbing was the change in Moscow's position regarding the conflict in the former Yugoslavia. Whereas during 1992 Russia had supported the Western position of condemning and isolating the Serbs, in the following year Russia's policy became distinctly pro-Serbian. In February 1993 Kozyrev presented an eight-point peace plan which stressed sanctions against Croatia in response to Zagreb's attacks on Serb-controlled enclaves in that republic (Adomeit 1995, p. 46), and by April Russia had reversed its previous support for economic sanctions against Serbia. Moscow also strongly opposed the use of air strikes against the Bosnian Serbs, and in February 1994 announced an agreement with Serb leaders to send Russian peacekeepers to Sarajevo, making the use of military measures against Serb positions in Bosnia even more problematic (Marantz 1994, p. 739). From the point of view of Russian policymakers, the benefits of this shift were twofold. First, it demonstrated that Russia was willing to distance itself from a policy already well established by the Western powers; and second, it played to the sympathy which many Russians were feeling for their fellow Slavs the Serbs. In addition to the ties of ethnicity and religion, there has been a widespread perception in Russia that the Serb leaders, in attempting to extend protection to a diaspora and resist the spread of the pernicious influence of Islam, are performing a task which Russia's leaders themselves may one day face.

Russia's attitude towards the expansion of the North Atlantic Treaty Organization (NATO) eastwards has similarly undergone a significant change. Although during 1992 and the first half of 1993 the Russian position on this issue was rather vague, neither Yeltsin nor Kozyrev expressed the outright opposition to the addition of Central and Eastern European states to the Western alliance which appeared in late 1993 and which has continued, with varying degrees of intensity (Marantz 1994, p. 744). From Russia's point of view, the desire of NATO's leaders to expand their alliance right up to the borders of the former Soviet Union, and perhaps even to the borders of Russia itself (if the Baltic states and Ukraine were to be considered as potential members) indicates that, at the very least, NATO continues to distrust Russia and Russian motives.[1] As one official of the Russian Foreign Ministry put it, '...preserving NATO in its present form means that it needs an enemy to contain, and Russia is the *only* realistic candidate' (Sokov 1994, p. 920, emphasis in original). In spite of high-flown rhetoric about Russia and countries in North America and Western Europe becoming partners, it is clear that, where security issues are concerned, the latter view the new Russia as simply the old Soviet Union in a different guise. In clinging to their Cold War era alliance and seeking to stretch it to encompass even more of Europe, Western leaders are demonstrating just how slowly their perception of Russia as a potential enemy will change.

As a result, the compromise put forward by NATO in January 1994, Partnership for Peace, was given a cool reception by Russia's leaders. Membership in Partnership for Peace is open to all the former communist countries in Central and Eastern Europe, including the Soviet successor states, and provides for a range of cooperative activities on military matters. But although there is no promise of NATO membership included in the package, Russia was quick to condemn the programme as merely the first step in the expansion of the Western alliance (Marantz 1994, p. 744). For several months after the programme was announced, Russia's leaders made contradictory statements regarding Moscow's intention of joining, although Russia did agree to join, in June 1994, in return for a vaguely worded declaration of Russia's important role in international affairs (Marantz 1994, pp. 746–67).

Rather than an expansion of NATO which leaves Russia on the outside, or a Partnership for Peace, which in Moscow's eyes simply represents a delayed, two-stage process leading to the same result, Russia would prefer any future security alliance in Europe to be created and conducted under the auspices of a much larger, international or multinational organization, such as OSCE or the United Nations. Russia presented a proposal to make OSCE the basis for a new organization for collective security.[2] This sort of collective security arrangement would not only include Russia, it would permit Moscow to have a genuine opportunity to influence its policies and operation.

Another area of Russia's national security policy which has undergone a significant shift is Russia's relations with Third World states, which have improved substantially, although in almost every case on the basis of trade in weapons or defence-related technology. In late December 1992 the Russian President Boris Yeltsin travelled to Beijing to sign an arms trade agreement. The weapons which Russia has subsequently sold to China include missile guidance systems, surface-to-air missiles and fighter aircraft. During his first visit to India in January 1993, Yeltsin stressed Russia's Euro-Asian nature and stated Moscow's intention of continuing to provide India with cryogenic, or low-temperature, rocket technology, although the Russians later reversed that decision under pressure from Washington, which is concerned about the proliferation of long-range missile technology (Marantz 1994, p. 741). Russia has similarly found a market in Iran for the products of its military industry, and has so far resisted considerable American pressure to halt the sale of Russian submarines and nuclear reactors to Teheran (Marantz 1994, p. 741).[3] Furthermore, since late 1994 there have been indications that Russia intends to re-establish links with Iraq which were broken by Gorbachev's support for the Western anti-Saddam alliance during the Gulf War in 1990–91. In December 1994 Iraq's Vice Premier Tariq Aziz visited Moscow, and statements by Aziz and Russian

Foreign Minister Kozyrev following their meeting suggested that Russia would be taking up Iraq's plea to lift economic sanctions imposed by the United Nations against Baghdad.[4]

In what Western leaders view as an alarming feature of the more independent Russian national security stance, Russia's continued adherence to arms reduction treaties has come under question. Western concerns have been raised, first by the Russian parliament's delays in ratifying the START II agreement, but more importantly by the reservations which have been expressed by Russia's political leaders about the terms of the Conventional Forces in Europe (CFE) treaty. The return of Russian troops from Eastern Europe and the Baltic states and the redeployment of forces to areas of existing or potential instability threatens to put Russia in contravention of the limits set by the CFE agreement, and therefore in October 1993 Russia asked the other signatories to consider changes to some of the treaty's limitations. Although this request was denied, Russian officials have subsequently repeatedly raised the issue, and from early 1995 began to argue that Russia's involvement in the war in Chechnya prevented Moscow from reducing its troops and weapons in that area to the levels required by the CFE treaty (Lepingwell 1994, pp. 82–3).

THE 'NEAR ABROAD'

Initially Russia's relations with its closest neighbours, the 'near abroad', scarcely figured at all in the plans of policymakers in Moscow. One indication of this is the fact that it took the Russian Foreign Ministry six months to establish a department to deal with relations with the other former Soviet states. During the course of 1992, however, Russia's political leaders, in particular Foreign Minister Andrei Kozyrev, increasingly came under criticism for neglecting the near abroad. The decline of Russia's Atlanticist foreign and national security policy has been accompanied by the emergence of a consensus, encompassing virtually the entire political spectrum, supporting the exertion of some degree of Russian influence over the territory of the former Soviet Union.

The formal beginning of Russia's relations with its neighbours in the near abroad can be dated from 8 December 1991, when the leaders of the three Slavic republics, Russia, Ukraine and Belarus, met in Brest to declare the creation of a new association superseding the USSR: the

Commonwealth of Independent States (CIS). The original Slavic union was quickly expanded to include eleven out of the fifteen former Soviet states (all except Georgia, which joined in the autumn of 1993, and the Baltic states of Latvia, Lithuania and Estonia), and the establishment of an association of Soviet republics as sovereign states brought an end to any chance of approval of the Union Treaty, which Mikhail Gorbachev had hoped to achieve even after the August 1991 *coup* attempt, and which was intended to preserve the Soviet Union from further fragmentation.

But for an organization with such an historic beginning, the development of the CIS has been remarkably uneven, proceeding in fits and starts and hampered by widely differing conceptions of its purpose. From the very beginning there has been a divergence of Russian and Ukrainian views about the Commonwealth. Kiev has argued for a loosely organized association, purely to smooth the transition to true independence and, in the words of one analyst, to 'be no more than a temporary mechanism for "civilised divorce"' (Morrison 1993, p. 688). Moscow, however, has favoured a permanent and much more tightly integrated organization, and probably one in which Russia takes the lead. The Commonwealth has, as a result, suffered from a lack of consensus on most issues, with a number of member states routinely refusing to sign agreements which are intended to encompass the whole of the CIS. The 15 May 1992 Treaty on Collective Security is a case in point. Although it formally created a mutual defence treaty, more than one-third of the members of the CIS (Ukraine, Belarus, Moldova and Azerbaijan) have refused to participate in it (Kuiper 1993, p. 565). CIS agreements and relations have therefore had to be augmented on many issues by bilateral treaties, usually between Russia and one of the other former Soviet states. Early attempts were made to establish joint control over strategic forces in the Commonwealth, but they were shortlived. A CIS joint armed forces command was created and the last Soviet Minister of Defence, General Yevgeni Shaposhnikov, was appointed as its chief. Strategic nuclear forces were to be maintained under the CIS command, with any decision to use them to be taken by the four nuclear weapons states (Russia, Ukraine, Belarus and Kazakhstan), after consultation with the other members of the Commonwealth. Peacekeeping operations in the CIS were also to be placed under its control according to the provisions of a protocol signed at the Bishkek CIS summit in the autumn of 1992 (Shashenkov 1994, p. 53). But the existence of national armies in each of the CIS member states, together with the absence of strong commonwealth structures, created enormous difficulties for the operation of a joint command which effectively had no forces at its disposal. In June 1993 the CIS joint armed forces command was disbanded by Russia, which was by this time the sole *de jure* nuclear weapons state remaining in the commonwealth. This means that when the transfer of the former Soviet strategic nuclear weapons to Russia is completed, Moscow may, if it chooses, use these weapons for the defence of Russia, rather than for the provision of security for the entire CIS.

The most frequently cited justification for greater Russian influence in the near abroad is the need to protect the rights of ethnic Russians living outside the Russian Federation. The existence of approximately 25 million Russians in the other former Soviet states has become an emotional issue which many Russian politicians have been willing to exploit. In October 1992 Boris Yeltsin publicly criticized the Ministry of Foreign Affairs for failing to defend the rights of Russian minorities in the near abroad. An acknowledgement of this criticism was incorporated in the final draft of the Foreign Ministry's 'foreign policy concept' published in December 1992, which gave special emphasis to the observance of human and minority rights (Page 1994, pp. 799–800). Russia's military doctrine, formally adopted in November 1993, also stresses the importance of the rights of Russians outside Russia and asserts that the violation of such rights is a legitimate reason for military action.[5]

In the case of Russians living in the Central Asian states, the concern for minority rights is often combined with the fear of the emergence and spread of Islamic fundamentalism, although there is as yet no evidence for the existence of such a tendency within the former USSR. On the contrary, many of the indigenous peoples in this region tend to regard clan and regional loyalties as more important than religious affiliation. While ethnic Russians who live in Central Asia or the Caucasus are at risk from the general instabilities and conflict which occur in those areas, as, indeed, are the other inhabitants, there does not appear to be systemic abuse or denial of their rights. Similarly, in Moldova and the other Slavic states Russians are granted equal status under the law. The only examples of legally enshrined discrimination against ethnic Russians in the former Soviet Union are to be found in the citizenship and employment laws of Estonia and Latvia, which require those who live and work in those countries to demonstrate knowledge of the official language, although they provide for a gradual implementation over the course of several years (Melvin 1994, p. 23). Moscow's disapproval of these laws led to numerous threats of delays in the withdrawal of former Soviet forces from Latvia and Estonia, although in the end the operations were completed on time, by 31 August 1994.

In at least one case of Russia's military involvement in territorial disputes in the near abroad, the protection of the rights of ethnic Russians was the ostensible motive. A community of ethnic Russians in the Transdniestr region of Molodova sought to secede from Moldova, fearing that the leaders of that country intended integration with Romania, and conflict erupted between the 'Transdniestr Republic' and Moldovan forces in 1992. The former Soviet 14th Army, then stationed in the area, reportedly intervened on behalf of the Russian separatists, and by some accounts actively incited the Russians to rebel against Moldova's authority (de Nevers 1994, p. 54). The introduction of a CIS peacekeeping force composed of troops from the Russian, Moldovan and 14th Armies has since maintained a semblance of peace between the Moldovan authorities and the Russian community, although the continued presence of the 14th Army and its participation in the peacekeeping arrangements indicates that if violence erupts again the separatists could have a considerable advantage (Kuiper 1993, p. 567). The extent of Moscow's support for the actions of the 14th Army remains uncertain. One Russian analyst has suggested that initial support from the Russian leadership was quickly overtaken by the momentum of events in the region, and in particular by the forceful and charismatic leadership of the Army's commander General Aleksandr Lebed, who became the driving force behind the operation. Lebed gained the allegiance of troops and inhabitants of the region alike, and subsequently defied Yeltsin and the Russian government on a number of occasions.[6]

Russia has been heavily involved in peacekeeping in Tajikistan, where civil war has broken out between the supporters of the elected President, former Communist Party First Secretary in the Republic Rakhmon Nabiev, and opposition groups, including the Islamic Renaissance Party. Forces supporting the opposition have found refuge over the border in neighbouring Afghanistan, from which they are able make sorties and return to safety. The combination of factors present in this conflict epitomizes the threats to national security which Moscow sees in the near abroad: raging civil war practically on the borders of the Russian Federation; political and military opposition based on Islamic fundamentalism; threats to the safety of Russian minorities; and the involvement of countries outside the CIS. The Russian (former Soviet) forces stationed in Tajikistan reportedly remained neutral during the beginning of the civil war in 1992, but in July 1993 an attack on a Russian border guard post led to the formal decision by the Russian parliament to authorize a Russian division already based in the region to help in securing Tajikistan's borders against rebels based in Afghanistan. Although Uzbekistan has also contributed forces to the peacekeeping force in Tajikistan, formally under the auspices of the CIS, Russia is clearly playing the dominant role and is providing a significant amount of military and economic support for Nabiev's regime (Lepingwell 1994, pp. 77–8). In general the Russian philosophy of peacekeeping in the former Soviet Union emphasizes maintaining stability and defusing conflicts (Shashenkov 1994, p. 49), and is therefore closer in meaning to the Russian word which is used to describe it (*mirotvorchestvo* or 'peace creation') than to the definitions which are more widely accepted in the international community.

THE THREAT FROM WITHIN: CENTRIFUGAL FORCES

Policymakers in Moscow have become increasingly concerned about the threats to Russian national security which come from within the Russian Federation itself. There is a real prospect of the Russian Federation disintegrating into its constituent parts, much as the Soviet Union did, because of the existence of two tendencies, which often coexist and are mutually reinforcing: regionalism and ethnic nationalism.

The Russian Federation as it is currently geographically configured is not simply the old, pre-Soviet Russia recreated. The Tsarist Empire was much larger, encompassing parts of what are now other former Soviet states (Stern 1994, p. 42). Indeed, it is necessary to go back in history several hundred years to find a Russian state covering approximately the same territory as its present-day counterpart. As a result, there is a large degree of confusion and uncertainty among citizens and policymakers alike about where Russia's borders should be. Moreover, the Russian Federation is a complex mixture of more than 70 administratively and ethnically defined provinces, territories, republics and areas, with differing rights and legal status (Stern 1994, pp. 46–9). Just as authorities in the USSR's constituent republics began to take greater control over the affairs of their own areas during the late 1980s, a similar process began within Russia following the collapse of Soviet power. Many regional authorities, responsible now to the local electorate and not to central organs as during the Soviet period, are primarily concerned with local factors. They tend to view the policies announced in Moscow as irrelevant, and, increasingly, simply ignore them (Szajkowski 1993, p. 173). While an estimated 25 million Russians live in the other states of the former Soviet Union, approximately 30 million non-Russians live within the Russian Federation, which has a total population of 150 million. These non-Russian citizens of the Russian Federation represent over 100 ethnic groups, and four religions (Stern 1994, p. 47). The consciousness of their ethnic identities was fostered during the Soviet period by policies which promoted the preservation of national cultures and languages, created administrative divisions along ethnic or national lines, and gave ethnic groups preferential treatment in their own regions in terms of education, employment and advancement within local party structures (Stern 1994, pp. 50–51). As a result, many regions are dominated by one or another ethnic group, and the process of greater regional autonomy reinforces and is reinforced by aspirations for national separatism.

Several such regions have declared themselves independent of Moscow's rule, and enjoy varying degrees of autonomy. At least eleven republics, including Bashkortostan, Tatarstan, Ingushetia and Chechnya, have passed constitutions or major laws which declare the primacy of local laws over federal ones (Stern 1994, p. 57). Since the spring of 1992 the leadership of Bashkortostan has been involved in a serious dispute with the Russian Federation over economic relations, including the retention of the republic's natural resources and industrial output. Tatarstan declared its sovereignty in 1990, while the USSR was still in existence, and this declaration was overwhelmingly upheld in a referendum held in March 1992. The republic has subsequently conducted relations directly with other states, with President Mintimer Shaimiev signing an economic cooperation agreement with Hungary during a visit to Budapest in May 1993 (Szajkowski 1993, p. 174). The case of Chechnya is the best-known example of regional autonomy combined with separatism threatening the territorial integrity of the Russian Federation. Chechnya declared its independence from the Federation in the autumn of 1991, under the leadership of its elected President Dzhokhar Dudayev. The combination of the region's assertion of sovereignty, its strategic location and the fact that the region became a headquarters for organized crime made Chechnya a particular challenge to Russian national security. The reasons for the timing of Moscow's decision to use the armed forces against the Chechen leadership are still unclear, but sometime in late 1994 Russian policymakers evidently decided to tolerate Dudayev's defiance no longer. From at least November Russia's Federal Counterintelligence Service was hiring Russian servicemen to strengthen the internal resistance to Dudayev,[7] and military operations against Chechnya formally began on 11 December.

Russia's experience in the Chechen conflict has been mixed. On the one hand, the operation was badly planned and poorly executed, revealing serious shortcomings in the army and raising questions about the ability of the Russian armed forces to defend the country against threats to its national security. Russia's military involvement in Chechnya was widely opposed, both within the military leadership and among the population, who were horrified at the massive use of force against their fellow citizens. On the other hand, however, within a few months after the start of the conflict, the Russian army had evidently gained control of at least large portions of the region, with Chechen resistance dispersed to sparsely populated, mountainous areas. Although Boris Yeltsin's popularity plummeted as a result of the war, public outrage did not result in the fall of the Russian government or the resignation of senior political figures – or indeed, in bringing military operations in the region to a halt.

CONCLUSIONS

Since the collapse of the Soviet Union, Russian national security policy has moved away from its initial exclusively pro-Western orientation. This shift is the result of a complex mixture of factors, including the failure of a pro-Western policy to bring tangible political and economic benefits, which has strengthened the position of those Russian politicians and institutions favouring a more assertive stance. At the same time, Moscow's attention has increasingly been focused on national security issues close to home. Ethnic, territorial and political disputes within the former Soviet Union are sources of instability close to Russia's borders. Concern about these threats to Russia's national security has been combined with the emotional issue of the treatment of Russian minorities in other parts of the former Soviet Union and has created a powerful incentive for Moscow to use its position as the dominant political, economic and military power in the region in support of stability. The imposition of order on Russia's terms and by Russia's definition, especially through the use of the Russian armed forces as 'peacekeepers', however, could itself easily become a source of instability.

Russian national security policy by the mid-1990s presents a very mixed picture. The stance towards which Moscow has been moving is not a uniformly or irreversibly anti-Western one. Cooperation with Western governments and international organizations is continuing in a number of areas. But at the same time Russia has demonstrated an increasing willingness to use the military as a policy tool, both in the near abroad and within the borders of the Russian Federation against the separatist movement in Chechnya. The extent to which Moscow judges the Chechen operation to have been successful may determine whether it marks the beginning of a more aggressive phase in Russia's national security policy.

NOTES

1. 'What I would take to NATO', *Moskovskie Novosti*, 24, 12–19 June 1994.
2. 'Russia and NATO: Dangerous Games in a Verbal Mist', *Moscow News*, 13, 7–13 April 1995.
3. 'Kozyrev warns of Chill with US as Geneva Talks Fail', *The Times*, 24 March 1995.
4. 'Kozyrev, Aziz Discuss Lifting Sanctions', *Moscow News*, 50, 16–22 December 1994.
5. 'Fundamental Tenets of the Military Doctrine of the Russian Federation', *Krasnaya Zvezda*, 19 November 1993.
6. Personal interview with Nodari Simonia, Deputy Director of the Institute of World Economy and International Relations, Moscow, 10 April 1995.
7. 'Lubyanka hired servicemen for secret operations in Chechnya', *Izvestiya*, 2 December 1994.

3. Culture and conflict in the post-Cold War world

Alan Macmillan*

INTRODUCTION

Culture, hitherto a byword in the subject of International Relations,[1] is fast becoming a buzzword. Its progress from a 'forgotten' to a conspicuous variable, indicated by the increasing frequency with which reference is made to it in the literature of, and conferences on, International Relations,[2] accords with a 'turn to culture' which some (for example, Robertson 1992, especially pp. 32–48; Chaney 1994) have observed in the human sciences as a whole. Both Robertson (1992, p. 32) and Chaney (1994, p. 182) see this cultural turn as bound up with the condition of postmodernity. Postmodern attitudes, which stress plurality and particularities, as opposed to universalities, encourage the celebration of differences in the beliefs and values of local cultural units.

There are other, related, intellectual currents affecting both the human sciences and International Relations which have helped to turn the tide culture's way. Culture has been described (Walker 1990, p. 4) as 'one of the two or three most complicated words in the English language'. Difficult to define and to operationalize, culture is a nebulous concept representing 'everything that good, positivistically trained international relations specialists should hate' (Rengger 1992, p. 85). However, at a time when new perspectives on international theory are challenging positivist assumptions, the slippery concept of culture has more chance of flourishing. In addition, the breaking down of boundaries between disciplines advances the cause of culture within Interna-

*The author would like to thank Tammy Duffey of the University of Bradford, UK for bringing to his attention the work done on culture within the field of conflict resolution, and for passing on to him much relevant material on that subject.

57

tional Relations. In the past, for instance, the division of labour between International Relations and Sociology may have led to 'the neglect of national cultures, identities and traditions' in the former (Robertson 1992, p. 5). That situation is now changing, as International Relations scholars take more notice of the concerns of sociology and other disciplines such as Anthropology, in which culture is a key variable. The analysis of cultures is also consistent with critiques of the neorealist approach to International Relations, which oppose the 'black-boxing' of states, and endorse investigation of how their internal workings affect their external relations. Finally, international theory is growing more aware of its own cultural roots and biases, and so is becoming more sensitive to cultural differences (Booth 1995b, p. 333).

If recent trends in international theory are conducive to the study of culture, changes in the post-Cold War world demand that it be afforded greater emphasis. The ending of the Cold War presents us with a more fragmented world. All sorts of peoples in far-away places, about whom we previously knew little, have moved from the periphery to centre-stage in world politics. With power more diffused following the break-down of bipolar confrontation, Iraq has the freedom to act on its own initiative, where in the past it would have been wary of defying the superpowers (see Booth 1991b, p. xiii). Accounting for the behaviour of Iraqis, Serbs, Kurds, Chechens, and a host of others takes on new importance and entails understanding their culturally moulded values and beliefs.

In the context of changes in the state of the world and of international theory, the concept of culture has been applied in various fields of International Relations. This chapter focuses on the developing study of the relationship between culture and conflict. It begins by discussing Samuel Huntington's (1993a) controversial recent article, 'The Clash of Civilizations?'. Appearing in *Foreign Affairs*, than which there is no more mainstream journal of foreign policy studies, it is an influential piece which has further raised the profile of culture in International Relations and associated it with a distinctive line of argument. Huntington sees civilizations, defined as groups of states and peoples united by common cultural outlooks, as the main actors in future international relations. Conflict in the post-Cold War world will most likely occur over the incompatible values held by each civilization.

Culture has also begun to intrude into those sub-fields of International Relations more directly concerned with the study of conflict. The concept of strategic culture has put cultural analysis on to the agenda of

Strategic Studies, while scholars of Conflict Resolution are also bringing considerations of culture into their calculations. In each case the concern is with the beliefs and values of different cultural groupings with regard to conflict and violence, and how these beliefs and values affect the group's behaviour in the realm of conflict. The role of culture within each field is surveyed briefly before consideration, in the conclusion, of whether culture is indeed becoming a crucial variable in the study of conflict, either as it is used within Strategic Studies and Conflict Resolution, or by Huntington, with whom we begin.

CULTURE AND CIVILIZATIONS

Huntington's thesis (1993a and 1993b) is that International Relations needs a new paradigm to explain and predict conflict in the post-Cold War world. Until the end of the First World War conflict resulted from princes or nation-states seeking to expand their wealth and territories. From 1919, liberal democratic, communist and fascist states waged ideological conflict. Since 1989, however, we have moved to a new phase in the evolution of conflict. In this phase states will continue to be important, but Huntington, borrowing from, amongst others, Arnold Toynbee (1972, p. 15), regards them as 'fragments of something larger: a civilization'. This is 'the highest cultural grouping of people and the broadest level of cultural identity people have short of that which distinguishes humans from other species' (Huntington 1993a, pp. 22–4). Huntington identifies Western, Japanese, African, Latin American, Confucian, Hindu, Islamic and Slavic–Orthodox civilisations. Internally united, these groupings are divided among themselves by their incompatible beliefs and values on such fundamental matters as human rights, democracy, liberalism, free markets, individualism and the relationship between church and state.

   That the world can meaningfully be divided in this way does not make conflict between its units inevitable. As Huntington acknowledges, 'differences do not necessarily mean conflict, and conflict does not necessarily mean violence' (1993a, p. 25). Yet the question mark at the end of his title adds virtually the only crumb of comfort to an otherwise deeply pessimistic piece. Huntington advances a number of reasons which he believes make violent intercivilizational conflict probable. The differences between civilizations on the issues noted above are both 'real' and 'basic', he writes, and deeper than those between rival regimes or ideologies. The product of centuries, culturally shaped beliefs are harder to change or to reach compromise over than mere political or economic ones. Moreover, history shows that such cultural differences generate 'the most prolonged and the most violent conflicts' (1993a, pp. 25–7).

Recent changes in the world further increase the risk of clashes between civilizations. Increased economic regionalism results from, and also raises, civilizational consciousness, while greater interaction between peoples makes them more aware of 'differences between ... and commonalities within civilizations' and 'invigorates differences and animosities stretching or thought to stretch back deep into history'. Finally, the resurgence of religion and the growth of fundamentalism unite civilizations internally and widen the gulf between them (1993a, pp. 25–7). Huntington concludes that 'in the coming years, the local conflicts most likely to escalate into major wars will be those, as in Bosnia and the Caucasus, along the fault lines between civilizations. The next world war, if there is one, will be a war between civilizations' (1993a, pp. 38–9). In the meantime, the battle lines are already being drawn for the next war. In Europe, for example, the 'Velvet Curtain of culture has replaced the Iron Curtain of ideology as the most significant dividing line' (1993a, pp. 30–31).

As evidence of intercivilizational conflict, Huntington cites the tragedy of the former Yugoslavia. The current Balkan conflict is the result of the accident which placed representatives of different civilizations within the same state. In such circumstances violent conflict is likely. Legislation in Germany to reduce refugee intake, fighting between Russian troops and Mujaheddin guerrillas, even the voting 'along civilizational lines' to award the 2000 Olympics to Sydney rather than Beijing; all these events and many others 'fit the civilizational paradigm and might have been predicted from it' (1993b, pp. 188–9). There is also evidence that peoples within the different civilizations see themselves as engaged in such conflicts already. So, Islam faults the West for failing to aid Muslims in Bosnia while confronting Saddam Hussein in the Gulf War. Meanwhile NATO has begun to turn its attention to threats from the south. And those involved in conflicts try to rally support for their cause among members of their own civilization, as Saddam tried to characterize the Gulf War as an attack by the West on Islam.

For the West, now at the peak of its power, all this amounts to a serious threat. Previously major conflict has taken place between units within Western civilization, so that even the Cold War may be seen as a 'civil war'. Now, other civilizations will take part in international relations along with the West, not as the objects but as the 'movers and shapers of history' (Huntington 1993a, p. 23). They are rejecting Western values and returning to indigenous ones, in a process of 'cultural decolonization'.[3] They will challenge the values and interests which the West promotes as universal and to which it assigns global legitimacy through its domination of international institutions. Violence could break out. Huntington's prescription for the West is that it should endeavour to maintain its advantage in the short term, promoting internal unity and seeking allies from other civilizations, such as Japan and Russia. It should exploit the internal differences of competitor civilizations and limit their military expansion. In the longer term it may be necessary to accommodate other civilizations, to pursue profounder understanding of their beliefs and values, to identify areas of commonality: to learn to coexist.

Huntington's article has provoked criticism on various grounds (Ajami 1993; Bartley 1993; Binyan 1993; Joffe 1994; Kirkpatrick et al. 1993; Mahbubani 1993; Muzaffar 1994; O'Hagan 1995; Tarock 1995; Walcott 1993). Most pertinently, its novelty has been questioned (Rubenstein and Crocker 1994, p. 115; O'Hagan 1995). What Huntington refers to as the Cold War paradigm of world politics will be recognized by students of International Relations as largely synonymous with the realist approach which has for much of the postwar period dominated their discipline. Huntington modifies realism by taking civilizations rather than states to be the main actors in the international system and culture rather than 'interest defined in terms of power' as their main motivator. But just as realists see states, either through flawed human nature or the anarchical self-help nature of the international system, struggling for relative power, so too Huntington's civilizations seem trapped in a self-help world, forced to compete for power, unable to live in harmony, though perhaps able to coexist. Much of the language and tone of Huntington's article suggests continuity rather than a break with the past: the velvet curtain replaces the iron curtain; competition, and at best coexistence, at worst war, are unavoidable; and the West should contain other civilizations. 'The Clash of Civilizations?' looks back to the future. It is an X-Article for the 1990s, a warning to the West of the dangers to be faced, this time from multiple sources rather than monolithic communism.

By offering not a new paradigm but a modified version of political realism, Huntington is caught in a critical crossfire between realists who would stick to their guns and longstanding opponents of realism. One line of attack focuses on the units he identifies. Are civilizations really 'meaningful entities'? Critics point to the lack of unity and consensus within Huntington's civilizations. For instance, Walcott (1993) cites the Dalai Lama's condemnation of Chinese human rights beliefs as evidence of a lack of consensus on basic values within the Confucian civilization. Europeans and North Americans disagree with each other, nor is there yet a common European identity. Does it make sense to talk about the West, Islam, or Africa, as cohesive groups or monolithic political actors? Does the attempt to do so invite reliance on stereotypes and risk essentialism? Is there not considerable overlap between civilizations? Huntington scarcely investigates the cohesion of his civilizations, tending to reify them in the same way that realists reified states.

Even to the extent that civilizations are meaningful entities, are they the most important actors in the world? For realists, the state remains the most meaningful entity in world politics: states control civilizations rather than the reverse (Ajami 1993, p. 9). For others, the end of the Cold War opens up space for people to develop all sorts of identities other than civilizational ones (see Zalewski and Enloe 1995, especially p. 279). There are ethnic identities to consider at levels below the state or nation. Gender, sexuality and environmentalism link people across nations and civilizations. Even with conflict specifically in mind, it is far from certain that the civilization is the most appropriate unit to study. Critics (for instance, Joffe 1994) point to the conflicts occurring within civilizations. What about Iraq's wars with Iran and Kuwait, or the conflicts in Rwanda and Burundi? Huntington selectively instances conflicts which appear to support his thesis. Civil wars, wars between states from the same civilization, domestic and structural violence can all be identified as more pressing threats than intercivilizational conflicts. Inevitably Huntington's 'new' paradigm simplifies the world. But in omitting cultures and identities at levels below the civilizational which will be crucial sources of politics and conflict, he is guilty of massive oversimplification. The post-Cold War world looks like being far too complex to reduce to a simple theory.

A further question asked of Huntington is whether cultural incompatibility is a cause of whatever conflict there is between civilizations. In suggesting that conflict since 1919 has been generated by ideology, Huntington in fact departs somewhat from the realist model, in which ideologies were less a cause of conflict than a means of rationalizing and justifying the pursuit of power, of concealing it and making it 'psychologically and morally acceptable'; though ideologies could also be 'the ultimate objectives for the realization of which political power is sought' (Morgenthau and Thompson 1985, pp. 5 and 101–3). So Huntington is charged with overestimating the importance of cultural values by realists, for whom the war in the former Yugoslavia can be read as a dispute over power in which 'grand civilizational undertakings' are mere camouflage (Ajami 1993, p. 7). Culture can therefore be seen as a cloak for the pursuit of power, and international relations can continue to be seen as concerned with states maximizing power, but now using culture to legitimize the activity.

Other critics (Rubenstein and Crocker 1994) articulate a related critique. Asking why conflict between civilizations should occur, they argue that cultural differences alone are insufficient to explain conflict. The cause of conflict is not that others are different, but that others come to be seen as a threat. If peoples feel that 'their identities, liberties, and livelihoods are seriously and immediately threatened by powerful, culturally distinct outsiders', then conflict is likely (Rubenstein and Crocker 1994, pp. 114 and 125–6). If 'the West' faces a challenge by 'the rest' it is not because it is different to them but because it seems to deny their basic human needs. The problem is not that there is a clash of civilizations, but that there is a system of 'global apartheid' in which rich white people oppress poor others (see Richmond 1994). Emphasizing a clash between civilizations with incompatible value systems, about which little can, in Huntington's view, be done, not only misses the point, but distracts attention from the serious social, political and economic causes of conflict, about which much more could be done (see Esposito 1992, p. 179). What is important here is the politics of culture, the manipulation of ideas about culture to justify the maintenance of the status quo (see Lawson 1995, pp. 13–15).

Huntington's paradigm therefore fails to deal adequately with the question of *why* conflict takes place. Neither does it fully address the issue of *whether* conflict must occur. Huntington, sharing the realist assumption that conflict is inevitable, ignores other international theories which stress the potential for cooperation between peoples. The international society approach to International Relations sees a society of states, linked by shared values, norms and institutions, with the potential to live and interact together peacefully, regardless of differences in their internal make-up (see Jackson 1995). Theories of global society or world community argue further that as individuals we can and do perceive commonalities with other people everywhere, and that the forces of globalization can and do foster a global consciousness and the development of a world community or culture (see for instance Brown 1995; Scholte 1993; Shaw 1994). Particularistic loyalties need not disappear, but may continue to exist alongside global ones. Local differences within global limits are possible (Booth 1995b, p. 342). International society and world community theorists therefore emphasize what unites civilizations, states and peoples. Viewed from the perspective of an international society theorist, for example, the Gulf War provides evidence not for the clash of civilizations, as it does for Huntington, but for the existence of an international society. The near global condemnation of Saddam shows that all states agree with the United Nations Charter position that it is wrong to use force against the territorial integrity of another state (see Jackson 1995).

Different theories of International Relations thus take different positions on the question of whether conflict and violence will occur. It may be, finally, that the answer to that question depends in some measure on which theory gains widest acceptance. A criticism of realism is that it did not merely describe the Cold War world, but also helped to construct that world and to legitimize a hostile US policy towards the Soviet Union (see Tarock 1995, p. 5; Wendt 1992). The danger is that Huntington is doing for the post-Cold War world what realism did after 1945. His professed aim is 'to set forth descriptive hypotheses as to what the future may be like' (1993a, p. 48). But his hypotheses ignore contradictory evidence and are based on events capable, like the Gulf War, of alternative interpretation by traditional realists, international society theorists and others. The danger is that this leads to a self-fulfilling prophecy (Rubenstein and Crocker 1994, p. 128). If we believe ourselves to be part of a meaningful entity called 'the West' (which may itself be a cultural construction) and, buying into a theory of the inevitable clash of civilizations, undertake actions to secure its position relative to others, it may well fuel their insecurity. If we support undemocratic governments against fundamentalist Islamic groups, as we supported them against communists in the Cold War; if we use force against Arabs in Iraq but not whites in Yugoslavia; then we shall encourage Muslims to denigrate 'the West', further confirming the clash of civilizations thesis, and returning us to Cold War security dilemmas.

Rather than digging in for the inevitable clash of civilizations, we might be trying to avert it and seeking ways 'in which cultures might meet in a creative dialogue about future possibilities' (Walker 1984, pp. 2–3). Rather than searching history for evidence of civilizational conflict, we could be focusing on the constructive interactions between civilizations in the past (Muzaffar 1994, p. 25). Rather than accepting that increased interaction between civilizations raises consciousness of difference, we could ask whether it shows commonalities across civilizational boundaries. If we don't accept the inevitable as inevitable, we don't have to bow to it.

CULTURE AND STRATEGY

Whether conflict occurs may then be decided in part by the theories people hold about its inevitability. Such theories can vary across cultures, as can beliefs and values regarding the utility and desirability of the use of force. In his recent book *A History of Warfare* (1994), John Keegan offers an illustration of such variation. Keegan interprets the Gulf War not so much as a clash of civilizations but 'as a clash of two quite different military cultures'. Each of these cultures has deep historical roots and is shaped by the broader cultural setting in which it has developed. The West, drawing on Clausewitz, emphasizes directness in the attainment through military means of political objectives. In so doing it believed that it had thoroughly defeated Saddam Hussein in the Gulf War. Saddam, however, did not accept that he had been comprehensively beaten. Instead he had 'recourse to a familiar Islamic rhetoric that denied he had been defeated in spirit', and so the West's victory lost its political point. This was, Keegan argues, 'a striking exemplification of the inutility of the "Western way of warfare" when confronted by an opponent who refuses to share its cultural assumptions' (1994, p. xi).

What Keegan refers to as military culture is increasingly being investigated within Strategic Studies under the heading 'strategic culture'. Operating at the level of nations and states rather than civilizations, advocates of the study of strategic culture propose that the distinctive strategic and political development of a state within its particular geographical setting will shape unique 'traditions, values, attitudes, patterns of behaviour, habits, symbols, achievements and particular ways of adapting to the environment and solving problems with respect to the threat or use of force' (Booth 1990, p. 121). The values, attitudes and so on which constitute a state's strategic culture will influence, though not necessarily determine, its strategic behaviour.

That different nations should develop distinctive beliefs about the use of force is not a new idea. Indeed, it is suggested by the ancient military principle 'know your enemy'. However, this principle seemed to have been forgotten by many exponents of Strategic Studies until Jack Snyder (1977) coined the term 'strategic culture'. Hitherto many strategists in the United States had assumed that their counterparts in the Soviet Union would share their views on nuclear strategy. They assumed that there existed a universal strategic rationality, that 'any player who had his wits about him' would act in the same way when developing nuclear strategy (Snyder 1990, p. 3). Snyder questioned this assumption, asking whether the distinct political and strategic experience and development of the Soviet Union and the United States might have led them to quite different beliefs about the use of force. United States nuclear strategy, he argued, would have to take account of Soviet strategic cultural beliefs if it was not to be flawed, perhaps fatally.

Snyder's phrase gave focus to writers who shared the concern that an ahistorical and acultural Strategic Studies was problematic. Many have taken up the study of strategic culture. Some, like Colin Gray (1986), operate within the tradition of Strategic Studies, characterized by Bernard Brodie as the how-to-do-it guide. Gray argues that US policy towards the Soviet Union must be informed by an understanding of each state's strategic culture. If Gray challenges the black-boxing of states and asserts the importance of cultural beliefs and values, he does not question the inevitability of conflict between states in an anarchic system. Other analysts (Booth 1990; Booth and Macmillan 1994a and 1994b), however, have used strategic culture in a rather different way. They do question the inevitability of conflict and war. As well as looking at how cultures make war, they also examine beliefs affecting why, when and whether they fight. The beliefs of different cultures about the nature of security, the utility of force, the nature of the international system and international relations all influence their conflict behaviour, it is claimed. Conflict, violence and war can therefore be seen not as inevitable but as cultural phenomena or learned behaviour, opening up the prospect of further cultural change in the direction of peaceful strategic cultures, or pacific cultures. The study of strategic culture therefore becomes not a how-to-do-it but a how-to-avoid-it guide. At the very least, sensitivity to the peculiar security concerns of different groups can avoid conflicts and security dilemmas based on misunderstanding and misperception and assist in the building of trust and security communities.

CULTURE AND CONFLICT RESOLUTION

Conflict is studied not only within Strategic Studies, of course, but also in the fields of Conflict Resolution and Peace Research, which stem from quite separate traditions and have, during the Cold War, had little contact with Strategic Studies (see Dunn 1991). Interestingly, culture is increasingly becoming a concern of Conflict Resolution as well as Strategic Studies. Cultural anthropologists Avruch and Black (1991) in particular have opened up 'the culture question' to serious discussion. As Jack Snyder questioned the existence of a generic strategic man, so Avruch and Black are reacting against the search for a culture-free, generic theory of Conflict Resolution. They reject both the views that conflict behaviour exhibits 'invariant features that will allow universal (acultural) prescriptions for its management or resolution', and that it is 'essentially idiosyncratic ... with no comparable significant features from one case to the next'. They focus their attention instead on middle-range explanations, where they look for regularity in conflict behaviour among groups, short of all of humanity. And in this range, they see the culture question as among 'the two or three most important questions facing conflict resolution theory' (Avruch and Black 1991, pp. 22–6).

Conflict occurs everywhere, but there is considerable variation in how much conflict occurs in different societies and how it is dealt with. Cultural differences play a part in explaining this. The culture of a group 'consists of both explicit rules, beliefs, values and symbols, and implicit, unrecognized sets of meanings, metaphors, stories, and discourses through which experience is interpreted and which are unconsciously reproduced as part of social life' (cited by Duffey 1994, p. 4). Within Conflict Resolution the referent group may be a pre-industrial society or a modern nation or ethnic group, and its rules, beliefs, values and so on regarding conflict are of importance in understanding and resolving it. Groups develop their own understandings of, and assign their own meaning to, conflict, and they develop different negotiating and bargaining styles and approaches to resolving conflict. Some cultures have developed more effective means of dealing with conflict, such as the Norwegians, who are said to seek to avoid conflict situations or develop non-violent responses to conflict. Those with less effective means of handling conflict could well learn from studying them (see Ross 1993, especially pp. xi–xii, 161–4).

Cross-cultural learning is therefore one reason to study conflict within different cultures. Another reason is that conflict between groups who hold different views of what it means may be particularly intractable, especially as ways of resolving conflict, perhaps based on understandings of it, may also differ. In his work on the Egyptian–Israeli conflict, Raymond Cohen (1990) argues that a mutual lack of cultural understanding prolonged the conflict between these states and hindered the search for solutions. Therefore those who would intervene to resolve conflicts will need to try to see the conflict as the parties involved do if they are to promote its resolution. They cannot simply apply theories of conflict resolution assumed to have universal validity. Very often, as with strategic theories, supposedly universal theories turn out to be rooted in particular Western beliefs and values, for Conflict Resolution has in common with Strategic Studies its 'Western' intellectual origins (see Duffey 1994, p. 1).

Cultural analysis has a number of adherents, but in neither Strategic Studies nor Conflict Resolution has it established itself firmly. Avruch and Black's (1991, p. 26) comment of Conflict Resolution that 'there are strong indications in the still-sparse literature that culture *matters* in some way that has yet to be precisely determined' echoes Colin Gray's (1986, p. xii) remark that scholars of strategic culture know it is important, 'but they are not sure *how* important'. Much work remains to be done to give 'empirical flesh and theoretical shine' to cultural studies (see Booth 1990, p. 126). Within both Conflict Resolution and Strategic Studies there is an awareness among scholars working on cultural analysis of its inherent complexities and difficulties (see for instance Avruch and Black 1991, pp. 41–2; Gray 1986, p. 35). Within each there are passionate critiques of cultural analysis (see for instance Snyder 1990; Zartman 1993). But within each, there is also a sense among advocates that it is too important to be ignored and that it represents 'a set of ideas ... whose intellectual time [has] finally come' (see Booth 1990, p. 122). No one claims that understanding culture alone is sufficient in the analysis of conflict. It is, however, regarded as necessary.

CONCLUSION

The work being done on conflict as part of a cultural turn in International Relations sees culture as a cause of conflict, and as an important consideration for understanding conflicts, prosecuting them efficiently, resolving and avoiding them. Samuel Huntington's promotion of culture as a key concept is commendable but his use of it is unsatisfactory.

Huntington seeks a parsimonious theory to explain conflict in the post-Cold War world. But the theory he produces at best explains only certain world events while claiming to explain many, and forces other events into an inappropriate conceptual straitjacket. It constructs and legitimizes while purporting to describe. Parsimony is no virtue in a theory if it denies the complexity of the world. Understanding culture is important, but it is important at all levels, not just the civilizational, and it needs to avoid stereotypes and artificial constructions. It is necessary not just to assume the inevitability of conflict and violence, but to look at evidence of cooperation, and also to seek to understand the social, political and economic causes of conflict and violence. Huntington fails to do so.

For some, Huntington's article has already enjoyed much more publicity than it deserves (see Lawson 1995, p. 13). Yet Huntington is a well-known and respected academic, writing in a journal at the heart of the American foreign policy process. That his theory simplifies the world to a distorting extent does not mean it will not win the favour of peoples and politicians. If 'The Clash of Civilizations?' indeed resembles George Kennan's X-Article, it is worth recalling the impact of that earlier *Foreign Affairs* essay. In his memoirs, Kennan (1967, pp. 294–5 and 356) records his own surprise at the sensational effect of both his famous long telegram and the X-Article in the United States, galvanizing opposition to the Soviet Union and heating up the Cold War. 'More important', Kennan observes, 'than the observable nature of external reality, is the subjective state of readiness on the part of Washington officialdom to recognize this or that feature of it.' Huntington provides a way of looking at the world which appears to explain some of its novel features within a familiar framework – a continuation of the Cold War with a new enemy. This could well strike a chord with policymakers in the United States, and then Huntington's clash of civilizations could come closer to realization.

This essay was written shortly after the Oklahoma City car bomb which destroyed a government building, claimed many lives, and which simultaneously exploded the myth of the invulnerability of the United States. With the trial of Muslims accused of bombing the World Trade Center in New York underway, and immediate reports of 'Middle East' suspects in the Oklahoma case, it briefly appeared that conditions were ripe for the clash of civilizations to grip the imagination of middle America and shape how politicians in the United States viewed the world. Had Muslims indeed been responsible, and had links between the bombers and any particular Middle East state been uncovered re-taliatory military action would have been hard for President Clinton to resist, even if he had wanted to. That in turn would have provided further evidence to Muslims of the hostility of 'the West'. In this respect it is fortunate that the perpetrators appear to have been home-grown. Muslim commentators noted nonetheless how quickly 'Islamic terrorists' were suspected, and how, once they were cleared, the word 'terrorism' was replaced with 'political violence'. Moreover, where an attack by Muslims would have been portrayed by some as an act of terror in a war of civilizations between 'Islam' and 'the West', an attack by white US citizens was an outrage committed by a few madmen. Indigenous bombers are characterized as alien to the culture of the United States, while Muslim bombers would have been representatives of their culture.

It is all too easy to see how the clash of civilizations thesis could take root and how self-fulfilling it could become. Moreover, the United States could offer particularly fertile soil for this thesis, and for cultural reasons. Observers point to repressive tendencies within the culture of the United States, to an 'intolerance of difference' and a 'propensity to perceive every challenge as a Manichean clash of civilizations' (Hughes 1994, p. 44; Walcott 1993, p. 7). Walcott notes that 'militant Islam and the workaholic Orient' easily replace communism as the new global threat, and Robert Hughes vividly conveys how this process can work. For Hughes, the Gulf War is the climax of the United States' 'long-implanted habit of hostile ignorance about the Arab World'. The media portrayed Muslims and Arabs as 'basically a bunch of volatile religious maniacs, hostage-takers, sons of thornbush and dune whose whole past disposed them against intercourse with more civilized states' (1994, p. 84). Little indication was given of past and present diversity within Islam which might puncture the stereotypes. 'The Clash of Civiliza-tions?' could well be a product of one element of the culture of the United States and could well find adherents there. It is therefore neces-sary to challenge Huntington's thesis.

Clashes between civilizations and other cultural units will surely occur in the post-Cold War world. What form such conflicts take, however, and whether they are resolved peacefully or violently, de-pends in part on the values and beliefs of these groups regarding the use of force and resolution of conflict. The study of conflict as cultural behaviour, taken up within Strategic Studies and Conflict Resolution, cannot alone answer all our questions, but it does offer hope of better understanding of conflict and security and some prospect of avoiding war or resolving conflicts peacefully. It may be that in the post-Cold War world the study of culture has come of age, as conflict between all sorts of cultures becomes possible, and further proliferation of nuclear weapons and ballistic missiles increases the dangers of such conflict. This belief informs recent work on the Asia–Pacific region which tries to link culture and conflict, and to explore how peace can be achieved in a potentially dangerous area.[4] Within Strategic Studies and Conflict Resolution, culture looks set to play an increasingly active part.

That both Strategic Studies and Conflict Resolution, still largely isolated from one another, have around the same time and for some similar reasons begun to consider cultural questions, indicates the importance which such questions are currently being assigned. It also suggests an area where fruitful collaboration might be possible between the two. Differences exist between the study of culture within Strategic Studies and Conflict Resolution which reflect their origins in different traditions. For example, the work on culture within Conflict Resolution deals with ethnic groups and pre-industrial societies as well as states and nations, while strategic culture takes the latter as its primary referent group, in line with realist Strategic Studies. In other respects, some strategic culture advocates move away from realism. The view that violence is learned rather than natural behaviour shifts strategic culture away from Strategic Studies and closer to Conflict Resolution. It remains to be seen whether these approaches can be combined effectively. But culture offers an arena in which Conflict Resolution and Strategic Studies might meet and develop links which could spread more widely. These different approaches to conflict had unhealthily little to say to one another during the Cold War. They now seem to be converging somewhat (see Dunn 1991, p. 69). In the post-Cold War era, a pooling of effort seems both appropriate and important, and culture offers a potential launch pad for it.

NOTES

1. I shall use the capitalized form 'International Relations' to refer to the academic discipline rather than the realm of activity between units in world politics.
2. Culture is characterized as the 'forgotten variable' by Bonthous (1994). Rengger (1992) notes that until recently culture was largely absent from the indexes of International Relations textbooks. Increased mention of culture is to be found in recent textbooks (Baylis and Rengger 1992; Booth and Smith 1995), while *Millen-*

nium (1993) has devoted a recent special issue to culture in international relations. Sessions on culture have been held at the 1994 annual conference of the British International Studies Association, a 1993 conference at Keele University on 'New Directions in International Relations', and the 1987 International Studies Association annual conference. The papers presented at the latter formed the basis of a significant recent book on culture and international relations (Chay 1990).

3.   The phrase is from Wallerstein (1991, p. 237).

4.   At a conference in August 1994 in Malaysia, papers were presented on the strategic cultures of various states in the Asia–Pacific region. These will be published by Macmillan and will represent the first large-scale comparative study of strategic cultures. The *Pacifica Review* (1994) includes papers from a conference on culture and conflict resolution in the Asia–Pacific region held, coincidentally, around the same time in Malaysia.

4. The security of Arab Gulf states and the end of the Cold War: external security versus internal stability

Clive Jones

INTRODUCTION

It is perhaps ironic that following the end of the Cold War, threats to the stability of the Arab Gulf states, not least from internal factors, have increased, rather than decreased, with the apparent demise of super-power competition. While the Gulf crisis of 1990–91 demonstrated the direct threat posed to the territorial integrity of Kuwait, the crisis itself has helped to exacerbate social, religious, ethnic, and economic tensions that now challenge the consensual base of support previously enjoyed by many regimes in the region. The rise of a vocal Islamic opposition to the autocratic leadership of the House of Saud; violent protests in Bahrain; the brief but vicious internecine conflagration in Yemen, provide some examples of a wider political dynamic that now threatens the stability of individual states on the Arabian Peninsula.

Indeed, the efficacy of the oil-rich states in using their accumulated wealth to buy security has now to be questioned at both the strategic and societal levels. Iraq's invasion demonstrated that loans and contributions made to Baghdad by the Gulf states did not translate into regional stability, while the decline in revenue from oil has led to increased levels of internal economic anomie which opposition groups, many centred upon an Islamist agenda, have used as platforms for political opposition. This has been compounded by the fact that ultimately, the Gulf states remain dependent upon the West, and in particular the United States, for their external security. Such reliance upon direct American military aid provides a powerful means to challenge the legitimacy of the self-proclaimed 'Servant of the two Holy Places', King Fahd of Saudi Arabia. Although the positioning of non-Muslim troops on Saudi soil during the crisis was condoned by a *fatwa* issued by the chief Saudi religious authority, Shaykh Abdul Aziz Bin Baz, wider Islamic sentiment condemned as apostasy such an overwhelming presence and an overt attempt by the West to occupy the 'Muslim Heartland' (Piscatori 1991, pp. 9–10).

Reliance upon the West remains, nonetheless, the most salient means to ensure the territorial integrity of the Gulf states. But the pursuit of external security has clearly impacted upon the internal stability of these regimes. The states of the Gulf Co-operation Council (GCC) – Saudi Arabia, Kuwait, the United Arab Emirates (UAE), Oman, Bahrain and Qatar – have consistently failed to develop a common defence structure, a failure which is a product of inter-state rivalry as well as fears over Saudi dominance of such a bloc. Continued investment, however, in high-technology weapons systems, coupled with the massive payouts in reparations to coalition partners, have continued to drain Gulf currency reserves. This problem is particularly acute for Riyadh which has seen such reserves fall from a peak of $121 billion in 1984 to an estimated $7 billion a decade later.[1] While unwilling to impose substantial levels of direct taxation on Saudi society – a characteristic of rentier states – cutbacks in funding to state institutions, the largest employers in the Saudi economy, have necessarily seen levels of unemployment rise. This has not only stoked the fires of Islamic opposition to the House of Saud, but also produced similar patterns of dissent in Bahrain, Oman and Kuwait where moves towards a more representative form of government are viewed with some concern in Riyadh.[2] Attempting to coerce or accommodate these conflicting demands, while maintaining the stability of state institutions, is the pressing challenge that now faces the Gulf states as they approach the millennium. In short, the perceived external threats facing the region can no longer be divorced from the internal challenges – an interdependence that continues to have important implications for the West.

THE DOMESTIC CHALLENGE: THE CASE OF SAUDI ARABIA

That Islamic opposition exists at all in the Gulf states is a source of much disquiet, not least to the House of Saud. Because the kingdom is run according to Islamic law, the *Shari'a*, leading defenders of the regime argue that opposition to the state on Islamic grounds is meaningless. The Islamic legitimacy of the ruling order remains based on its adherence to the orthodox Wahhabi interpretation of Sunni Islam. Wahhabism has traditionally been marked by an emphasis on 'Islamic devotion, purity, simplicity and egalitarianism as they are perceived to have existed in the days of the Prophet' (Faksh and Faris 1993, p. 287). The rapid rate of modernization experienced by the country after the discovery of oil, however, meant that Wahhabism was used increasingly to sanctify political decisions already taken by the ruling élite, rather than having a direct Islamic bearing on the process of decision-making itself. Accordingly, the Senior Committee of *Ulama*, consisting of government-appointed clerics and lawyers, became the bastion of theological legitimization for policy decisions already taken by King Fahd. The *fatwa* issued by Shaykh Bin Baz condoning the presence of non-Muslim troops on Saudi soil provides one obvious example.

In the wake of the Gulf crisis, the subservience of this relationship has been brought into sharp relief following the resurgence of what perhaps can be termed neo-Wahhabism, concentrated particularly among the Islamic state universities of the Najd region. The call for the restitution of strict Wahhabi practice in the governing of the kingdom has proved of particular concern to the Saudi élite: not only did the House of Saud originate from the Najd, but the theological basis of the regime, Wahhabism, remained a largely Najdi phenomenon. The emergence of such an opposition is therefore the cause of increased anxiety to the Saudi monarch since it suggests theological recidivism on the part of the Royal Family.

The opposition of students and graduates to the Saudi government falls within the wider remit of Najdi discontent and the faltering performance of the Saudi economy. It has been estimated that upwards of 150 000 graduates, many of them educated at the Islamic state universities such as the Imam Bin Saud University, remain either under- or unemployed. As one commentator observed:

> Islamic universities have loomed disproportionately large in the phenomenal growth of Saudi education. They award Ph.Ds by the hundred for flimsy dissertations on subjects such as divorce under Islam. A kind of professional religious class is being created which is largely unemployable, dominated by those whose pretensions outweigh their abilities, and who are therefore natural recruits to any subversive cause that can advance them.[3]

These 'subversive causes' are most forcefully served by a new generation of young, highly educated academics and clerics. Because of their strict adherence to Wahhabism, they have proved difficult for the government to silence. In short, their allegiance to the religious base of the Saudi state helps legitimize their dissent. This had already been expressed in May 1991 by a number of *ulama* who, in a petition to the king, outlined a comprehensive reform programme that repeated the call for the creation of a consultative council, *majlis al-shura*. Such a council had been promised by the ruling al-Saud family intermittently over the past 35 years but had never been established.[4] It was suggested that membership of such a council should be based on ability rather than social status or gender, with the petition also embracing the view that the judiciary, media and economy should be subject to tighter Islamic control. The petition ended with a call for Saudi Arabia to refrain from concluding non-Islamic alliances in future crises, a clear reference to Saudi Arabia's continued dependence upon Western military aid (Piscatori 1991, p. 10). This argument was put most forcefully by Dr Safir al-Hawali and Shaykh Salman Auda. Both men were vociferous in their denunciation of Saudi arms purchases, their cost being thought to be disproportionate to the actual security accruing to the state. But such spending was also thought to suggest that faith in weapons systems bought from the West superseded a firm belief in the central tenets of Islam as *the* safeguard of both the spiritual and physical well-being of the kingdom.[5]

King Fahd outlined the official channels where dissent could be openly expressed. In March 1992, he issued three statutes that carefully outlined the limits of civic debates in Saudi society. The first of these not only established the right of succession to the Saudi throne, but also enshrined a code of civil liberties under Saudi law as well as the right to own private property. The second statute authorized the establishment of the *majlis al-shura* . Nonetheless, clear limitations were put upon its advisory powers with the king retaining the right to appoint and dismiss its constituent members. Moreover, the council was denied the right of veto over legislation proposed by the king or the Saudi government. The final statute was a devolution of additional power to the royal princes appointed by the king to govern the kingdom's provinces (Faour 1993, p. 43). Though not an official constitution, the statutes were an attempt to conflate pressure for greater political participation in government with existing Wahhabi interpretations of the *Shari'a*.

Despite this, implementation of the statutes, particularly the establishment of the *majlis al-shura*, remained stalled. Indeed this proclamation failed to address the growing demands for greater participation in the political process and decisionmaking of the kingdom. Furthermore, the advent of the fax machine, as well as the mass production of cassette tapes questioning the Islamic credentials of the Royal Family, made it increasingly problematic for the Saudi authorities to control the growth in political dissent throughout the kingdom.[6] In an effort to assuage growing pressure for political reform the king announced in March 1993 the 'imminent implementation' of the new *majlis al-shura*. Yet this failed to forestall the establishment of the Committee for the Defence of Legitimate Rights (CDLR) on 7 May 1993. The CDLR was set up by six prominent Saudi academics, three of whom, Shaykh Abdullah al-Mas'ari, Shaykh Abdullah al-Tuwaijari and Sulayman al-Rushudi, issued an immediate statement detailing their agenda. This centred on a need to confront human rights abuses throughout the country and called upon members of the Saudi public to inform the committee of any injustices suffered at the hands of the authorities. The CDLR programme also embraced calls for reform of the Saudi judicial system, labour laws, and endorsed free elections to a representative assembly.[7]

The roots of the CDLR lay in the *nasiha* or advice, a manifesto signed by 109 Najdi *ulama* and academics in July 1992. In effect this was a wide-ranging critique of the economic, social and political development of Saudi Arabia since the end of the Gulf crisis. It recommended that existing implementation of Saudi laws be reviewed, in effect declaring that non-compliance with the dictates of the *Shari'a* was responsible for the perceived anomie now facing the kingdom. Declaring that the role of the *ulama* had been marginalized in the actual running of the state, the *nasiha* concluded with a call for all government departments to appoint a qualified Islamic scholar in an attempt to equate policy implementation with religious orthodoxy. While partly a means to check the influence of non-Muslim actors in the affairs of the Saudi state, the suspicion remained that the Najdi *ulama* held wider political motives. Mas'ari and Abdul Rahman Jibrin, both founding members of the CDLR, were signatories to the manifesto.[8]

The influence of the *nasiha* was reflected in the programme of the CDLR as it attempted to embark upon a political discourse over the heads of the ruling élite, dismissing as it did the efficacy of Fahd's statutes in the process. But liberals in the kingdom remained wary of the exact agenda pursued by the CDLR. Some viewed it as no more than a front for fundamentalist clergy from the Najdi city of Qasim. Indeed, the beliefs held by leading committee members placed clear limitations on what the CDLR construed as legitimate rights. Jibrin, himself a leading Saudi cleric, was known to regard Saudi citizens of the Shi'a faith as 'apostates who merited death', while the leading spokesman for the group, Mas'ari, had condemned women who had openly defied the ban on female drivers during the Gulf crisis as little better than prostitutes.[9] For the liberal opposition, progress on issues of gender was a benchmark by which the CDLR was to be judged. Failure by the committee to address the styptic nature of present Saudi norms on the rights of women was seen as indicative of the CDLR's real agenda. This agenda had little to do with promoting greater pluralism throughout the kingdom; rather, it was more concerned to further strict adherence to a neo-Wahhabi agenda throughout the Royal Family and Saudi society.[10]

The response of the Saudi government revealed a fist within a velvet glove. Ghazi Gosaibi, Riyadh's ambassador to London, indicated that the *majlis al-shura* would be formally established soon. While insisting that the 60-member council would function 'like an elected government', Gosaibi attacked the theological basis of the CDLR, noting that the existing *Shari'a* courts throughout the kingdom were the legitimate guardians for the protection of Saudi human rights.[11] In support of this position, King Fahd was quick to enlist the support of the Senior Committee of *Ulama*, who promptly issued a *fatwa* on 12 May 1993 denouncing the committee and its self-proclaimed agenda as illegitimate under existing Saudi laws.[12] The following day, having gained the necessary religious approval, the Saudi authorities moved swiftly to ban the CDLR, dismissing the six founding members from their jobs, mainly as lawyers and academics, and closing down their offices in the process.

Nonetheless, the government remained acutely aware that the CDLR represented the vocal expression of theological dissent among growing numbers of the religious right in Saudi Arabia. The response of the king appeared to reveal a twofold strategy: on the one hand, the inauguration of the *majlis al-shura* on 29 December 1993 was clearly a move designed to appease the growing pressure upon the Saudi monarch for greater government accountability. On the other, King Fahd made it clear that the proceedings of the council would be strictly limited to an advisory capacity and subject to an official interpretation of the *Shari'a*.

It was becoming noticeable that strict application of the *Shari'a* in administering legal punishment had resulted in a dramatic rise in the number of public executions throughout the kingdom. The period 1992 to 1993 witnessed 105 such executions for offences ranging from apostasy to drug trafficking, rape and murder. This, according to Amnesty International, represented a fourfold increase over the period 1991 to 1992. The suspicion remained that irrespective of guilt, the increase in such executions allowed the Saudi government to reaffirm its Wahhabi credentials in the administration of public justice.[13] Against this background, however, repressive action against the founders and supporters of the CDLR continued apace. Families were prevented from visiting those placed in detention, while over 60 academics, having signed a petition calling for the release of the CDLR detainees, were prohibited from travelling overseas. Proscribed as a legal organization in Saudi Arabia, the CDLR eventually established itself in opposition in London under the leadership of Mas'ari in April 1994.[14]

The measures adopted, combining apparent accommodation with coercion, went some way to relieving the immediate challenge to the established order in Saudi Arabia. But the very growth in such opposition groups as the CDLR was linked clearly to the state of the kingdom's economy. The closed nature of the Saudi government placed obvious restrictions on accurate economic data, but it was estimated by one source that realizable assets in 1993 were between $12 and $15 billion, compared to over $100 billion ten years earlier. Remittances to Gulf War allies accounted for approximately $52 billion, while $25 billion was estimated to have been spent on vast arms purchases from Western Europe and the United States.[15] It was also disclosed that the king had made available loans worth $23 billion to Baghdad during the course of the Iran–Iraq war. In present circumstances it would appear unlikely that Riyadh will ever see repayment of that debt.

Ostensibly, such expenditures appeared within Saudi means: the kingdom's reserves of oil account for a quarter of all such known deposits in the world. But falling world oil prices have raised doubts about the continuing ability of the Saudi economy to indulge in the widespread subsidies and financial relief provided to the rest of Saudi society. While clear asymmetries always existed between the accumulated wealth of the ruling élite and the wider populace, the provision of a modern state infrastructure, interest-free loans for the purchase of housing, and freedom from direct taxation, have nurtured a popular acceptance, though grudging in some quarters, of the existing political order.[16]

The decline in oil revenue, however, has forced the kingdom into a greater dependence upon loans, totalling $19.5 billion for 1993 if present commitments on welfare spending were to be met.[17] Indeed, the state of the Saudi economy highlights the acute security dilemma facing King Fahd. Drastic cuts in defence expenditure, amounting to $16 billion from a total state budget of $52 billion for 1993, would have released money for welfare expenditures but at the perceived cost of weakening Riyadh's military capability *vis-à-vis* Baghdad and Tehran. But with plans announced to establish six new colleges, 800 new schools, and 500 health clinics nationwide in 1994, any interruption to such projects risked incurring popular discontent, fuelling the already tangible rise in opposition to the Saudi government, not least among the growing numbers of unemployed graduates. Cutbacks imposed in the public sector, particularly in the state oil industry, had already adversely affected career opportunities in the kingdom's largest employer. In an attempt to compensate, Interior Minister Prince Nayif Bin Abd al-Aziz announced a review of employment patterns in the kingdom, the intention being to promote greater private sector involvement in graduate recruitment.[18] The sagacity of this strategy remained uncertain, however, not least because the economic difficulties facing Saudi Arabia negate any immediate improvement in private sector growth and investment.

An alternative lay in the application of direct taxation to help alleviate an internal public debt totalling $40 billion in 1993. Yet according to William Quandt of the University of Virginia this course of action remained proscribed, largely because the imposition of taxes would entail calls for greater popular participation in the political structures of the country. Moreover, such action would signal the demise of what one commentator has termed the 'ruling bargain' in Saudi Arabia, by which 'Arab rulers promised social welfare and job security in return for the populace's pledge not to engage in autonomous political action' (Blumberg 1991, p. 188). The rise in political opposition to the ruling élite came, however, after relatively minor cutbacks in public sector funding. These developments could only have discouraged the Saudi government from taking more radical economic measures, believing that such action would probably fuel the domestic challenge to the existing order.

The defection of two high-ranking diplomats from Saudi missions in the United States has only served to increase the urgency for restrictions to be placed upon access to information regarding state capabilities. Both Mohammed al-Khilawi, First Secretary to the Saudi mission to the United Nations, and Ahmad Zakrani, Vice-Consul to the Saudi Arabian Consulate-General in Houston, made clear that their respective requests for asylum had been driven by the climate of repression that now permeated Saudi society. Moreover, al-Khilawi was reported to have in his possession documents accumulated during the course of his diplomatic career detailing extensive corruption and mismanagement on the part of the Royal Family. Drawing inspiration from the creation and activities of the exiled CDLR, al-Khilawi revealed in July 1994 details of the huge financial investment that Saudi Arabia had made in Iraq's nuclear weapons programme between 1985 and 1989, totalling, it was alleged, $5 billion. In the light of such disclosures, both men made it clear that the kingdom of Saudi Arabia would face religious, economic, and political turmoil if extensive structural reforms to the decisionmaking process were not forthcoming.[10]

THE DOMESTIC CHALLENGE: KUWAIT, BAHRAIN AND OMAN

The rise of an opposition movement to an established regime has not, however, just been confined to the realm of Saudi politics. The post-Gulf crisis period has seen the emergence of similar movements in Kuwait, Bahrain, and to a lesser extent Oman. Such opposition, often centred around an Islamist agenda, has nonetheless, widened the debate concerning the efficacy of a civil society emerging within an essentially dynastic milieu. No precise definition concerning the parameters of civil society exists but it can be said to include organizations, groups and individuals who 'provide a buffer between the state and citizen' (Norton 1993, p. 211).

While such a buffer has yet to acquire any tangible meaning within the Saudi political milieu, developments in Kuwait since the conclusion of the Gulf crisis offer the best illustration to date of the genesis of such a civil society, and one capable of challenging a political domain that has been previously the preserve of the al-Sabah family. Political dissent is not new to Kuwait: the decision of the emir, Shaykh Jaber al-Ahmed al-Sabah, to suspend the short-lived national assembly in July 1986 was motivated by the apparent popularity registered at the polls by the Democratic National Alliance of Dr Ahmed al-Khatib. The alliance agenda, based as it was upon a pan-Arab, pro-Palestinian platform, struck at the heart of the al-Sabah sensibilities: considerable sums, accumulated from the 'rent' derived from oil sales, had been invested by the family overseas, while the Palestinians, the backbone of the labour force, formed a disenfranchised yet substantial minority (Whitley 1993, p. 40).

The aftermath of the Gulf crisis transformed Kuwait's political landscape. In part a product of successive United Nations resolutions that had emphasized the liberation of Kuwait, the flight of leading members of the al-Sabah family to Riyadh at the onset of the crisis did much to discredit the regime in the eyes of those Kuwaitis who had to endure the Iraqi occupation.[20] Under pressure from a loose alliance of opposition groups – both secular and Islamist – who in April 1991 issued a manifesto calling for a free press, an independent judiciary, freedom of assembly, and the legalization of formal political parties, the emir tried to reassert his authority by arresting five members of the Islamic Constitutional Movement. Such measures, however, did little to assuage growing popular discontent, particularly among the armed forces, the security services, and influential merchant groups in Kuwait city itself (Deegan 1993, pp. 41–2). Perhaps with this in mind, elections to a new national assembly were eventually called for 5 October 1992.

Despite the restrictive nature of the elections – voting was confined to male citizens over 21 who could trace a continuous family connection to Kuwait before 1921 – opposition candidates won 35 of the 50 available seats to the assembly. Moreover, the Sunni-dominated Islamic Heritage Society and Social Reform Society, and the Shi'i Islamic Cultural and Social Society polled particularly well.[29] Despite this result, Shaykh Jaber al-Ahmed still believed he could dictate the terms of political discourse in Kuwait. He refused opposition demands to separate the position of crown prince and prime minister, hoping to ensure the continued dominance of al-Sabah rule although six members of the new assembly were appointed to the new cabinet.

It is becoming clear, nonetheless, that economic conditions inside the emirate are pushing forward a process of greater politician accountability. As with Saudi Arabia, the Gulf crisis had a disastrous impact upon the Kuwaiti exchequer, with the value of overseas holdings slashed from $100 billion to an estimated $35 billion as the costs of postwar reconstruction soared. In total, it has been estimated that Kuwait has spent over $100 billion on reimbursing coalition allies for military assistance, continued defence spending, and the need to rebuild a shattered infrastructure. In 1994, the government was forced to take out a loan of some $5.5 billion to cover the cost of ongoing reconstruction. Such levels of borrowing have seen growing calls for state subsidies to be cut, not least from the governor of the Central Bank and member of the ruling family, Shaykh Salim Abd al-Aziz al-Sabah. The favoured means to achieve this remains greater private sector involvement in state utilities such as water, electricity and telecommunications as well as the strategically vital oil industry (Collett 1994, p. 17).

Such measures, favoured by the World Bank and the International Monetary Fund, pose a particular dilemma for all sections of Kuwaiti society. Private sector involvement, particularly from foreign investors, clearly weakens the ability of the al-Sabah family to manipulate the economy for political purposes. While political opposition has always been a feature of the Kuwaiti milieu, the generous provision of an advanced social welfare system, funded by oil revenue, did much to induce an acceptance of the prevailing political order. Moves towards privatization can only undermine this particular form of social contract, prompting further demands for more power to be vested in the national assembly (Collett 1994, pp. 17–18).

This desire to harness private investment in an effort to underpin Kuwait's economy also poses a dilemma for the opposition. While welcoming any moves that devolve greater power to the assembly, the speaker of the parliament, Ahmad Sa'dun, voiced concern that privatization necessarily entailed widespread job losses as part of the process of rationalization. Given that the state employs 95 per cent of all Kuwaiti nationals, the sentiment expressed by Sa'dun was reflective of a wider concern over the impact government proposals would have on societal security. Indicative of this was the cabinet decision in October 1994 to withdraw a proposal for direct taxation over a six-month period for all Kuwaiti nationals and expatriate workers. Moreover, Islamist groups, fearing that foreign investment would only lead to a new form of 'neo-colonialism' of Kuwaiti assets, have made clear their opposition to the privatization proposals (Collett 1994, p. 18).

Clearly, the contradictory demands of economic expediency and domestic stability are challenging the political *status quo* within Kuwait itself. Moreover, the pressure upon the al-Sabah family to accommodate these conflicting pressures has been exacerbated by Saudi concern that elections to the Kuwaiti assembly have set a dangerous regional precedent. This concern was amplified by the outbreak of widespread and violent protests on the oil-rich island of Bahrain in December 1994 and January 1995. The root cause of the trouble lay in agitation by sections of a disenfranchised majority, some 385 000 Shi'a, for the restitution of a short-lived national assembly that had been dissolved by royal decree in 1975, on the orders of the ruling Sunni Arab family, the al-Khalifa.[21]

Most of the reported violence was in response to the arrest of a young Shi'i cleric, Shaykh Ali Salman, who openly supported calls for political reform. Unrest centred mainly upon Shi'i villages on the main island of Bahrain, but some reports also spoke of protest flaring in the poorer Sunni districts of the Bahraini capital Manama itself.[22] The response of the authorities was unequivocal: five demonstrators were killed, 1600 were arrested, while Salman and two other leading Shi'i clerics, Shaykh Hamza al-Deiri and Shaykh Sayed Haidar al-Setri were eventually deported to London. While Salman declared his intent had been to reform the system rather than overthrow the family, cassette tapes of his sermons circulating among Bahrainis were alleged to have called for the removal of the al-Khalifa as a precursor to the establishment of an Islamic government.[23] Whatever the truth, it was clear that the scale of the rioting, continuing well into January 1995, provoked deep unease in Riyadh. It was reported that members of the Saudi National Guard were despatched to Manama to help control the rioting, while Saudi prisons were used to detain those arrested by the Bahraini authorities (Jarrah 1995, p. 12).[24]

In explaining the cause of such widespread disturbances, Crown Prince Hamed bin Issa al-Khalifa remained keen to apportion blame on 'saboteurs', most notably the foreign media and Iran. That the Iranians should be suspected of inciting rebellion came as little surprise. Although Iran, under the shah, formally abandoned claims to Bahrain in 1971, irredentist sentiment, based upon ethnic and religious ties to the islands, remains strong in Tehran. Nonetheless, the undoubted antipathy between the dynastic order in Bahrain and the Islamic Republic of Iran appears to present a convenient scapegoat that masks wider structural faults within Bahraini society. The fact that civil disorder encompassed both Sunni and Shi'a communities suggests a wider unease over the economic anomie now facing Bahrain.[25]

In this sense, the opposition movement in Bahrain is a product of similar economic factors at work in both Kuwait and Saudi Arabia, with whom Manama shares its main oil field at Abu Safa. The ability of the Bahraini state sector to support an inflated bureaucracy as part of the governing contract has been punctured by the decline in oil revenue. A clear correlation exists between the growth in the level of unemployment in Bahrain and the rise in open protest against the ruling order. As with Kuwait, Manama is also trying to attract foreign investment as a means to alleviate the immediate burden on the state sector, although deficit funding appeared set to account for 15 per cent of

GDP, some $650 million, for both 1995 and 1996.[26] Yet while the desire to harness inward investment was tacit recognition that unemployment remained the root cause of widespread civil dissent, all demands for political reform have been eschewed by the al-Khalifa. The sagacity of this strategy remains a moot point. Certainly, Saudi influence is strong in Manama, not least because Riyadh wants to pre-empt such discontent spreading from Bahrain to its own Shi'i minority in its eastern province. However, despite an apparently efficient and loyal security service, failure to address the underlying cause of popular Bahraini discontent can only undermine the process of inward investment that Manama so desperately seeks.

The need for inward investment is also fundamental to the economic development of the sultanate of Oman. Again the ability of the sultanate to sustain high levels of expenditure on the public sector has been questioned, not least by the World Bank. Accordingly, economic planners in Muscat, the Omani capital, have begun to propose the sale of public utilities to the private sector, proposals that include reform of the country's tax laws to attract overseas investment. Against this background, protests against the regime of Sultan Qabus bin Said have been reported, although the cause of such dissent remains unclear. The sultan retains absolute power, combining the positions of prime minister, foreign minister and defence minister under the monarchy. The only forum for debate remains the State Consultative Council, whose members are nominated, rather than elected, by the sultan. Like Bahrain and Kuwait, Oman is a heterogeneous society, although its long history of independence, dating back 350 years, has meant that societal dissonance based upon ethnicity has remained muted. Indeed, as one observer noted: '[A] distinguishing feature of Oman is that its majority population, as well as its ruling family, are Ibadi Muslims, a sect generally considered separate from mainstream Sunnism. Sunnis make up about 25 per cent of the population of 1.6 million, but no overt discrimination or unrest among them has been reported' (Whitley 1993, p. 45).

Without doubt, Sultan Qabus has enjoyed widespread support among the Omani people since he came to power in July 1971. It came as a shock, therefore, when reports of an attempted *coup* against the sultan in June 1994 came to light. A terse statement released by Muscat on 28 August declared that 'it had dismantled a foreign network of foreign sponsored Islamic militants', although the identity of both the 'militants' and the alleged overseas patron remained undisclosed.[27] It did emerge, however, that some 200 people were arrested, many of them students, academics and army officers. By placing blame on the outside interference of a third party, the Omani Minister of Palace Affairs, General Ali Bin Majid al-Ma'mari, clearly hoped to allay suspicions that unrest has been conditional upon internal problems associated with the regime. Yet according to one source, the arrests, coming as they did against a background of declining oil revenues, coupled with the world's second highest birth rate, had more to do with allegations of government corruption and nepotism than any overt Islamist threat to the established order (Rathmell 1995, p. 24).

The ability and willingness of all Gulf regimes to countenance meaningful political reform remains, however, in doubt, not least because they continue to reject any challenge, Islamic or otherwise, that questions the legitimacy of present state structures. If the political and economic consequences of the Gulf crisis disabused the ruling dynasties of any reliance upon the efficacy of 'riyal politik' in ensuring internal stability, recourse to more draconian measures has, with the possible exception of Kuwait, become a depressingly familiar pattern. This reassessment has not just been confined to the realm of domestic politics. Conscious of the limited security economic aid to Baghdad actually bought the region as a whole, a state-centric paradigm has emerged that now defines the conduct of inter-state relations in the aftermath of the Gulf crisis.

REGIONAL SECURITY IN THE AFTERMATH OF THE GULF CRISIS

Failure of established institutions to mediate an effective Arab solution to the Gulf crisis has since influenced regime perceptions of regional security in the aftermath of the conflagration. Moves towards a foreign policy based upon national self-interest are the product of failure by collective organizations, most notably the Arab League and the GCC, to conclude regional solutions to regional problems. The support of Jordan, Yemen, and the PLO for Baghdad's action, support based largely upon these states' own particular geopolitical interests, was seen by Gulf states as a direct affront in light of the financial aid bestowed on Amman, the Palestinians, and Sana'a over nearly two decades. While most remained neutral, the perceived alliance between the PLO Chairman Yasser Arafat and Saddam Hussein resulted in over a quarter of a million Palestinians being forced to leave Kuwait at the conclusion of hostilities (Mattar 1994, p. 41). If anything, Iraq's invasion of Kuwait demonstrated that the main threat to regional order came not from the West, or indeed Israel, but from within the Arab and Islamic world itself.

This assessment clearly conditioned inter-Gulf relations in the aftermath of the crisis. Not surprisingly, Iraq continued to be the subject of the most extreme Saudi and Kuwaiti vitriol although this tended to concentrate on the persona of Saddam Hussein rather than on the structures and institutions of the Iraqi state itself.[28] Nonetheless, the mass troop deployment by Baghdad close to the Kuwaiti border on 2 October 1994 only served to reinforce an inherent xenophobia among Kuwait's citizens towards non-Arabian peninsular Arabs.[29] No clear rationale for Saddam's 'sabre-rattling' was immediately apparent, although frustration at the continued imposition of United Nations sanctions – not least Saudi and Kuwaiti support of measures that limit Iraqi oil production to a level sufficient only to purchase essential medical supplies and foodstuffs – undoubtedly informed at least part of Baghdad's calculations (Rouleau 1994, pp. 10–11).

The prompt despatch of Western forces to Kuwait in response to the crisis did much to diffuse the immediate prospects of a new conflagration. Under threats of renewed military action by Washington, issued under the auspices of UN Resolution 949 that demanded a complete Iraqi withdrawal, Baghdad backed down. Indeed, within one month of the crisis abating, the Iraqi government had formally recognized the 'sovereignty, integrity, and independence of Kuwait' as well as the legality of the new border between the two states drawn up by the UN border commission in April 1992. This in effect moved the Kuwaiti border northwards, forcing Baghdad to cede several oil wells from the Rumaila field to the Kuwaitis along with control of its former naval base at the port of Umm Qasr (Marr 1993, p. 123).

However, distasteful, Saddam Hussein realized that compliance with the dictates of the international community remains the only viable option if sanctions are to be lifted in the short to medium term. Yet the issue of Kuwait is a truly national issue for Iraqis that goes beyond the purely naked ambitions of their current president. Ever since it was established as a nominally independent state in 1921, all Iraqi regimes, be they royalist or republican, have coalesced around the legitimacy of a claim that regards Kuwait as a province of Iraq. In this the respect the security threat that Iraq presents to its southern neighbour cannot be finite, simply because irrendentist sentiment, nurtured by a particular cultural and historical milieu, can never compromise over a claim viewed as a matter of national honour. As one commentator noted:

> Although the work of the UN commission may be technically impeccable and legally binding on Iraq, its disregard for Iraq's political sensitivities seems likely to make the new border a source of enduring contention. By imposing its decision, backed by the weight of the Security Council enforcement mechanisms ... the United Nations provoked outrage among Iraqis, a sentiment that may well outlast Saddam. (Faour 1993, pp. 96–7)

Though keen to maintain UN sanctions against Baghdad – not least because their removal would further depress world oil prices as Iraq resumed production, thereby exacerbating the economic difficulties of the region still further – other Gulf states still view their erstwhile protagonist as a necessary evil against Shi'i fundamentalism spreading from Iran. The fact that Washington offered moral support and little else to the Iraqi Shi'a insurgency in the south of Iraq following the conclusion of hostilities with Baghdad was attributed to pressure from a Saudi government, unwilling to accept the establishment of a Shi'a entity on its immediate border and adjacent to Saudi Arabia's own oil fields in the eastern province of al-Hasa (Faksh and Faris 1993, p. 281). The establishment in 1979 of an Islamic republic in Iran reinforced the official prejudice against the Saudi Shi'a not least because they were viewed as a potential 'fifth column'. Indeed, such suspicions continue to inform Saudi policy towards its immediate neighbours, as evidenced by its response to the Shi'a inspired demonstrations in neighbouring Bahrain (Whitley 1993, p. 42).

The perceived threat from Iran is twofold, combining territorial claims with religious aggrandizement. Both, seen from Riyadh and Manama, have the potential to destabilize the two main pillars of the House of Saud: access to the wealth contained in the vast reserves of oil, and the religious legitimacy of King Fahd's claim to be the sole protector and servant of the 'two holy places'. Tehran's occupation of the islands of Abu Musa and the Greater and Lesser Tunbs in the Straits of Hormuz, an action taken over the protestations of the United Arab Emirates who claim sole sovereignty, justifies the perception that the Iranians continue to harbour ambitions of dominating the Gulf. This suspicion had already marked bilateral relations before 1979 with the revolution merely exacerbating an already entrenched nervousness in Riyadh about Iran's hegemonic aspirations.[30]

Fears over Iranian intent, coupled with ongoing concern regarding Iraqi ambitions, has not been sufficient, however, to lay the foundations of a secure pan-Gulf defence structure. The 'Damascus Declaration' of 6 March 1991 was an attempt to construct such a regional security framework largely independent of Western support. The declaration offered Egypt and Syria a security role in the Gulf in conjunction with the member states of the GCC. In return, both Cairo and Damascus were to receive substantial economic aid from Council members. Although it was an attempt to eschew overt reliance on military support from the West, the venture was soon fraught with difficulties. Although GCC Secretary-General Abdallah Bishara spoke of a new 'Arab order', divisions over the precise security structure quickly emerged. No consensus could be reached regarding the size and composition of the pan-Arab force, while failure by Kuwait to award Egypt with what Hosni Mubarak regarded as a proportionate share of contracts for reconstruction work in the emirate, saw Cairo, closely followed by Damascus, withdraw all troops by the middle of May 1991. There also remained a deep-seated suspicion among the smaller GCC states concerning Riyadh's natural dominance within any new security structure: an unease based upon a series of long-simmering border disputes.[31]

The conflicting claims between Bahrain and Qatar over control of the strategically important Hawar group of islands remains a case in point. While both claim sovereignty, the decision of Doha to pursue its claim through the International Court of Justice in the Hague was driven by a well-founded suspicion that, close ties between the al-Saud and al-Khalifa notwithstanding, the continuing dispute over border demarcation between Qatar and Riyadh undermined objective mediation within the confines of the GCC. A *fatwa* issued by Shaykh Bin Baz declaring the inadmissability of non-Muslim courts ruling over disputes between Muslim countries was a clear reflection of Saudi displeasure at Qatari Crown Prince, Shaykh Hamad bin Khalifa al-Thani. Yet the Saudi position remains inconsistent on this score, not least because it supports the United Arab Emirates in its claim over possession of Abu Musa and Greater and Lesser Tunb, a claim that Sharjah wishes to press through the UN Security Council (Jarrah 1995, pp. 14–15).

At a more prosaic level, it remained questionable whether the GCC states could actually afford the cost of maintaining a token pan-Arab force to counter security threats to the region. Though the GCC signatories to the Damascus Declaration made a pledge of $15 billion to

Damascus and Cairo, the exigencies facing their respective economies due to depressed oil prices saw this figure reduced to $6 billion little under a year later. Internal division over the scope of the declaration among GCC states undermined further a coherent strategy towards collective security. Though ostensibly aimed at Iraq, Tehran voiced disquiet at an organization that precluded an Iranian role in future Gulf security, regarding the declaration as antithetical to its regional interests. Some sympathy with this position was expressed by Kuwait, keenly aware that Iran remains a powerful bulwark against Baghdad, while Doha, because of its territorial claims, has deliberately set out to court influence in both Iran and Iraq against the express wishes of Saudi Arabia. Competing interests, coupled with simmering border disputes between member states of the GCC, has therefore precluded any effective defence and diplomatic cooperation. Failure to agree a collective stance regarding Iranian intent in the Straits of Hormuz remains the most salient example, but Saudi actions with regard to Yemen provides yet another (Faour 1993, p. 88; Chubin and Tripp 1993, pp. 8–12).

In the brief but vicious civil war that ravaged Yemen between May and July 1994, Riyadh's approbation clearly rested with the socialist leader of the South, Ali Salem al-Baidh. The unification of the country in May 1990 did little to assuage underlying tensions between Sana'a and Aden, a product largely of ongoing tribal, ethnic, and ideological loyalties that unification had failed to ameliorate. The decision of the Yemeni State President and leader of the North, Ali Abdullah Saleh, to support the Iraqi invasion of Kuwait was greeted with dismay in the South. The resulting mass expulsion of Yemeni workers from Saudi Arabia adversely affected remittance payments, sorely needed by the South following the collapse of ideological and material support of the Soviet Union. Free elections in 1993 only served to highlight the differences between North and South. Taken as a popular mandate by the Southern leadership to reintroduce socialist planning and move away from a single unitary state, Sana'a reportedly unleashed death squads to eliminate socialist politicians, claiming 157 lives in the process. This provided the spark that engulfed Yemen in a wider conflagration as the army began to split along lines of ethnic affinity and tribal loyalty.[32]

While Riyadh remained keen to appear balanced in its diplomatic approach to the conflict, material aid was reportedly offered to the South, including the loan of 178 battle tanks.[33] But such largesse remained conditional on wider Saudi policy objectives. As with Kuwait, the establishment of a multi-party system in Yemen, whatever its flaws, was seen as setting a potentially subversive example for the rest of the Arabian Peninsula. Moreover the 1934 Taif agreement that set *de facto* frontiers between the two states was due for renegotiation. Not only did Riyadh continue to press longstanding territorial claims, but the suspicion remained that such demands were a means to a wider strategic end.

> Potentially, Saudi oil exports are vulnerable to a blockage, since tankers have to pass through one of three narrow waterways, none of which the Saudis control directly: Suez and the Bab al-Mandab at each end of the Red Sea, and the Strait of Hormuz in the Gulf. An outlet southwards, direct to the Indian Ocean, would provide greater security, but a mere pipeline would not suffice – it would have to be a corridor of sovereign Saudi territory. Oman rejected the idea some years ago, which now leaves Yemen as the only possibility. (Whautaker 1995, p. 11)

The support offered to the South was therefore functional, meeting as it did several complementary foreign policy requirements. The Northern victory was consequently a severe setback for the Saudis, and provided the background for the border clashes between Riyadh and Sana'a in January 1995.[34] While both sides have since agreed to accept third party mediation, a resolution to the dispute appears fraught with difficulties given the overlap of competing territorial claims with a legacy of historical antipathy.

SAUDI ARABIA, IRAN AND THE STRUGGLE FOR REGIONAL HEGEMONY

It is the relationship between Saudi Arabia and Iran, however, that continues to dominate the political agenda in the Gulf. Conflicting regional ambitions, interwoven with competing claims over Islamic legitimacy, have long soured ties between Riyadh and Tehran. The 1980s witnessed a series of demonstrations by Iranian Shi'a pilgrims during the course of the annual *hajj*, demonstrations that attacked continuing Saudi control over the two holy shrines. The resulting clashes with Saudi security police resulted in the abrogation of diplomatic ties in 1987. Only with the defeat of Saddam Hussein, and the common desire to thwart any future aggrandizement on the part of Baghdad, were relations restored in March 1991 (Vaziri 1994, p. 1).

While Tehran adopted a strict stance of military neutrality throughout the Gulf conflict, this did not prevent scathing attacks on King Fahd for allowing the presence of Western troops on soil sacred to the whole Islamic world. Such condemnation, though not surprising, represented a continuation of populist themes that had both legitimized and solidified the Iranian revolution during the reign of Ayatollah Khomeini. The Saudi regime had long been regarded as blasphemous, not least because the al-Saud were viewed as being 'proponents of American Islam'. Therefore, despite calls for greater pan-Islamic unity as a precursor to tackling the economic problems facing all the Gulf states, the role of fundamentalist clerics in defining Iranian foreign and domestic policy continued to cause considerable disquiet among the Gulf states (Vaziri 1994, p. 4).

In the aftermath of the conflict concern has centred once more upon the numbers of Iranian pilgrims allowed to make the annual *hajj*, and the open demonstration of Shi'i religious rites that previously all too often developed into anti-Saudi protests. During the course of the *hajj* in May 1993 and May 1994, reports of clashes between Saudi security police and Iranian pilgrims emerged following the latter's insistence on demonstrating against the 'infidels'. Though aware that Iranian proselytizing in part reflected the ongoing debates surrounding policy direction within Tehran, the attacks upon the Saudi state, particularly the legitimacy of the House of Saud itself, appeared to intensify in the aftermath of the *hajj* in May 1994. The deaths of 'hundreds of pilgrims' in a stampede during the course of the pilgrimage provided a platform from which radical clerics in Iran poured scorn upon the very basis of the Saudi regime.[35] On 10 June, Ayatollah Ahmed Jamatti used a sermon delivered at Tehran University to launch a scathing attack upon both the ability of Saudi Arabia to manage the *hajj*, its refusal to allow Iranian pilgrims to conduct ceremonies freely in accordance with Shi'i practice, and its overt reliance upon the United States.[36]

Such themes were not new, least of all the perceived influence of Washington on Saudi decisionmaking. But Riyadh remained sensitive to such charges. Such remarks were clearly intended to de-legitimize the House of Saud, chiding, as they did, King Fahd for his reliance upon the 'Great Satan', and accusing Riyadh of merely being the instrument of American designs throughout the Gulf.

Despite the hyperbole involved in such pronouncements, the Gulf crisis did in fact expose both the military vulnerability of the kingdom and its ultimate dependence on the United States for security guarantees. Several factors would suggest that this dependence, however distasteful, seems set to continue. The failure of the signatories to the Damascus Declaration to implement an effective Gulf security regime, coupled with Tehran's pre-emptive action over Abu Musa, could only have served to undermine the practical utility of collective Gulf security measures. Furthermore, in spite of the massive purchases of high-tech weaponry from London, Paris and Washington, the ability of the Gulf states to defend the region effectively remained a moot point. Partly, this is due to the demographic asymmetries that states such as Saudi Arabia face with regard to their immediate neighbours: a population of 17 million is dwarfed by that of Iran, over 60 million, while Baghdad was estimated in 1993 to be able to mobilize 1 million troops from a total population of some 18 million people (Cordesman 1993, p. 15). Against this, the optimal strength of the Saudi armed forces was placed in 1993 at 95 000 men, with a further 50 000 enrolled as part of the paramilitary National Guard.

This 'division of military labour' is deliberate. Although the National Guard's primary function concerns internal security – it was used to suppress the 1987 Iranian Shi'a riots in Mecca – its primary role has been to deter any *coup* attempt on the part of the regular armed forces. Accordingly, the defence capabilities of the kingdom remain dependent upon a logistical and technical expertise furnished by Western powers. As one commentary noted, 'the regime [Saudi monarchy] has preferred to see the fingers of apolitical and trusted US personnel resting on the triggers of Saudi big guns, especially if the fingers can be well hidden' (Faksh and Faris 1993, p. 279).

ARMS SALES AND THE SECURITY DILEMMA

The ability of Saudi Arabia to keep US military influence 'well hidden' remains, however, open to some doubt. Fears over the regional ambitions of both Baghdad and Tehran continue to dominate strategic analysis in Riyadh. The steady expansion in Iran's military capability, particularly its acquisition of aircraft and submarines from the former Soviet Union, and advances in the field of ballistic technology and missile production, saw Saudi arms purchases from the West increase steadily in the aftermath of the Gulf crisis.[37] In October 1992, Riyadh concluded a deal with France worth $3.9 billion for the construction and delivery of three frigates plus support services. The following

January, agreement was reached with the United Kingdom for the sale of 48 Tornado aircraft within the framework of the ongoing al-Yamamah project, as well as the purchase of 72 F-15 aircraft from the United States.[38]

These deals proved contentious for all concerned, not least because the scale of such arms transfers made a mockery of President George Bush's announcement on 29 May 1991 regarding the need to impose a moratorium on the sale of arms to the Middle East. Between 2 August 1990 and 25 September 1992, it was estimated by one source that total US arms sales to Riyadh alone stood at $25 billion.[39] In the immediate aftermath of the Gulf crisis, Washington did put forward several proposals concerning future security arrangements for the Gulf. Of these, both the State Department and the Pentagon favoured the pre-positioning of US military equipment in the kingdom sufficient to equip 9000 men. The Saudis rejected the proposal, citing fears of a fundamentalist backlash over the continued presence of non-Muslim troops needed to maintain this equipment (Abir 1993, pp. 208–9). Yet this position contained an inherent contradiction. The very complexity of these defence systems purchased for the Saudi Armed Forces requires a Western presence given the limitations on the size and technical ability of the Saudi armed forces. The employment of 3500 British aerospace workers on secondment to the Royal Saudi Air Force remains a case in point.[40]

Such arms transfers neatly highlight the security dilemma facing all the Gulf states: how to ensure territorial integrity without undermining regime legitimacy as governments struggle to meet the cost of defence requirements. A report in the *New York Times* on 23 August 1993 detailed the difficulties the Saudis faced meeting repayments on weapons already ordered and delivered.[41] Indeed, by the beginning of 1994 the crisis facing the Saudi economy had forced a revision in Riyadh's programme of arms purchases. Reliance upon credit to meet defence expenditure commitments was supplemented by an agreement with US military manufacturers that spread the cost of repayments beyond the normal two years. The deal was condoned by Washington, realizing it had little option if wholesale redundancies throughout American industry were to be avoided.[42] Yet the security dilemma facing the kingdom again becomes all too apparent: on the one hand, the need to sustain a high level of public sector investment for reasons of internal stability; on the other hand, continued fears over regional security are seen to justify high levels of defence expenditure.

This situation is not unique to Saudi Arabia, as the case of Kuwait demonstrates. However, unlike the House of Saud the advent of a more open form of government in Kuwait has pushed the al-Sabah family into accepting parliamentary scrutiny regarding levels of future defence spending. Kuwait has set aside some $11.7 billion for defence expenditure over the next decade. Nonetheless, the demands of reconstruction have provoked questions regarding this fixed level. Such concerns are amplified by the knowledge that given size, geographical location, and demographic limitations, the emirate will never be in a position to resist an external threat of any sustained magnitude as the Iraqi invasion so clearly demonstrated. The Kuwait Air Force does not even have enough trained pilots to fly the 40 F/A-18 fighter aircraft recently purchased from the United States.[43]

In addressing these shortcomings, Kuwait has become the leading exponent of defence treaties with major powers, in itself a clear indictment of the Gulf states' inability to coalesce around an agreed security regime. Ten-year bilateral treaties have been concluded with Washington, London, Paris and Moscow, which represent a clear diplomatic strategy to tie in the permanent members of the UN Security Council to the defence of Kuwait. This strategy bore fruit in October 1994, following the movement of Iraqi troops towards the Kuwaiti border. The prompt despatch of Western troops, able to utilize pre-positioned military supplies in accordance with the bilateral agreements, appeared to mitigate the threat of any immediate confrontation with Baghdad. Nonetheless, the cost of deploying Western troops – estimates have varied between $500 million to $1 billion – has imposed further pressure upon Kuwait's economy, not least the attempt to control its budget deficit (Collett 1994, p. 17). In turn, such pressure can only narrow further the consensual base surrounding the constitutional power of al-Sabah family rule as, once more, internal need conflicts with external exigency.

CONCLUSION

Attempting to trace the course of developments in any closed societies remains a hazardous venture. The availability of limited material, often ambiguous in its presentation, can only suggest changing patterns of state behaviour within such a constrained milieu. This chapter is no exception, and as such, can only present a partial analysis, much less draw definitive conclusions.

Mindful of such limitations, it has been argued, nonetheless, that the Gulf states face difficult decisions as they attempt to maintain stability in the face of conflicting demands. While undoubtedly possessing a momentum of its own, the growth in religious dissent appears linked to the financial exigencies now facing the region. Failure to realize sustained economic growth would suggest a recourse to further draconian measures if the stability of present state structures is to be assured. Further restrictive measures, coupled with increased borrowing, seem likely to distinguish internal state policy in the forthcoming years; all may hope for an upturn in oil prices to deflate domestic pressure, but the failure of OPEC to fix, let alone adhere to, agreed oil quotas continues to depress the world market.[44]

The dynamics now shaping the internal politics of the Gulf states cannot, however, be divorced from the conduct of regional relations. Wider Islamic sentiment throughout the *umma* voiced concern at Riyadh's relationship with Washington, a process that called into question the religious credentials of the kingdom. While remaining sensitive to such charges, regional developments in the aftermath of the crisis exposed the limitations in establishing effective Gulf security regimes. Accordingly, the United States remains the main guarantor of regional territorial integrity, as well as the main supplier of weapons systems.

Yet such weapons sales have continued to expose the Gulf states, not least Saudi Arabia, to accusations that the cost of strategic security inhibits the development of societal security in an era of increased economic stringency. While this may appear to resemble a choice between 'guns or butter' the implications for the Gulf as a whole remain far more profound, not least because they nourish an opposition that flourishes on social disaffection. In short, the perceived external threats facing the region can no longer be divorced from internal challenges. The defeat of Saddam Hussein may have removed the most extreme threat yet to the security of the Gulf, but the forces unleashed in its aftermath may prove more demanding. Attempting to coerce or accommodate these forces, while maintaining the stability of present state institutions, is the urgent challenge the Gulf crisis has imposed upon the region.

NOTES

1. 'Saudi Stability Hit by Heavy Spending Over the Last Decade', *New York Times*, 22 August 1993.
2. 'Saudis Break the Silence', *London Review of Books*, 22 April 1993.
3. 'The Kingdom Where God is Everywhere', *The Guardian*, 16 August 1993.
4. *Arab Monitor*, 2 (3), March 1993.
5. *The Guardian*, 16 August 1993.
6. 'Saudis Break the Silence', *London Review of Books*, 22 April 1993. One such cassette attacked the king's favourite son, Abdulaziz, declaring him to be uneducated and unfit to rule.
7. 'Saudis Form Embryo Opposition', *The Guardian*, 8 May 1993.
8. 'Human Rights Group Founder Resigns: Interior Minister Criticizes Western Media', *British Broadcasting Corporation – Summary of World Broadcasts (BBC–SWB)*.
9. *The Guardian*, 16 August 1993.
10. 'Saudi Human Rights Committee Banned', *The Guardian*, 14 May 1993.
11. *The Guardian*, 14 May 1990.
12. 'Senior Ulama Council says Self-Formed Human Rights Committee is Illegitimate', *BBC–SWB*, ME/1688 A/4, 14 May 1993.
13. 'Saudi Executions Increase', *The Independent*, 1 July 1993.
14. 'Academics Reportedly Punished for Petition to Release Human Rights Activists', *BBC–SWB*, ME/1764 A/9, 11 August 1993; 'Opposition Group Moves to London', *BBC–SWB*, ME/1978 MED/12, 22 April 1994; 'Islam Finds Cracks in Saudi Rule', *Independent on Sunday*, 24 April 1994.
15. 'Heads in the Sand', *The Guardian*, 14 August 1993.
16. *New York Times*, 22 August 1993.
17. 'Saudis Tighten Belt After Oil Price Fall', *The Jerusalem Post*, 5 January 1994.
18. 'Saudi Ministers Consider Ways of Employing Saudis in the Private Sector', *BBC–SWB*, ME/1575 A/3, 31 December 1992.
19. 'Saudi Defectors Request for Asylum Embarrasses Britain', *The Times*, 30 June 1994; 'Saudi Envoy Pleads for Political Asylum', *The Sunday Times*, 12 June 1994; 'Britain's Gulf Ally Helped Saddam Build Nuclear Bomb', *The Sunday Times*, 24 July 1994.
20. 'Father of all Peace Plans', *The Guardian*, 4 July 1994.
21. 'Bahraini Security Forces Detain 1,600 Dissidents', *The Independent*, 21 December 1994.
22. *The Independent*, 21 December 1994; 'Bahrain Presses for Hurd Talks on Asylum Seekers', *The Times*, 21 January 1995.
23. 'Bahrain Anger at Islamists in UK', *The Guardian*, 27 January 1995.
24. 'Saudi Riot Police Reportedly Helping Bahraini Forces in Clashes with Protestors', *BBC–SWB*, ME/2203 MED/4.
25. 'Bahrain Source Rejects "Baseless" AFP, Iranian Reports on Continued Demonstrations', *BBC–SWB*, ME/2190 MED/10.
26. 'Government Targets Bahraini Jobs', *Middle East Monitor*, 5 (3), March 1995.
27. '"Secret Organization" with "Foreign Links" Uncovered', *BBC–SWB*, ME/2087 MED/9.
28. 'Saudis Papers Say Saddam Hussein Responsible for Iraqi People's Problems', *BBC–SWB*, ME/1588 A/11, 16 January 1993.
29. *Middle East International*, no. 488, 18 November 1994.
30. *Financial Times*, 22 December 1993.
31. 'The Land of Crisis and Upheaval', *Jane's Defence Weekly*, 30 July 1994.

32. 'Arab Leaders Fight Proxy War in Yemen', *The Observer*, 22 May 1994.
33. *The Observer*, 22 May 1994.
34. 'Troops Clash in Saudi-Yemen Dispute', *Jane's Defence Weekly*, 14 January 1995.
35. 'Hundreds Die as Pilgrimage Turns to Tragedy', *The Independent*, 25 May 1994.
36. 'Ayatollah Jamatti Attacks Saudi Arabia on the Issue of the Hajj', *BBC–SWB*, ME/2020 MED/5, 13 June 1994.
37. 'Iranian Navy Takes Delivery of New Submarine', *BBC–SWB*, ME/1546 i, 24 November 1992; 'Iranian Pavilion Displays Domestically Produced Weapons', *BBC–SWB*, ME/1615 A/3, 17 February 1993.
38. 'Three Frigates and Support Services Reportedly Purchased From France', *BBC–SWB*, ME/1519 A/8, 23 October 1992; 'King Fahd Receives John Major: Saudi Arabia Announces the Purchase of 48 Tornadoes', *BBC–SWB*.
39. *Jane's Defence Weekly*, 30 July 1994.
40. 'Behind the Desert Shield', *Panorama: BBC–TV*, 7 January 1991.
41. 'US–Saudi Deals in '90s Shifting Away From Cash to Credit', *New York Times*, 23 August 1993.
42. 'Saudis Near a Deal on Slowing US Arms Payments', *International Herald Tribune*, 19 January 1994.
43. *Jane's Defence Weekly*, 30 July 1994.
44. See for example, 'Saudi Oil Minister Says Iran is Exceeding its Quota, not Saudi Arabia', *BBC–SWB*, ME/1749 A/5, 24 July 1993.

5. 'The perils of prosperity?' Security and economic growth in the ASEAN region

Amitav Acharya and Richard Stubbs

The argument of this chapter is that regional security issues cannot be divorced from regional economic issues. They are inextricably inter-linked. One cannot be examined without an appreciation of the other. While the overarching Cold War structure, which emphasized the division of the world into two armed camps, tended to mask the complex interrelationship between changes to a region's economy and regional security issues, the post-Cold War world has made the importance of the relationship readily apparent. As Barry Buzan has argued, now that the 'security obsession with the nuclear balance and ideological rivalry has faded into the background, a much wider debate about the economic, societal, and environmental aspects of security has developed' (Buzan 1994, p. 94).

The linkages between economic change and regional security are complex. Depending on how they affect each country, regional security structures can either undermine economic growth or provide the preconditions for economic prosperity. Similarly, changes in a region's economic well-being can either enhance or diminish regional security. Moreover, the interconnectedness of economic and security issues often means that a virtuous or a vicious circle can be generated. Hence, regional stability can promote economic growth which in turn promotes further stability and so forth or, alternatively, instability can prompt economic decline which in turn contributes to further regional insecurity and instability.

One area where the linkages between regional security issues and regional economic issues have become clearly discernible in the post-Cold War era is the region covered by the members of the Association of Southeast Asian Nations (ASEAN) – Brunei, Indonesia, Malaysia, the Philippines, Singapore, Thailand and Vietnam. Of these countries, Singapore and the tiny but oil-rich Brunei are considered high-income economies; Indonesia, Malaysia and Thailand are considered newly industrializing economies (NIEs); and the Philippines and Vietnam are expected to quicken their so far relatively poor pace of development in the next few years (World Bank Report 1993, pp. xv–xvii and pp. 1–4). In other words the ASEAN members have shown a remarkable capacity for economic growth over the last decade or so. Yet the cause and effect linkages between security and economic growth in the ASEAN region are not always as straightforward as might be predicted.

REGIONAL CONFLICT AND ECONOMIC GROWTH

While stability and security are generally seen as prerequisites for economic growth, ironically, the economic success of the ASEAN states owes much to the fact that they are located in a region of the world which has experienced a great deal of instability and insecurity. Most importantly, East and Southeast Asia were pivotal arenas in the US-led fight against Asian communism. Two major wars – the Korean War and the Vietnam War – as well as a number of insurgency wars meant that during the Cold War conflict has been an unwelcome but persistent characteristic of the region. Yet, perhaps somewhat surprisingly, these wars and the associated sense of insecurity which went along with them also had a positive impact on the economies of the region.

First, the Korean War, which lasted from June 1950 to July 1953, led to both sides in the Cold War building up their stocks of strategic commodities. Fear that the fighting might extend to Southeast Asia meant that the demand for natural rubber and tin, two of the region's main commodities, immediately increased dramatically. The price of rubber quadrupled and the price of tin doubled. As a consequence the government's revenues in Malaya – as Malaysia was known at the time – then the world's largest producer of rubber and tin, and Singapore, the premier trading port for both commodities, doubled. Spurred on by the need to undermine the guerrilla threat posed by the Malayan Communist Party, the windfall revenues in both countries were put to work refurbishing and developing the economic infrastructure, expanding the education system, and enlarging and training the bureaucracy (Stubbs 1989). All this laid a solid foundation for the later development of the Malaysian and Singaporean economies.

Second, the Vietnam War, which started to heat up in the early 1960s, reached its peak in the late 1960s and ended in April 1975 with the North Vietnamese entering Saigon, prompted the US government to spend vast amounts of money in the region as it sought to contain Asian communism. One of the main beneficiaries was Thailand, a front-line state in the battle against Indo-Chinese communism into which the Americans began to funnel aid from the mid-1950s onwards. As the Vietnam War gathered momentum so American aid increased. By 1975 the United States had spent nearly $3.5 billion in military and economic aid in Thailand (Girling 1981, pp. 235–6; Economist Intelligence Unit 1968). The economic infrastructure was greatly improved, especially the highway system and key ports and airports, and the Thai bureaucracy, which had a long tradition of being at the centre of power in the country, was expanded and strengthened (Nuechterlein 1967; Caldwell 1974; Muscat 1990).

Another beneficiary was Singapore, which was separated from Malaysia and became an independent state in 1965. Singapore became the regional petroleum refining centre providing petroleum products for the American military campaign in Indo-China, and its traditional entrepôt trade rapidly increased as US spending generated greater regional prosperity. Singapore also became a destination for US servicemen on leave in the region. The income generated for the Singapore economy by these developments allowed the government to put in place its economic and social infrastructure programmes and to shift over to an export-oriented development strategy (Stubbs 1989, pp. 529–60). Moreover, support among Singaporeans for a strong, interventionist government in the city-state was reinforced by the perceived threat posed by communism, both inside Singapore and neighbouring Malaysia, and on its doorstep in Vietnam.

Third, the Vietnamese invasion of Cambodia in December 1978 and the subsequent fears in the region of Vietnamese expansionism prompted the Japanese, spurred on by the Americans, to increase their aid to the ASEAN region. Hence, for example, during the height of the Cambodian conflict from 1982 to 1986, the four largest ASEAN states – Indonesia, Malaysia, the Philippines and Thailand – together received nearly $1 billion in development assistance from Japan. For the government of Japan this was the best way of ensuring that a region which was increasingly vital to Japanese companies seeking lower-cost sites for producing manufacturing goods for export to the United States and Europe, and which sat astride key sea-lanes linking Japan to Europe and the Middle East, was kept relatively stable. Hence, once again security issues paved the way for the injection of capital into the ASEAN region which in turn promoted economic growth.

Overall, then, the impressive economic growth rates – at times during the last decade reaching over 9 per cent per year in Thailand, Singapore and Malaysia – of the ASEAN members can be attributed in good part to the impact that security issues have had on the region's economies. The Korean War, the Vietnam War and the Vietnamese occupation of Cambodia have all produced much-needed external funds which helped to create a relatively prosperous region. At the same time the pervasive communist threat also encouraged the emergence of relatively strong institutional states to which the general publics of the various ASEAN members – except notably the Philippines – were generally willing to cede considerable authority in order to ensure a stable and secure society (Stubbs 1994, pp. 370–71).

However, especially since the end of the Cold War, the economic success of the ASEAN states has had consequences for the security of the region. For Southeast Asia the end of the Cold War came in 1989. In September 1989 the Vietnamese withdrew the bulk of their forces from Cambodia and set in train the events which culminated in the May 1993 Cambodian elections. It became obvious that Vietnam was no longer a significant external threat. In December 1989 an agreement was signed by the Malaysian government, the Thai government and the Communist Party of Malaysia – formerly the Malayan Communist Party – which ended the over 40-year guerrilla struggle to overthrow the Malayan/Malaysian government. This clearly signalled the decline of internal communist subversion within the region. These two events, when combined with other events around the world, such as the Tienanmen Square incident, which placed Chinese communism under a considerable cloud, and the fall of the Berlin Wall, which heralded the end of communism in Europe, required the governments of the ASEAN states to reassess their approach to security in the region. This re-evaluation was spurred on by the US withdrawal, in 1992, from their bases in the Philippines. Economic issues became more salient. For example, safeguarding trade routes and the security of the economically important South China Sea emerged as significant issues for the ASEAN states. Moreover, there was new interest in multilateral approaches to security issues. But, most importantly, underlying all these changes in attitude towards regional security has been the rapid growth in the region's economies.

THE PERILS OF PROSPERITY

Generally, ASEAN's remarkable prosperity has been thought of as having a positive influence on the region. However, there are a number of ways in which ASEAN's economic growth can be said to have increased tensions and decreased regional security. First, economic growth has encouraged what some have characterized as a regional arms race. Until recently, the ASEAN states had largely abstained from the kind of wasteful diversion of national resources to defence that was characteristic of other parts of the Third World. But the end of the Cold War has seen an unprecedented scale of defence modernization in the region.

According to one estimate, the arms spending of the six members of ASEAN (excluding Vietnam) increased more than 77 per cent in 1993 to $11.5 billion, compared with $6.6 billion in 1980–81.[1] Among individual ASEAN states, Thailand increased its defence budget by more than 50 per cent in 1992. Even more striking is the case of Malaysia, a star economic performer within ASEAN. Malaysia's total defence spending doubled in 1994 to about $1.5 billion and is expected to continue at a level equivalent to 4 per cent or 5 per cent of gross national product for the next ten to fifteen years.[2] Indonesia's defence budget for the 1995–96 fiscal year is estimated to rise by about 24 per cent.[3] Singapore has been one of the heaviest spenders on defence in ASEAN with its 1985 defence budget rising by about 20 per cent to S$5.6 billion (Singaporean dollars).[4] In the Philippines recent tensions in the South China Sea – over China's placement of 'sovereignty markers' on several atolls claimed by the Philippines – has galvanized the Philippine Congress into approving a US$2 billion modernization programme.[5] Even Vietnam, which became the newest member of ASEAN in 1995, and whose recent economic performance has been remarkable even by East Asian standards, has joined the trend by increasing its defence budget by a massive 50 per cent in 1994.[6]

All the ASEAN countries have acquired increasingly sophisticated defence equipment. Indonesia, Thailand and Singapore have acquired the high-performance fighter aircraft, such as the F-16 or the *Hawk*, while Malaysia is buying a comparable aircraft, the F-18 from the United States, as well as MiG-29 fighters from Russia. A second key trend has been the acquisition of a variety of weapons systems designed to give ASEAN states the capability of moving beyond the strategy of simple coastal defence. The headline-grabbing purchase by the Indonesians of the entire East German navy has underscored the moves by regional governments to bolster their naval capabilities. Thailand is acquiring the ASEAN region's first helicopter carrier, while submarine acquisitions are in prospect for Malaysia and Thailand.

Hence, the ASEAN members have been able to begin the task of reconfiguring their defence capabilities because of their relative prosperity. As the Singapore Defence Minister has noted, 'with the rapid economic growth that they [the ASEAN countries] have enjoyed over the last several years, they now have more money available to modernise and improve the capabilities of their navies, air forces and armies'.[7] Indeed, several studies have indicated a strong positive correlation between economic prosperity and defence spending within the developing world in general and especially within the ASEAN grouping (Harris, 1987; Denoon 1987, pp. 48–71; Ross 1989, pp. 1–41). Moreover, the highest increase in defence spending has occurred in Singapore, Thailand and Malaysia – countries that have experienced the most spectacular rates of economic growth.

Yet claims that regional prosperity has fuelled an arms race have to be treated with some scepticism. For example, of the two potential regional powers, Indonesia and Vietnam, neither has given any indication that they seek greater regional influence through an expansion of their respective military establishments. If the past record of government choice between defence and development is any indication, the defence programmes of ASEAN states can be expected to remain subject to the fluctuations in the national economic cycles. In this context, it is noteworthy that while pursuing a vigorous military modernization drive, the ASEAN states remain generally sensitive to the issue of the defence burden. Indonesia's leaders, for example, have acknowledged that 'ever increasing purchases of arms merely divert sorely needed resources from national development efforts without necessarily resulting in greater security'.[8] Certainly, at present there appears to be no political will in the region to engage in an arms race.

Second, rapid economic growth has bred new security challenges relating to issues of sustainable development and ecological degradation (Homer-Dixon 1991, pp. 76–116). Traditionally, the major security problems in the ASEAN region, most notably those associated with insurgency warfare, were rooted in conditions of poverty and underdevelopment. With some exceptions, this is no longer the case. Now, new forms of insecurity are arising as a result of reckless growth, which has taken place without sufficient regard for its environmental consequences.

These run the danger of producing serious conflicts within and between states. Certainly, there is increasing evidence that the security of the ASEAN region, and indeed the wider Southeast Asian region, is being compromised by environmental problems caused by growth.

Economic growth is also usually accompanied by a host of societal and demographic changes affecting the environment. Changes such as urbanization and mass internal movements of people, as have taken place in Thailand and Indonesia, for example, damage stable ecosystems and the social–political relationships built around them. The result is often a greater level of social tension and political instability. Environmental degradation caused by economic development also creates transboundary refugee flows as people losing their traditional lifestyles and habitats attempt to move to new areas for sustenance. Such refugee movements are a potential source of inter-state friction. In particular, Malaysia has experienced an inflow of illegal migrants from neighbouring parts of Indonesia which has caused problems for both governments.

Another environmental consequence of rapid economic growth is the depletion of natural resources such as fishing grounds, agricultural land, rain forests and fossil fuels. As these resources become scarcer, competition for them intensifies within and between states. In Southeast Asia, competition for fishing rights and maritime areas with deposits of petroleum has become particularly strong in recent years. Encroachment by foreign fishing vessels into waters claimed by a particular state has, on occasion, led to war-like tensions between Malaysia and the Philippines as well as between Thailand and Cambodia. The Spratly Islands provides a clear example of how militarized territorial disputes can be aggravated because of their potential for hydrocarbon resources, the demand for which has increased significantly due to rapid economic growth. In addition to this, certain types of environmental hazards, such as major oil spills and forest fires (both common occurrences in Southeast Asia), have transboundary effects. They affect entire sub-regions or regions, often raising inter-state tensions and undermining the potential for regional cooperation.

Similarly, the aggressive pursuit of logging rights by Thai companies (after having already exhausted domestic resources) in neighbouring states is fuelling insurgencies within Burma and Cambodia. These insurgent groups support themselves principally by controlling the right to award concessions. A particularly disturbing example of this is the illegal gem and logging trade across the Thai–Cambodian border, which is the lifeline of the Khmer Rouge. This not only contributes to continued regional instability, but also tensions between governments as Cambodia's leaders accuse the Thai military of complicity with the lucrative Khmer Rouge trade. All this underscores the point that increased economic activity has environmental consequences which in turn can produce problems for regional security.

Third, rapid economic growth has led to an increased possibility of regime instability and domestic disorder. Although economically induced instability in the Third World has been traditionally viewed as a function of underdevelopment, such instability is becoming associated just as much with the strategies for, and the achievement of, success in economic development. In Africa, 'structural adjustment' and growth-oriented economic liberalization mandated by lending agencies such as the IMF and the World Bank has led to acute political strife and regime insecurity. On the other hand, many of the successful developing countries of East and Southeast Asia today exhibit the 'performance paradox'. In these cases, authoritarian regimes find that although their position is strengthened by increased prosperity, it is at the same time undermined by demands for greater participation and more transparency in politics as the middle class grows and the economy becomes more complex (Morley 1993).

Hence the democratization process fuelled by rapid economic growth could cause instability by empowering social groups seeking a greater role in the political process. Throughout ASEAN, an expanding middle class and the emergence of interest groups creates the basis for challenges to the ruling élite's hold on power. Certainly in the ASEAN states the size of the middle-class population has grown substantially. This has led to demands for political change, since opportunities for political participation are no longer adequate within the framework of existing authoritarian regimes. The middle class is thus potentially the main agent for political change, although its size and clout remain relatively small, except in Singapore and Malaysia, and its desire for political change is tempered by the substantial benefits it continues to derive from the ruling regimes.

Although the current climate of rapid economic growth benefiting large sections of the society has allowed the ruling élite to contain demands for liberalization by projecting a common stake in prosperity, in times of economic downturn this may no longer be possible. The global democratic revolution that accompanied the end of the Cold War, and associated changes in the policies of Western powers seeking

to promote democratization around the globe have given encouragement to pro-democracy groups in the region, including segments of the
civil society pressing for greater respect for human rights. Democratization could also fuel ethnic strife, as marginalized minorities excluded
from the benefits of economic growth may seek political autonomy as
the basis for a fairer distribution of wealth and political power concentrated in the hands of the dominant majority community.

At the same time, while the pace and scope of political change in
Southeast Asia has been far less dramatic than in Eastern Europe, there
is concern about the possibility of violence resulting from leadership
transitions, particularly in the context of increased demands for greater
political openness in authoritarian polities. Leadership change has already produced conflicts in the Philippines, during the transition from
Marcos to Aquino as a result of the 'People's Power Revolution' in
1986, and in Thailand, during the Bloody May 1992 episode when the
Thai armed forces cracked down on pro-democracy crowds protesting
the army commander General Suchinda Kaprayoon's accession to the
post of prime minister even though he was not elected in the preceding
general elections. In Indonesia, the declining legitimacy of the Suharto
regime has led to similar concerns about a violent process of leadership
transition. This is fuelled by memories of the last leadership transition
in the country, from Sukarno to Suharto, one of the bloodiest events in
its history. The concern here, then, is that future upheavals and possible
problems associated with leadership succession might spill over and
create regional tensions which would, in turn, have ramifications for
regional security.

INTERDEPENDENCE AND SECURITY

Yet, overall, there is ample evidence that the rapid economic growth
that has characterized the ASEAN region has, on balance, increased
regional security. First, in all developing countries, economic growth is
vital to domestic stability. Development and security are closely linked
not only because 'a semblance of security and stability is a prerequisite
for successful economic development', but also because 'it is also
generally understood within the Third World that economic development can contribute to national security; an economically weak nation
can be exploited or defeated more easily by foreign powers and may be
exposed periodically to the violent wrath of dissatisfied citizens'

(Rosenbaum and Tyler 1975, pp. 243–74). Rapid economic growth helps to address the sources of insurgency and rebellion. In this vein, the Indonesian analyst, Hadi Soesastro, has drawn attention to a 'virtuous cycle of national economic development, regional economic integration and security in the Asia Pacific region'. As he puts it: 'economic inter-dependence and integration in the region contribute to economic growth and development of the region as a whole. As people's well-being in the region increases the region becomes more stable; this in turn im-proves the region's security' (Soesastro 1994, p. 1).

A second, and related point, is that economically dynamic growth triangles are emerging which serve to knit the ASEAN region more closely together and to reinforce efforts to bring about domestic stabil-ity in the ASEAN states. Growth triangles link capital, management and technical expertise, and knowledge of international markets to be found in major urban centres with cheap and abundant land and rela-tively skilled labour to be found in more economically marginalized regions surrounding the urban centres. Importantly, growth triangles can cut across state boundaries. The model is the growth triangle that links Singapore to the Malaysian state of Johore and the Indonesian province of Riau. Other possible triangles would link Penang in the northern part of peninsular Malaysia with southern Thailand and north-ern Sumatra and Davao in the southern Philippines to Sabah in eastern Malaysia and Sulawesi in eastern Indonesia (Milne 1993, pp. 300–301). In a similar vein an extended sub-region which would make Bangkok the economic centre of mainland Southeast Asia has also been mooted. Significantly, these growth triangles or sub-regional economic zones are helping to reintegrate areas that were traditional economic systems but which have in the recent past been divided by colonially imposed state boundaries.

Importantly, by stimulating economic growth in areas that have tra-ditionally been marginalized, these triangles have the potential to un-dermine support for destabilizing insurgency groups. These include the Muslim separatists in southern Thailand, the Moro rebels in southern Philippines and the Aceh separatist movement in northern Sumatra. Moreover, the shared commitment of the governments of the states involved to supporting the development of growth triangles suggests, at the very least, that the traditional element of the region's high politics is no longer a sufficient barrier to serious attempts at economic regional-ism. As Malaysia's Deputy Prime Minister, Anwar Ibrahim, put it, 'Instead of talking about border disputes, we are now promoting economic cooperation through growth triangles and other cross-border linkages.[9]

Third, economic growth leading to transnational economic linkages can enhance regional security. It is a major argument of liberal international theory that growing economic interdependence reduces the utility of force in international relations (Keohane and Nye 1977). All forms of transnational economic activity have the potential to promote peaceful inter-state relations. Robert Scalapino, a long-time analyst of Asian security, has argued that 'The intricately interwoven economic ties binding states together will reduce incentives to resort to violence in resolving inter-state disputes. Given the disruptions that would occur to each state's economy, the costs of regional conflict are growing rapidly.' He goes on to argue that 'Today and in the future, any war conducted with one's neighbours will penetrate deeply into the very marrow of one's own economic system' (Scalapino 1994, p. 50).

This is important because a number of the ASEAN states were bitter enemies in the not-too-distant past. For example, who in 1964 at the height of Indonesian President Sukarno's *Confrontasi* policy, could have imagined that Singapore, Malaysia and Indonesia would become such close partners in search of common prosperity? Even today, several of the ASEAN states remain mired in a number of territorial disputes with one another (Acharya 1993). Singapore and Malaysia contest sovereignty over the Pedra Branca Islands while Indonesia and Malaysia dispute the Sipadan and Ligitan Islands. Malaysia, Brunei, the Philippines and Vietnam are parties to the Spratly Islands dispute (along with China and Taiwan). The fact that the member states continue to express a strong belief in ASEAN as a regional forum for the peaceful resolution of disputes, as well as a renewed commitment to implementing the ASEAN Free Trade Area proposal and a promise to develop various growth triangles, suggests that these bilateral problems have been significantly muted by a shared quest for prosperity: a quest in which they have been conspicuously successful.

Fourth, the rapid economic growth of the ASEAN region has provided the governments of the member states with the resources to sponsor a series of conferences, seminars and workshops at which informal discussions of a number of security issues have taken place. This Track II process, as it has come to be called, allows government officials, acting in their private capacity, government advisors and academics to get to know each other on a personal level and to explore ways of dealing with security problems without governments having to lose face if a particular approach fails to gain the necessary consensus. There are now more than 30 sets of such meetings around the Asia–Pacific region with many of them centred on the ASEAN region. Perhaps the best known is the Kuala Lumpur Roundtable which meets every year in the Malaysian capital and which has become the focal point for discussions of a broadening array of security issues including human rights, environmental degradation, and the impact of economics on security.

Significantly, out of this process came the inauguration of the ASEAN Regional Forum (ARF) on political and security matters in Singapore in July 1993. The ARF is made up of the seven ASEAN members, ASEAN's seven dialogue partners (Australia, Canada, the European Union, Japan, New Zealand, South Korea and the United States), two official ASEAN observers (Laos and Papua New Guinea), and ASEAN's two 'consultative partners' (China and Russia). Representatives from Cambodia and Burma attended the inaugural meeting as guests of the ASEAN foreign ministers. The ARF deals with a wide range of security issues including matters well beyond the borders of the ASEAN region, but it is important to note that it has been ASEAN around which the institutionalization of Asia–Pacific regional security has been developed. ASEAN's economic success, its tradition of consensus building and its relative neutrality in international affairs have made it an obvious candidate for leadership in dealing with Asia–Pacific regional security issues.

This leads directly to the final point. ASEAN's obvious economic success has earned it not just the attention but also the respect of the major powers around the world. Transnational economic activity, such as that which has burgeoned in the ASEAN states, increases the stakes of the world's major powers in the stability and well-being of the region. In Southeast Asia as elsewhere in the developing world, great power interventionism and rivalry have often undermined regional stability. But in an era when geoeconomics is taking precedence over geopolitics, the ASEAN region's economic growth offers outside powers strong incentives to view the region as a theatre of economic opportunity, rather than as an object of their power politics. The experience of the former Soviet Union and pre-reformist China suggests that true great power status cannot be attained without a strong and open economy, one that both exploits and participates in the transnational movement of capital. Moreover, with the demise of the Soviet Union as a superpower, the world's major powers (including China) today display a convergent approach to economic development which recognizes the importance of transnational production.

In addition, just as transnational economic activity reduces the propensity for military conflict among the weaker powers, it also constrains the desire and ability of great powers to pursue unilateral measures in relation to weaker and more vulnerable states. For example, fear of upsetting mutually beneficial economic linkages is a significant factor inhibiting the unilateral and aggressive pursuit of human rights objectives in the policies of external powers, especially the United States. This became evident in the Clinton administration's decision to revoke the linkage between human rights and most favoured nation status in relation to China. Without an expanding web of transnational economic activity, it is quite likely that the political and security relationship between the major powers on the one hand and the regional countries on the other could have become considerably worse. Similarly, in Northeast as well as Southeast Asia transnational economic linkages remain an important barrier to the potential for Chinese and Japanese hegemonism in the region. This is a crucial factor in regional security in view of the fact that many ASEAN countries remain very apprehensive about the desire and ability of the major Asian powers to step into the strategic void caused by superpower retrenchment.

CONCLUSION

Clearly, economic issues and security issues are intertwined in the ASEAN region. During the Cold War period American concerns about regional security in the face of an apparently expanding Asian communism led the United States to pump huge amounts of money into Southeast Asia. This influx of funds was one of the main factors in the rapid economic development of the ASEAN region in general, and Singapore, Malaysia and Thailand in particular.

In turn the increased prosperity of the ASEAN member states has had both a negative and a positive impact on the security of the region. The problems have started to become obvious in the last few years. Rapid economic growth has allowed for a rapid increase in defence budgets, and therefore defence acquisitions, creating the impression of an incipient arms race. Both rapid industrialization and increased patterns of consumption have put pressure on the environment. Issues associated with environmental degradation run the risk of spilling across borders and creating security incidents. And regional prosperity has also given a boost to social and political groupings which may generate problems for governments of the region as they attempt to deal with transitions in leadership and calls for greater political transparency. Possible domestic instability may create regional security problems.

Yet overall the ASEAN region's economic success has had beneficial consequences for regional security. Compared with the recent past the members of ASEAN are experiencing domestic stability and they are increasingly interdependent because of the emergence of growth triangles and production complexes. Moreover, they are increasingly tied economically to other economies in the Asia–Pacific region. Expanding government revenues have also meant that the large number of informal security negotiations that have characterized the region in recent years could be supported and encouraged. This has led to the formation of the ASEAN Regional Forum which has helped to stabilize regional security relations. And perhaps most importantly, the great powers now woo ASEAN members as economic partners rather than seeing them as proxies in a global fight for supremacy.

NOTES

1. L. Makabenta, 'South-east Asia: newly-rich nations arming up', *Inter Press Service Dispatch*, 7 March 1994.
2. 'As Asia navies grow, fears of a broader arms race mount', *International Herald Tribune*, 21 January 1994.
3. '24 pc hike in defense spending proposed in Indonesia', *Xinhua News Agency Dispatch*, 14 September 1994.
4. 'Budget 95', *The Straits Times*, 4 March 1995.
5. 'A Line in the Sand', *Far Eastern Economic Review*, 6 April 1995.
6. 'Military Wins Big Boost', *South China Morning Post*, 22 October 1994.
7. 'Lean, Mean SAF by 2000', Interview with Defence Minister Dr Yeo Ning Hong, *The Straits Times*, 1 July 1993.
8. *International Herald Tribune*, 29 October 1992.
9. 'Malaysia: Use ASEAN Spirit as Basis – Anwar', *Business Times* (Malaysia), 7 June 1994.

6. The United Nations: collective security and individual rights

Justin Morris*

INTRODUCTION

The end of the Cold War transformed international politics and in particular the way in which the United Nations Security Council (UNSC) functioned. These changes have led some politicians, journalists and academic commentators to suggest that the United Nations is now functioning as the drafters of the charter originally intended, promoting the values outlined in the preamble of the charter and policing international affairs accordingly. Recent UN action in Iraq, Yugoslavia, Somalia, Rwanda and Haiti are cited to support this claim. However it is far from clear that these cases actually do provide such support, indeed an underlying theme of this chapter will be the assertion that the UNSC is now acting in a manner that was never intended by the drafters and which was actually rejected by the delegates of those nations which met in San Francisco five decades ago. The chapter will attempt to locate recent UNSC actions within an historical and constitutional framework, and in so doing will assess the implications for the future of the UN of recent interventionary activity.

THE UNSC AND THE GUARDIANSHIP OF INTERNATIONAL PEACE AND SECURITY

The drafters of the charter of the United Natons, determined not to repeat the mistakes of its predecessor the League of Nations, set for themselves the task of creating an organization which would be able to

*The author would like to express his appreciation to Nicholas Wheeler for the many helpful comments which he made throughout the writing of this chapter.

maintain international order. Initially a concert-style approach was favoured as the means by which this end would be achieved, with the United States, the USSR, the UK and China adopting the roles of the so-called 'four policemen'.[1] However this original idea underwent substantial amendment, with the 'four policemen' eventually being expanded into an eleven-member Security Council,[2] the inclusion of non-permanent members on the Council helping to assuage the lesser states which accepted the system as the price to be paid for operational efficiency. Nevertheless the great powers of the day – the United States, the USSR, the UK, China and France – were still guaranteed positions of such privilege through their permanent membership of the UNSC that their participation was secured and thus the hurdle of great power membership, at which the League of Nations had so fatally stumbled, was safely navigated. To ensure clearly defined areas of constitutional competence there would be a clear separation of functions and power, with the Security Council demarcated as the organ with primary concern for the maintenance of international peace and security. Finally the jettisoning of the unanimity rule, which many claimed had undermined the ability of the League of Nations to operate effectively, would expedite the decisionmaking process within the Council, enabling it to react rapidly when threats to international peace arose.[3]

The Security Council was also provided with remedies to overcome many of the other problems which had plagued the League. It was granted the ability to impose not only economic but also military sanctions, thus providing it with far greater *utility* than the League Council had enjoyed.[4] Furthermore the council was granted a wide discretion in determining that the conditions existed under which it should sanction collective action, though having made such a determination it was under an absolute duty to take steps to remedy it. Thus the Council simultaneously retained considerable flexibility of response while embodying a high degree of *certainty*, underpinned by an implicit assumption that the great powers in particular would work in unison to preserve international peace and security.[5]

The centrality of the Security Council is fundamental to the UN system. Member states confer upon the Council 'primary responsibility for the maintenance of international peace and security' and agree that in this respect it will act on their behalf and they will abide by its decisions (Arts 24 and 25). The Security Council's substantive powers are found in Chapters VI and VII of the charter. The former deals with the pacific settlement of disputes, while Chapter VII provides for extensive powers of coercion, including the power to impose economic sanctions (Art. 41) and, where these have proved inadequate, or are in the opinion of the UNSC likely to prove inadequate, the power to impose military sanctions (Art. 42).

The primary restraint upon Security Council action is that it can only become involved in situations which either 'endanger the maintenance of international peace and security' in the case of Chapter VI or where, under Article 39 of Chapter VII, it determines that there exists a 'threat to the peace, [a] breach of the peace, or [an] act of aggression'. The charter provides no guidance as to what constitutes such situations, and it is clear that the drafters intended that the Security Council should have a wide discretion in determining them. Proposals to include a definition of aggression in the charter were rejected, reflecting the reluctance of states to place undue parameters on the Council's ability to act. More significantly, the decision reflected the fact that the UNSC was intended to act as a political rather than a judicial body, and therefore legalistic definitions were viewed as inappropriate. However, as noted above, freedom of action was limited in so far as once a determination that a situation represented a threat to international peace and security was made, the Council was under an obligation to remedy the problem.[6]

The Security Council's role was further constrained in that it was only mandated to respond to situations of an international nature. The Security Council's unique ability to intrude into the internal affairs of member states was made subject to the strict proviso that it could only do so where their internal activities threatened peaceful inter-state relations (Art. 2(7)). While it was left to the Security Council to decide when such a situation had arisen, it was clearly envisaged that the UNSC was not to concern itself with the internal use of force by member states. Furthermore Article 2(4) re-emphasizes this point, prohibiting member states from using force 'in their *international* relations', thus by implication not applying where force is being used internally, for example to suppress revolution or – of considerable significance at the time of drafting – colonial uprisings.

This restriction is symptomatic of an international community which views the concept of security in essentially statist terms. In particular the manner in which sovereign governments behave toward their citizens was not perceived as being a matter of legitimate concern to the Security Council unless and until it acquired external implications. The issue of human rights proved to be a thorny one from the time of its introduction by the United States during preliminary negotiations over the establishment of the United Nations. The Americans had to contend with the opposition of both the USSR and Britain, the former insisting that human rights had no place within an organization essentially dedicated to the maintenance of international peace and security, while the British more specifically feared that in the absence of any universal agreement as to what constituted human rights, their inclusion within the United Nations framework might lead to the organization interfering in their colonial affairs (Hilderbrand 1990, pp. 83–107).

Eventually both the British and the Soviets relented and accepted the inclusion of general references to the promotion of respect for human rights and fundamental freedoms. However in practice it was believed that these would be of only limited consequence since the two organs with responsibilities in this area – the General Assembly and the Economic and Social Council – lacked obligatory powers, and both were subject to the prohibition of intervention in the domestic affairs of member states. The articles of Chapter VII which relate to the Security Council's enforcement powers make no mention of human rights, and at no point was there any suggestion that human rights could in themselves constitute a security issue giving rise to utilization of the organization's collective security mechanism. This statist concept of security was, however, to evolve over time, with human rights steadily gaining in importance, and consequently the strict dichotomy between situations of an international and a domestic nature was to be substantially eroded.

THE EVOLVING NATURE OF SECURITY IN THE COLD WAR ERA

The notion that the organs of the United Nations should not interfere in the domestic affairs of member states is based upon a premise which is as old as the concept of state sovereignty: states as sovereign independent entities are entitled to organize their internal behaviour as they choose; such behaviour only warrants international attention when it affects or effects inter-state relations. This position is reflected in the United Nations Charter, but in practice both the General Assembly and the Security Council have eroded what Article 2(7) refers to as being 'essentially within the domestic jurisdiction' of a state, and have thus enlarged their own operational competence.[7]

For the Security Council the first step along this route was taken less than a year after the signing of the charter when it met to consider the so-called 'Spanish question'. In conjunction with the cases of Southern Rhodesia and South Africa this is commonly cited as evidence of this process of erosion and expansion (Harris 1991, pp. 874–91; Higgins 1963, pp. 77–106; Wellens 1993, pp. 122–33 and 203–39).[8] However while these cases attest to the existence of such a process, their specific facts are such that caution must be exercised to ensure that the extent of the practice is not exaggerated. In the first of these cases the UNSC addressed a Polish claim that the nature of the Franco regime in Spain led to 'international friction and endangered international peace and security'. It found, despite British and Dutch claims to the contrary, that the situation represented a 'potential menace to international peace' and therefore Article 2(7) did not preclude Security Council consideration. However the Council rejected claims that the regime constituted a threat within the meaning of Chapter VII, instead opting to utilize the charter's provisions providing for the pacific settlement of disputes. Thus while the Council accepted that the nature of a government may be an issue of international concern, it rejected arguments that it should employ its enforcement powers in dealing with it.

In its deliberations over Southern Rhodesia the Security Council found that the situation in the territory constituted a 'threat to international peace and security', sanctioning the use of force to prevent the delivery of oil to the territory in contravention of a UN embargo, and eventually imposing stringent and wide-ranging mandatory economic sanctions.[9] However while the Council criticized the nature of the 'racist settler minority' which seized power, its determination was premised on the fact that control of territory had been illegally wrested from the hands of a member of the United Nations. Thus the case, particularly in its initial stages, offers little support for the argument that the Security Council was attempting to broaden its operational remit to allow for the censorship of governments or to cover human rights. Furthermore Britain, the member state in question, chose to reverse its position regarding the applicability of Article 2(7) and instead actively sought UN involvement, thus further undermining the claim that the UNSC was seeking to expand its jurisdictional competence.

In responding to requests that it consider the situation in South Africa, the Security Council passed a resolution in which it '[r]ecognis[ed] that the situation ... is one that has led to international friction and if continued might endanger international peace and security' and went on to '[d]eplore … the policies and actions of the Government of the Union of South Africa which have given rise to the present situation'.[10] However it was a further seventeen years before the Security Council finally accepted that the situation in South Africa constituted a threat within the meaning of Article 39, this determination being based upon consideration of the build-up of arms which had taken place within the country rather than the nature of the apartheid regime. Furthermore, in imposing mandatory sanctions the exercise of the veto by the three Western permanent members ensured that punitive measures were limited to the establishment of an arms embargo.[11] The Western powers argued that the imposition of economic sanctions was likely to prove ineffective, but more fundamentally asserted that the situation in South Africa did not represent a threat to international peace within the meaning of Chapter VII. With considerable justification proponents of sanctions – in particular the post-colonial African states, the USSR and China – rejected both lines of reasoning, insisting that reluctance to support sanctions was simply grounded on a fear of undermining economic interests in the region.

Countering these allegations the Western states, again with considerable justification, accused those who sought only to castigate South Africa of hypocrisy. On a continent in which governmentally orchestrated human rights violations were almost endemic, concentration upon the behaviour of white racist regimes to the exclusion of all others appeared to pay little heed to genuine concerns for human rights. Factors which elicited Western support in the case of Southern Rhodesia did not exist in the case of South Africa, and thus the latter appeared to some, including the three permanent Western members of the Council, to be no different to the multitude of other governments which abused human rights. However the majority of the international community supported the imposition of mandatory economic sanctions. For most states the crucial factor in the debate – distinguishing the South African and Southern Rhodesian regimes for censure – appears not to have been their record on human rights, but rather the manner in which these regimes obstructed the process of decolonization which had swept the remainder of continental Africa. This right had both implicitly and explicitly been a feature of resolutions on South Africa and Southern Rhodesia, suggesting that UN sanctions would not have been forthcoming other than within the context of the process of decolonization.[12]

In terms of human rights, proponents of sanctions against South Africa may have been guilty of hypocrisy, but in truth few if any members of the international community had clear consciences over the issue. While the United Nations reacted in the cases of Southern Rhodesia and South Africa, these were the exception rather than the rule, for in other cases where human rights abuses of equal and greater magnitude occurred, it strenuously avoided any involvement. As many as one million people may have died in late 1965 during civil conflict in Indonesia, but the international community failed to respond or to object when the country declared its wish to 'resume full co-operation with the United Nations' (Franck and Rodley 1973, p. 295). Similarly when Burundi's Tutsi minority embarked upon the systematic slaughter of the country's Hutu population killing tens of thousands of innocent people, the UN effectively remained passive and the Organization of African Unity (OAU), while simultaneously advocating sanctions against South Africa, insisted that the events in Burundi were of a purely internal nature and therefore not open to international scrutiny (Umozurike 1979, p. 199; Kuper 1981, pp. 162–5).

The United Nations' response to India's 1971 intervention in East Pakistan, Vietnam's 1978 intervention in Cambodia and Tanzania's 1979 intervention in Uganda also demonstrate the inability (or unwillingness) of the Security Council to deal with cases of gross human rights abuses other than within the context of the process of decolonization. These three cases bore marked similarities: first they involved governments which were pursuing genocidal policies; second these governments were overthrown by neighbouring states; third, none of the intervening states claimed to be motivated primarily (if at all) by humanitarian concerns; and finally, the international community, having failed to prevent the bloodshed, condemned – to a greater or lesser degree – the governments which chose to intervene. The UN's response to each of these cases was determined more by the political and strategic imperatives of the Cold War than by concerns for human rights. Thus where armed intervention was arguably most justifiable on humanitarian grounds – Vietnam's intervention to overthrow the Pol Pot regime in Cambodia – the intervening state received the greatest censure. In contrast, Tanzania's overthrow of Idi Amin received little more than ritualistic public denunciation from the Cold War protagonists. With the exception of the majority of African states which roundly condemned its actions, the rest of the international community reacted in a way which amounted to what Caroline Thomas has described as 'almost tacit approval' (Thomas 1985, pp. 113 and 122–3).[13]

The inability of the Security Council to utilize its coercive powers to solve the problems that these situations represented is indicative of the dangers of attempting to expand a security system beyond its original remit, and of the problems associated with a collective security system lacking *certainty* and dependent upon the political judgements of member states. Direct control of domestic behaviour had been deliberately excluded when the charter was drafted on the grounds that it was not possible to reach agreement as to what constituted acceptable and unacceptable behaviour. A 'minimum of political solidarity and moral community' is an essential prerequisite for collective security to function successfully,[14] and in the case of the United Nations Security Council this could only be attained at the level of inter-state relations where a minimum compact of coexistence premised upon the non-use of force and non-intervention received consensual backing. The expansion to include – even indirectly – issues of human rights placed too great a strain on the system, and the onset of the Cold War and the communist revolution in China served only to intensify the problem as ideological and political rivalries destroyed any vestiges of cooperation. This led to inaction not only because of a lack of consensus amongst the veto-bearing powers, but because each sought to use its position to promote its own political objectives.

THE EVOLVING NATURE OF SECURITY IN THE POST-COLD WAR ERA[15]

The end of the Cold War heralded the possibility of great power collaboration akin to that envisaged when the United Nations was established. While political ideology remained a dividing factor, the end of East–West antagonism meant that the Security Council was now better placed to perform its intended function than at any other time in its troubled history. The first test for this new-found spirit of cooperation came when Saddam Hussein invaded Kuwait in August 1990. Through the use of UN-mandated economic sanctions and military force, Iraq was forced to withdraw from Kuwait. The Gulf conflict was extolled as a classic example of collective security: an act of inter-state aggression, a clear violation of the pre-emptory norms of international society, had been addressed in the most forthright manner possible, and in a wave of self-congratulation US President George Bush declared the dawning of 'a New World Order'.

This new-found optimism was immediately put to the test when, spurred on by Saddam's defeat and the encouragement of Western governments, the Iraqi Kurdish population in the north of the country and the Shi'a Moslems in the south rebelled against the central authorities. Despite its recent defeat the Iraqi army retained an overwhelming military advantage *vis-à-vis* the Kurds and the Shi'a and the uprisings were suppressed with characteristic brutality. The resulting humanitarian disaster received extensive media coverage, eventually prompting Western governments to react by establishing 'safe havens' in the north of Iraq and a protective 'no-fly zone' in the south (Wheeler and Morris, forthcoming 1996). The Western allies involved in establishing the former[16] claimed that the Security Council, in passing Resolution 688,[17] had provided legal authorization for their actions and furthermore that, in so acting, members of the Council had been unanimous in their commitment to intervene to protect the Kurds. However analysis of the Security Council meeting held on 5 April 1991 before the passing of Resolution 688 indicates that the degree of consensus was far more limited.

In draft form the resolution was sponsored by four states, each of which adopted subtly different positions during the debate. France argued, without reference to the principle of non-intervention, that the Kurdish crisis constituted a matter of 'international interest' because Iraqi human rights violations had assumed 'the dimension of a crime against humanity'.[18] In contrast the United States insisted that it was 'not the role or the intention of the Security Council to interfere in the internal affairs of any country' but that action had to be taken because the refugee flows caused by Iraq's mistreatment of the Kurds threatened regional peace and stability. Britain and Belgium both drew attention to Iraq's obligations under international humanitarian law, and noted that its human rights abuses had led to a population exodus which threatened international peace and security. Ironically, given its role, Britain also cited the precedent of South Africa in support of its argument that human rights violations could in themselves give rise to international repercussions.

Those states which supported the resolution[19] all adopted a similar line of reasoning, namely that while it is imperative that the United Nations respect the sovereignty and territorial integrity of member states, Article 2(7) of the charter did not apply in this particular case since the flow of refugees caused by Iraq's repression of its Kurdish population constituted a 'threat to international peace and security'. Thus even those states which supported the resolution demonstrated a clear reluctance to internationalize human rights to the extent that the

Security Council could intervene where they were being violated other than when such a threat existed.

China chose to abstain on Resolution 688, explaining its position in a short and somewhat ambiguous statement. While voicing concern over the situation in Iraq and the refugee flow into Turkey and Iran, the situation was described as one of an essentially internal nature and thus covered by Article 2(7). Without addressing the question of whether the current situation represented a threat to international peace and security, the Chinese representative stated that 'the international aspects involved ... should be settled through the appropriate channels' and that humanitarian assistance should be rendered 'through the relevant organisations'.[20] The meaning of this remains unclear, but in abstaining on the vote it is apparent that China did not view the Security Council as either an 'appropriate channel' or a 'relevant organisation'. The Indian representative, having expressed concern over the plight of the Iraqi Kurdish population, explained his country's abstention by stating that the Security Council should concern itself solely with issues of international security. The resolution was unacceptable because in addition to addressing the security aspect of the problem, it went on to 'prescribe what should be done', thus impinging upon Iraq's internal affairs, violating 'a cardinal principal in international relations'.[21] Cuba, Yemen and Zimbabwe voted against the resolution, basing their position on a narrow interpretation of Article 2(7). Each claimed that the relationship between the Iraqi government and its Kurdish population was a purely internal matter. Since there was no conflict or war between Iraq and any of its neighbours, international peace and security were not threatened and thus any Security council involvement would exceed its operational competence.

Being able to secure only ten positive votes in favour of Resolution 688 provided its sponsors with little diplomatic room to manoeuvre.[22] With many supporting governments showing only cautious enthusiasm, the sponsors were unable to attain as forthright a mandate as they wished. Despite declaring that the refugee problem on the Iraqi–Turkish border constituted a 'threat to international peace and security' and employing pre-emptory language in 'insisting' that Iraq allow UN relief agencies to operate inside its territorial borders, and 'demanding' that the Iraqi government stop repressing its people, the resolution was not passed under Chapter VII of the charter. It made no reference to the Council's collective security powers and failed therefore to provide a mandate for the military mission which the Western allies undertook in its name.[23] It seems almost certain that a more forthright resolution specifically invoking the Council's coercive powers would have faltered at the voting stage for, while China's contribution to the debate over Resolution 688 was notable by its brevity, Beijing clearly indicated its willingness to veto any resolution which went beyond mere declaratory condemnation. Furthermore, states such as the USSR, Romania and Ecuador, which were prepared to support a draft resolution that specifically referred to Article 2(7) but made no mention of Chapter VII, would have been alienated by the inclusion of more stringent measures and thus even if China had not exercised its veto, the resolution would probably have failed to attract the requisite number of positive votes.

Resolution 688 fits uneasily within the evolutionary process by which the Security Council's comprehension of the notion of security has been gradually expanded. It is a retrograde step in the sense that, unlike the cases of Southern Rhodesia and South Africa, the Security Council failed to specifically authorize the use of coercive measures. In common with these cases the Council relied upon the existence of a factor other than the abuse of human rights to justify its finding that a 'threat to international peace and security' existed. In the light of this, Resolution 688 represents a progressive move given that 20 years earlier the Council had rejected Indian claims that a refugee flow resulting from human rights violations could constitute such a situation. The real significance of Resolution 688, however, lies in the fact that for the first time in its history the Security Council had dealt with a situation involving gross human rights violations without the permanent members using the issue to score political points against one another.

This cooperation reached its zenith as the Security Council sought to respond to the human tragedy which befell Somalia during 1991–92. The chaos which gripped the country resulted from a series of uprisings against the government of President Siad Barre in December 1990 and January 1991. As the central government collapsed a variety of disparate groups competed for control of the country. The conflict, compounded by drought, led to a catastrophic famine. Regional attempts to bring stability to the country failed and eventually in January 1992 the UN became involved, with the Security Council unanimously adopting Resolution 733. This delcared that the conflict in Somalia constituted 'a threat to international peace and security', established an arms embargo under Chapter VII of the charter, and called for an increase in humanitarian assistance.[24]

Despite the establishment of a 3000-strong UN peacekeeping force[25] the situation in Somalia continued to deteriorate. Resolution 794, which under Chapter VII of the charter authorized member states to 'use all necessary means to establish … a secure environment for humanitarian relief operations in Somalia', was the Security Council's final attempt to respond to the human suffering in the country.[26] The resolution marked a fundamental shift in the UNSC's approach to the crisis. Resolution 733, and those which had followed it, determined that the conflict posed a threat to regional stability, but in Resolution 794 the Council took the radical step of stating that the 'magnitude of human suffering caused by the conflict' and obstacles to the delivery of aid constituted a threat to international peace and security. The resolution must therefore be seen as a ground-breaking attempt to broaden the concept of security to include individual and intra-state issues, thus rejecting the traditional state-centric approach. This is not to suggest that states in adopting this resolution were necessarily motivated solely or even primarily by humanitarian sentiments, but the willingness of members to see the Council's operational remit expanded in this way is revolutionary judged against the historical backdrop outlined above.

Given that the resolution was passed unanimously it appears at first sight that the Council may have been signalling a major and irreversible reorientation in terms of how it viewed its security mandate. However, closer scrutiny of the resolution and of the statements made before its adoption suggest otherwise. During the Security Council debate several states referred to the fact that intervention to provide humanitarian aid was in their view permissible given that the central government in Somalia had collapsed. States such as China, India and Zimbabwe, which had refused to support intervention in Iraqi Kurdistan, emphasized this and declared that the unique position in which this placed Somalia required an exceptional response. The Zimbabwean representative stated that the resolution only set a precedent for 'operations under equally unique circumstances',[27] while India stressed that in its view no precedent for future action was being set.[28] In response to these concerns the preamble of the resolution recognizes 'the unique character of the present situation in Somalia and [is] mindful of its deteriorating, complex and extraordinary nature, requiring an immediate and exceptional response'. Inclusion of the word 'immediate' appears to refer to the fact that the United States was to be mandated to undertake the operation, a measure which China and India in particular referred to with some concern, though both stated that in the circumstances they were prepared to accept an essentially unilateral approach as opposed to collective action given the necessity of an immediate response.

Resolution 794 must therefore be viewed with caution if one is seeking to demonstrate a willingness on behalf of the Security Council to act to protect human rights. While adopting an individualist rather than a statist approach to security, it does so within carefully defined parameters. First, if it sets any form of precedent, this only extends to cases in which the political infrastructure of a state has collapsed. Emphasizing that the Security Council was taking 'exceptional' steps to deal with a 'unique situation' was crucial to ensuring support for the resolution. In situations where no government exists states concerned at the erosion of the principle of non-intervention are able to maintain their position by simply asserting that rather than intervention against the will of a government, action is being taken in the absence of any form of recognizable government. Many states placed such emphasis on this characteristic in the case of Somalia that one must assume that in different circumstances they would be unwilling to support direct intervention. The conspicuous absence throughout the debate of references to Article 2(7) or to the competence of the Security Council to deal with issues of a humanitarian nature – contrasting sharply with the debates over Southern Rhodesia, South Africa and Iraqi Kurdistan – would also appear to be attributable to this. Second, the willingness of states to acquiesce in mandating intervention which is to be undertaken by a single state or a small group of states appears limited. This is problematic since while certain states may prefer that the Security Council maintain operational control, those states prepared to contribute forces are likely to oppose such a position.

The next humanitarian tragedy to come before the Security Council concerned Rwanda, a country long racked by conflict between its Hutu and Tutsi population. Under international pressure the two sides signed a peace accord and the Security Council despatched a 2500-strong peacekeeping force, the United Nations Assistance Mission for Rwanda I (UNIMAR I) to monitor the fragile ceasefire.[29] Despite the presence of UN personnel the situation exploded in April 1994 when the country's Hutu president was killed, sparking an orgy of violence in which the Hutu-dominated government forces killed approximately 500 000 Tutsis and moderate Hutus and a further million were forced to seek refuge in neighbouring Zaire. Having initially prevaricated in its response,[30] the Council met against a backdrop of continued killing to consider a proposal that it authorize the deployment of a French force which would undertake the task of stabilizing the country until a strengthened UN force (UNAMIR II) could assume its allotted role.

The meeting culminated in the adoption of Resolution 929, but in a voting pattern reminiscent of Resolution 688 and in stark contrast to that leading to the adoption of Resolution 794, only ten positive votes were cast, five states choosing to abstain.[31] In explaining the proposal the French representative insisted that the initiative was 'exclusively humanitarian' and would be impartially conducted.[32] By coincidence Rwanda held a seat on the Security Council at the time of the debate and in supporting the French scheme, the Hutu government representative also chose to emphasize the humanitarian aspect of the crisis. However, with the Tutsi Rwandan Patriotic Front in control of the majority of the country and given that France had intervened unilaterally to support Hutu client regimes in the past, many suspected that the French initiative was primarily driven by strategic concerns. The abstentions of China, Brazil and Nigeria appear to be grounded in such fears: each expressed the view that unilateral intervention by France was inappropriate and that the UNAMIR II framework should be utilized to achieve a solution to the problem. Even some of the states which supported the resolution appear to have harboured concern regarding the possibility that the proposed intervention might serve to promote the interests of the Hutu faction in Rwanda, but French assurances to the contrary, coupled with the specific wording of the resolution, allayed these fears. The Russian and Argentinian representatives in particular appear to have attached great significance to a preambular paragraph which 'stress[ed] the strictly humanitarian character of [the] operation which shall be conducted in an impartial and neutral fashion, and shall not constitute an interposition force between the parties'.[33]

Much of the debate surrounding the adoption of Resolution 929 centred upon the relationship between France and Rwanda, with many states apparently basing their voting strategy upon their perception of the geopolitical implications of a French military deployment in this region of East Africa. Nevertheless the resolution has significant implications in terms of the progression of Security Council activity which is the focus of this chapter. As it had in the case of Somalia, the Security Council determined that 'the magnitude of the humanitarian crisis in Rwanda constitutes a threat to peace and security in the region' and acting under Chapter VII of the charter it authorized the use of 'all necessary means' to assure the delivery of humanitarian assistance. What is striking about the cases of Somalia and Rwanda is that despite their essentially humanitarian nature, no member of the Council asserted that Article 2(7) prohibited their consideration, the link between human suffering and the existence of a 'threat to international peace and security' was never disputed, and at no time was it suggested that the Security Council lacked the constitutional competence to deal with the crisis. In part this can be attributed to the fact that in neither case was the Security Council taking action *against* the will of a sovereign government. In the case of Somalia there was no government; in the case of Rwanda the *de jure* government consented to the intervention. However, considering the pre-eminent position which questions of constitutional competence and jurisdiction had enjoyed in previous debates, it may also be that Somalia and Rwanda provide evidence – however slight – that members of the Security Council now perceive its guardianship of international peace and security in terms which exceed the classical inter-state paradigm.

The depth of this change was questioned in the case of Haiti for here the issue before the Council was one of political as well as human rights. Direct United Nations involvement in the case began in October 1990 when, at the request of the country's Provisional President, Ertha Pascal-Trouillot, the General Assembly established the United Nations Observer Group for the Verification of the Elections in Haiti.[34] Along with representatives of the Organization of American States (OAS) and a variety of non-governmental organizations, this group monitored the elections held in December 1990. In what was judged to be a remarkably peaceful, if somewhat confused ballot, Jean-Bertrand Aristide was elected as the country's new president. He took office on 7 February 1991, but within eight months was overthrown by a *coup d'état*, headed by the army's Commander-in-Chief General Raoul Cedras[35] (Morris 1994, pp. 40–68).

In early October the French representative on the UNSC requested that it meet to consider the situation in Haiti. However, despite a personal appeal for assistance from President Aristide, it failed to respond other than issuing a presidential statement condemning the *coup* and calling for Aristide's return to power. A more assertive stance was blocked by the Chinese representative who, with the support of India, insisted that the *coup* was a domestic matter and that UN involvement was therefore prohibited by Article 2(7). The General Assembly in conjunction with the OAS was therefore burdened with initial responsibility for finding a solution to the problem. However in June 1993, the ousted Aristide government once again requested Security Council involvement, calling upon the Council to impose a mandatory and universal trade embargo on Haiti.

On this occasion the Security Council accepted responsibility for dealing with the crisis, a change of heart ostensibly motivated by a growing refugee problem which was determined under Article 39 to be a 'threat to international peace and security'.[36] In response to the threat and in an attempt to secure the reinstatement of President Aristide, the Council imposed a mandatory oil and arms embargo on the country although it stopped short of including any enforcement provisions. The resolution, which eventually gained unanimous support in the Council, was the result of diplomatic moves on the part of the United States, France and Venezuela. Active support from the latter, an influential member of the Non-Aligned Movement, provided the resolution with a more balanced political foundation, and thus helped to nullify the objections of states such as China, who were concerned that the UNSC – at Washington's behest – was attempting to dictate the domestic political agenda of UN member states. In furtherance of achieving as wide a support as possible for the resolution, the Security Council also resorted to a tactic first seen in the case of Somalia. To placate fears that taking action over Haiti would establish a general precedent for the future, the resolution stated that the threat posed by the situation in Haiti resulted from a combination of 'unique and exceptional circumstances' and that these gave rise to the actions taken under Chapter VII. Resolution 841 marked the beginning of a process during which the Council would employ the whole array of measures at its disposal, culminating in the sanctioning of military intervention.

The pressure brought to bear by the Security Council initially appeared to be paying dividends when negotiations between Aristide and Cedras led to the signing of the Governor's Island Agreement which provided for Aristide's return to power along with the removal of sanctions and an amnesty for leading members of the military regime. Further limited progress toward a settlement resulted in the suspension of sanctions, but with the continuation of political violence, and the failure of the Cedras regime to honour its Governor's Island commitments, the Council was forced to apply greater pressure, reimposing sanctions and authorizing a military blockade to enforce them.[37] With Cedras still firmly entrenched, the Security Council imposed more extensive sanctions including a comprehensive trade embargo, the freezing of foreign assets and the introduction of travel restrictions, but despite this the junta showed no signs of relinquishing power.[38] Consequently President Aristide wrote to the Secretary-General and, reversing his original position, called for military intervention.[39] In response

to the letter the Council passed Resolution 940 which under Chapter
VII reaffirmed that the situation in Haiti constituted a 'threat to international peace and security' and authorized 'Member States to form a
multinational force under unified command and control and, ... to use
all necessary means to facilitate the departure from Haiti of the military
leadership'.[40]

Despite President Aristide's backing for the plan, the decision to
sanction military intervention pushed the consensus within the UNSC
and the wider international community to near breaking-point. Having
passed Resolution 940, the president of the Council issued a statement
saying that its adoption was warranted by the exceptional and unique
situation in Haiti and that it should not be regarded as setting a precedent, a point reinforced by a point within the text of the resolution.[41]
These concessionary steps were an attempt to pacify those states which
had voiced concern over the use of force to resolve what they perceived
to be an essentially internal matter. While no state voted against the
resolution, China and Brazil abstained and Cuba, Mexico, Uruguay and
Venezuela – addressing the Council in pursuance of their rights under
Article 32 – all spoke out against the resolution.[42] Beijing, which had
so far judiciously supported the UN's actions against Haiti's military
leaders, was unwilling to veto the resolution for fear of alienating
Western leaderships, but it was also unwilling to actively support direct
military intervention.[43] The Chinese representative stated that in his
country's view the situation in Haiti constituted an 'element of instability in the region' and on that basis it had supported economic sanctions.
However he would abstain here on the grounds that 'resolving problems such as that of Haiti through military means does not conform
with the principles enshrined in the United Nations Charter and lacks
sufficient and convincing grounds.[44] Similar sentiments were expressed
by the representatives of Brazil, Mexico, Cuba, Uruguay and Venezuela. The Brazilian representative argued that while his country had
supported economic sanctions, he could not support the resolution under consideration because 'the defence of democracy should always be
consistent with principles governing relations between states and does
not entail the recourse to force...'.[45] Opposition to Resolution 940
centred upon the distinction between situations which warrant economic sanctions, and those where military measures are justified. However, the UN Charter makes no such distinctions in its Chapter VII
provisions and thus in constitutional terms the claim that the use of
military force would be *ultra vires* was mistaken, though it does illus-

trate the psychological chasm which exists between recourse to economic and military sanctions.

In relation to action taken in the other post-Cold War cases, Haiti represents yet another expansion of the interventionary role of the Security Council. In common with Kurdistan – but in contrast with the 1971 crisis in East Pakistan – a refugee flow was found to constitute a 'threat to international peace and security'. As with Somalia and Rwanda the Council emphasized that the situation in Haiti, and therefore its reaction to it, was 'unique and exceptional', a contrivance which was now becoming so familiar as to be meaningless. However, the most conspicuous aspect of the Security Council's deliberations over Haiti, particularly the debate over Resolution 940, was the manner in which it replicated the Security Council debate on the Kurds and more generally those of the Cold War era. Whereas the debates over Somalia and Rwanda were notable for their failure to address the issues of domestic jurisdiction and constitutional competence, in the case of Haiti these issues once again came to the fore. There are a number of possible explanations for this. Specific to the case in question, states may have been concerned by the prospect of the United States intervening in the Caribbean, having spent so many years trying to reduce the influence of the regional hegemon. Three more general factors may also have been influential. First, recent experience of states unilaterally intervening on behalf of the UN, as in Somalia and Rwanda, suggested that the approach was at best of limited efficacy, and at worst futile and counterproductive. Second, repeated assertions that precedents were not being set by UN actions became more difficult to sustain and thus states may have feared the consequences of eroding the principle of non-intervention. Finally, unlike any of the previous post-Cold War cases, Haiti involved intervention to promote political rights, for while violations of human rights were a significant factor, the restoration of a democratically elected government appears to have been the primary concern of the majority of UNSC members. In an international system in which agreement on political rights is far from universal, the prospect of militarily intervening to restore democracy may, for states such as China, have been one step too far down the evolutionary road.

CONCLUSION

Since its inception in 1945 it is irrefutable that the Security Council has progressively redefined the meaning of the term 'threats to international peace and security' as employed in Chapter VII of the UN Charter. Having initially denoted threats of a strictly inter-state nature, the post-Cold War cases in particular suggest that the term is now understood to encompass also certain aspects of individual security. What remains unclear however is first, how expansive the redefined term is, and second, how extensively it is supported by states other than the liberal democracies of the Western world.

As to the extent of what now constitutes 'security' within the UN system, the post-Cold War cases suggest that the organization's collective security machinery will be utilized to protect human rights, first, if human rights violations result in a flow of refugees which threatens regional peace and stability. In this situation intervention[46] can be justified on the traditional grounds of a 'threat to international peace and security', allowing the Council to (at least partially) side-step the thorny issues of human rights. Second, human rights will be protected if a state's central government has collapsed. Here intervention is permissible because it can be distinguished as action taken in the absence of, as opposed to against the will of, a government. Finally, protection will be given if the *de jure* government requests intervention. In this final instance there is no breach of sovereignty simply by virtue of consent, though where the *de jure* government lacks *de facto* control intervention is likely to prove problematic in practice if not in theory. If this is an accurate representation of the implications of these cases, then the prospect of widespread UN action to promote human rights remains a distant one. It would for example suggest that, in the absence of one of the above factors, the international response to the cases of Indonesia, Burundi, East Pakistan, Cambodia and Uganda may not be that different today from what it was during the Cold War. The post-Cold War cases suggest two further guidelines for future UN conduct. The Council is more likely to sanction intervention if it is to be carried out by a multinational force rather than by a single state or small number of states. Acceptance of a UN command structure answerable to the Security Council is likely to increase support still further. Second, intervention to safeguard political rather than human rights is less likely to attract international support, particularly if the use of military force is involved. The case of Haiti suggests the existence of widespread opposition to the use of military force for this purpose.

With regard to the extent to which the post-Cold War cases have enjoyed international support, there remains considerable doubt over the breadth of the underlying consensus. This problem remains particularly acute in the case of China, for not only does the country approach the question of human and political rights from a markedly different historical, cultural and ideological standpoint, but as a veto-bearing member of the Security Council it also possesses the ability to prevent UN action. At a recent UN meeting convened to discuss the Security Council's responsibilities for maintaining international peace and security, the Chinese representative commented that for China the 'core' principle in international relations was that of 'non-interference in each other's internal affairs'. In a thinly veiled criticism of the Council's Western members China insisted that:

> A country's human rights situation should not be judged in total disregard of its history and national conditions. It is neither appropriate nor workable to demand that all countries measure up to the human rights criteria or models of one country or a small number of countries ... [China] is opposed to interference in the internal affairs of other countries using the human rights issue as an excuse.[47]

If, as suggested earlier, collective security is dependent for its success upon a 'minimum of political solidarity and moral community', then the above quote suggests that the prospect of promoting human rights through the collective security mechanism of the Security Council is indeed limited. Since Chinese acquiescence is the least which is required if the Council is to utilize its powers under Chapter VII, then it is essential that the Western members of the UNSC do not attempt to pursue the human rights agenda to a point at which they undermine the consensus in the Council which exists over the policing of inter-state affairs. Agreement regarding the latter, the original goal of the Security Council, is closer now than at any other time during the history of the United Nations, but any attempt to expand the organization's collective security role to include individual security in the form of human and political rights is undertaken in the knowledge that it threatens the minimum compact which exists at the level of inter-state affairs.

NOTES

1. For a detailed discussion of collective security see Thompson (1953), Claude (1965 and 1984) and Kupchan and Kupchan (1991). For an historical account of the formative years of the United Nations see Goodrich and Hambro (1949), Luard (1982) and Hilderbrand (1990).
2. By an amendment adopted in 1965 Security Council membership was expanded to its current number of fifteen.
3. Security Council decisions were originally made by the affirmative vote of seven members (amended to nine when the Security Council was expanded in 1965), including on substantive mattes the affirmative vote of all of the permanent members – Article 27.
4. Here *utility* denotes the ability of a collective security organization to employ a wide variety of coercive measures. Preferably member states should be willing to resort not only to moral and diplomatic censure; they should also be prepared to employ economic and ultimately military sanctions.
5. Here *certainty* refers to the extent to which a collective security organization's constitutional framework obliges member states to act in order to oppose aggression by states.
6. See Goodrich and Hambro (1949, p. 265).
7. For reasons of space and because it has exclusive recourse to coercive powers, discussion in the remainder of this chapter will focus upon the activities of the United Nations Security Council. It should however be noted that the General Assembly also asserted its authority over issues traditionally viewed as of domestic jurisdiction.
8. For details of UN action in each of these cases see the relevant United Nations *Yearbook*.
9. UNSC Res. 217, 20 UN SCOR (1965) of 20 November 1965; UNSC Res. 221, 21 UN SCOR (1966) of 9 April 1966; UNSC Res. 232, 21 UN SCOR (1966) of 16 December 1966.
10. UNSC Res. 134, 15 UN SCOR (1960) of 1 April 1960.
11. UNSC Res. 418, 32 UN SCOR (1977) of 4 November 1977. The Western permanent members indirectly blocked draft resolutions intended to impose sanctions under Chapter VII on several occasions and exercised their veto power for the same purpose in June 1976, on three occasions in March 1977, in April 1987 and in March 1988 (Harris 1991, p. 891; Wellens 1993, pp. 201–39).
12. UNSC Res. 232, 21 UN SCOR (1966) of 16 December 1966; UNSC Res. 418, 32 UN SCOR (1977) of 4 November 1977. See Jackson (1990, pp. 102–8).
13. For a general discussion of the UN's failure to react to cases of gross human rights during the Cold War era, see Morris (1991) and Wheeler and Morris (forthcoming 1996).
14. See Thompson (1953, p. 761). It is crucial that the major powers within a collective security organization exhibit unanimity amongst themselves in the name of the organization and the particular peace which it serves. They must be willing to act together in the name of the international community which they lead, and they must be prepared to act in such a way that 'national self-interest becomes equated with, but not subjected to, the welfare and stability of that international community' (Kupchan and Kupchan 1991, pp. 124–5).
15. There is considerable debate regarding the legitimacy and utility of recent interventions undertaken by the United Nations. However discussion here will concentrate on the debates and discussions which took place in the Security Council regarding the sanctioning of such operations. For a broader discussion of humani-

tarian intervention in the post-Cold War era see Wheeler and Morris (forthcoming 1996).

16. Primarily the United States, Britain and France. Italy and The Netherlands committed resources on a smaller scale.
17. UNSC Res. 688, 46 UN SCOR (1991) of 5 April 1991.
18. S/PV. 2982, pp. 53–4.
19. Austria, Ivory Coast, Ecuador, Romania, the USSR and Zaire.
20. S/PV. 2982, pp. 55–6.
21. S/PV. 2982, p. 63.
22. Under Article 27 (3) Security Council decisions on substantive matters require nine positive votes including the concurring votes of the permanent members.
23. The issue of whether or not Resolution 688 provided a mandate for the 'safe havens' project became a matter of heated debate. See Wheeler and Morris (forthcoming 1996).
24. UNSC Res. 733, 47 UN SCOR (1992) of 23 January 1992.
25. UNSC Res. 751, 47 UN SCOR (1992) of 24 April 1992. See also White (1993, pp. 255–6).
26. UNSC Res. 794, 47 UN SCOR (1992) of 3 December 1992.
27. S/PV. 3145, pp. 8–10.
28. S/PV. 3145, p. 51.
29. UNSC Res. 872, 48 UN SCOR (1993) of 5 October 1993.
30. UNSC Res. 912, 49 UN SCOR (1994) of 21 April 1994; UNSC Res. 918, 49 UN SCOR (1994) of 17 May 1994.
31. Brazil, China, New Zealand, Nigeria and Pakistan.
32. S/PV. 3392, p. 6.
33. UNSC Res. 929, 49 UN SCOR of 22 June 1994.
34. UNGA Res. 45/2, 45 UN GOAR (1990) of 10 October 1990.
35. For the official UN account of the organization's involvement in Haiti, see 'Crisis in Haiti: Seeking a Political Solution', in *United Nations Focus*, New York: United Nations Publications, 1993.
36. UNSC Res. 841, 48 UN SCOR (1993) of 16 June 1993.
37. UNSC Res. 872, 48 UN SCOR (1993) of 13 October 1993; UNSC Res. 875, 48 UN SCOR (1993) of 16 October 1993.
38 UNSC Res. 917, 49 UN SCOR (1994) of 6 May 1994.
39. S/1994/905 of 29 July 1994.
40. UNSC Res. 940, 49 UN SCOR (1994) of 31 July 1994.
41. 'Crisis in Haiti' op. cit., note 27, p. 5.
42. In order to avert the antagonism of another veto-bearing member of the council, the United States was apparently also forced to make concessions to Russia. Moscow had been seeking the backing of the Security Council for its proposals to send a peacekeeping force to the neighbouring state of Georgia, but this had not been forthcoming. US appeals to the council for the sanctioning of military intervention in Haiti met with Russian demands that in exchange for support on this, Washington must use its political weight to help Moscow achieve its own aims. Hence a deal was reportedly struck whereby the two permanent members would provide reciprocal support for each other's proposals, provided each carry out their actions under UN supervision. 'US and Russia Broker Haiti invasion Deal', see *The Times* (London), 1 August 1994.
43. For a discussion of China's attitude to the principle of non-intervention, and her behaviour within the Security Council, see Wheeler and Morris (forthcoming 1996).
44. S/PV. 3413, p. 10.
45. S/PV. 3413, p. 10.

46. Intervention here denotes the imposition of economic sanctions as well as military measures.
47. S/PV. 3046.

7. Security, nuclear proliferation and the end of the Cold War

Nicholas J. Wheeler and Simon J. Davies

INTRODUCTION

The demise of bipolarity and the debates surrounding the fate of the Non-Proliferation Treaty (NPT) at the 1995 Extension and Review Conference have made nuclear proliferation an increasingly significant global security issue. The problem has attracted further prominence since the end of the Cold War as a result of the covert nuclear weapons programmes discovered in Iraq and North Korea, both of whom are members of the NPT and thus subject (at least in theory) to safeguards administered by the International Atomic Energy Agency (IAEA). Besides prompting a general re-evaluation of the policy measures that exist to retard the further spread of nuclear weapons, these events have also led to much speculative debate about the likely future course of proliferation, and the prospects for controlling or even reversing it in the next phase of international relations. This chapter makes a contribution to that debate: first, by critically reflecting upon the historical success of the global NPT regime,[1] and suggesting that lessons might be learned from this experience for future non-proliferation efforts; and second, by exploring the strengths and weaknesses of four alternative theoretical and policy approaches to proliferation in the post-Cold War world. We identify the main protagonists in the proliferation debate as 'fatalists', 'unilateral mitigators', 'cooperative mitigators' and 'abolitionists'. In addition to offering a comprehensive framework for future debates, we argue that nuclear proliferation constitutes the principal threat to global security and that future theory and policy should take seriously the goal of a nuclear-weapons-free world. To perpetuate the simple verities of our nuclear past offers little more than a counsel of despair.

The permanence of the nuclear condition is an inescapable reality of the world that we inhabit. This is not to say that nuclear weapons are a natural or inevitable feature of inter-state relations, for while it may be difficult, discomforting or simply beyond the capacity of some to contemplate a future without these weapons, there is no necessity about their continued physical existence. Rather, the notion of permanence associated with the nuclear condition resides in the idea, employed forcefully in the work of Jonathan Schell, that the *knowledge* of their invention cannot realistically be lost (Schell 1984). The realization of this crucial fact has prompted a diversity of reactions that is striking. For Colin Gray, the durability of nuclear knowledge is linked necessarily to the persistence and continued spread of nuclear weapons themselves (Gray 1994). Since tension, mistrust and even nuclear conflict are seen as the inescapable consequences of this view, Gray's position is one of fatalism. Conversely, for neorealists like Kenneth Waltz and John Mearsheimer, the likely continued existence of nuclear weapons is regarded as a cause for some optimism, because their perceived deterrent qualities provide good reason to welcome their 'measured spread' (Waltz 1981, p. 30; Mearsheimer 1990 and 1993). Finally, in Schell's work it is the very durability of our knowledge about nuclear weapons that is seen to make total nuclear abolition possible (Schell 1984).

That the single issue of nuclear proliferation can attract such extremes of response is endorsement of the simple yet compelling idea that we attribute different meanings to social problems and behaviour on the basis of subjective perceptions, values and beliefs. Our practices towards the problem of nuclear proliferation are therefore, like many others, the product of socially constructed theories (Berger and Luckmann 1966; Giddens 1979; Wendt 1992). With regard to the relatively short history of thinking about nuclear weapons proliferation since 1945, it is the bipolar structure of global security relations that has exerted by far the greatest influence in conditioning dominant perceptions of what the proliferation problem is and, consequently, informing the major policy responses to it. This is significant for, as the next section argues, the Cold War security structure exerted an adverse effect on thinking about proliferation, its likely causes, consequences and solutions.

Scrutinizing previous and existing approaches to thinking about nuclear proliferation can yield insight into how our evolving perceptions of what the problem is (if indeed they *are* evolving) can or should affect subsequent attempts to deal with it in the post-Cold War era. The departure of bipolarity and the subsequent decline of Cold War tensions present a significant opportunity to re-evaluate previous approaches for a number of reasons. First, the shift in system structure away from bipolarity has also signalled the demise of the Cold War security dynamic, which focused thinking about security globally around a dyadic competition between the superpowers. Though many characteristics of the order that is emerging after bipolarity remain uncertain and the subject of intense controversy, it is clear that the next phase in international relations will be one free from the influence of this previously overwhelming security structure. This provides a space within which to consider new or previously suppressed views about the causes and consequences of proliferation, and the direction in which future policy should evolve.

Second, the issue of nuclear proliferation is of substantial importance in the post-Cold War era since more states than ever before now have the technological opportunity to procure nuclear weapons. For a significant number of states, the issue of whether to 'go nuclear' now depends more on considerations of political and military necessity, than on technological possibilities (Spector 1995, pp. 70–71). If the recent example of Iraq's attempt at covert proliferation demonstrates anything at all, it is surely that a sufficient *political* motive to acquire nuclear weapons can in some cases overcome the considerable legal, financial and technological barriers to doing so. Realization of this is crucial to understanding why the predominantly 'supply-side' measures associated with the Cold War phase of non-proliferation policy must be considered at best as a partial success. The record of covert NPT proliferators such as Iraq and the Democratic People's Republic of Korea, in addition to prominent non-NPT signatories such as India, Pakistan and Israel, shows that attempts to restrict the supply of nuclear weapons technology, materials and information fail to address the underlying factors that prompt some threatened states to seek nuclear weapons. Supplier controls such as the Zangger Committee and the London Club have been aimed primarily at those states not operating IAEA safeguards, but technological denial has done little to resolve the factors that drive the *demand* for nuclear weapons (Simpson 1994, pp. 47–9).

COLD WAR SECURITY AND NON-PROLIFERATION POLICY, 1945–90

It is significant that the unprecendented development of a global bi-polar system after 1945 coincided directly with the first formal measures aimed at retarding the further spread of nuclear weapons. The centre-piece of these efforts was the Non-Proliferation Treaty, and strong arguments can be made to support the claim that the perspectives of its main architects (which is to say principally the two superpowers, in addition to the limited influence of other key nuclear states such as the United Kingdom) were consistently distorted by the adverse influence of the East–West security competition. Tracing the development of superpower thinking about nuclear proliferation during the Cold War illustrates vividly the distortive influence of bipolarity over US–Soviet non-proliferation policy. Peter Clausen has stated the problem clearly:

> For 45 years … nonproliferation policy was made and implemented in the shadow of the Cold War rivalry. The spectre of a nuclear-armed Soviet Union inspired the first US attempts to prevent the spread of the bomb; subsequent US policies on proliferation were often conceived and shaped according to Washington's preoccupation with the Soviet problem. Just as the Cold War largely defined US foreign policy throughout the decades following Word War II, *it also largely determined American perspectives on the nature of the proliferation threat, the range of choices for dealing with it, and the costs and benefits of alternative policies.* (1993, p. 184, emphasis added.)

A closer examination of the historical development of non-proliferation policy shows the superpowers to have pursued a sequence of divergent and (at times) contradictory policy objectives before 1970. Each shift in policy direction reflects closely the evolving conceptions of the key nuclear powers with regard to proliferation and the perceived strategic value of either sharing, restraining, promoting or denying the spread of nuclear information and technology. Indeed, the policy history shows cooperative strategies between them to have taken more than 20 years to emerge fully.

The mixed nature of early US attitudes towards proliferation was reflected in an effectively 'dual-track' policy strategy that sought to maximize the changes of a satisfactory resolution to the issue under conditions of great uncertainty, particularly with regard to possible Soviet capabilities and intentions (Clausen 1993, pp. 2–9; Gardner 1994, p. 38). The presentation of the Baruch Plan to the United Nations in

1946, proposing the international regulation of all nuclear activity and the eventual elimination of US atomic weapons, thus coincided directly with the introduction of the highly repressive Atomic Energy Act (or McMahon Act), that sought to maintain strict national control over US atomic secrets (Fischer 1971, pp. 21–2; Fischer 1992, pp. 31–3; Melissen 1993, pp. 1–5). Following Stalin's rejection of the proposals for international control and the subsequent testing of Soviet atomic and hydrogen (thermonuclear) weapons in 1949 and 1953 respectively, US disillusionment with the strategy of denial resulted in two key policy developments that reflected changing attitudes towards proliferation. The first was a dramatic relaxation in the terms of the Atomic Energy Act, initially following the Soviet fusion test of 1953 and then again after the launch of *Sputnik* prompted US fears about a possible 'missile gap' in 1958. The upshot of this policy adjustment was to allow selective 'nuclear-sharing' with key strategic allies and the deployment of US nuclear forces in certain of the NATO countries of Western Europe (Nye 1988, p. 339). The second development was the unveiling of Eisenhower's 1953 'Atoms for Peace' proposal, which sought to trade legitimate access to the peaceful benefits of nuclear energy for all states in return for commitments to accept safeguards against the military misuse of nuclear technology. Peter Clausen argues that, in effect, Atoms for Peace represented nothing more than an additional attempt by the United States to maintain global control over the spread of nuclear technology (Clausen 1993, pp. 43–54).

Soviet attitudes and policies towards proliferation over the same period underwent a remarkably similar process of development to those of the United States. This comprised an initial period of restrictive secrecy followed by a shorter period of limited nuclear-sharing with key allies up to the end of 1958, namely China and certain members of the Warsaw Pact (Fischer 1971, pp. 26–7). The decline of political control over China following the Sino–Soviet split of 1959, and an increasing sense of worry about the possible *de facto* spread of US nuclear weapons to West Germany pushed Soviet policy into a new confrontational phase with the West. This was given explicit and alarming focus in the Berlin crisis of 1958, through which it has been suggested by Joseph Nye that Khrushchev sought to win concessions over the German nuclear issue (Nye 1988, pp. 340–41). At the same time, US proposals in the United Nations regarding IAEA safeguards and a possible draft test ban treaty were rejected by the Soviet Union, thereby consolidating the position of stalemate through mutual confrontation.

By the mid-1960s, several policy developments suggested a growing realization that confrontation over the control of nuclear weapons was proving to be a less than optimal strategy for both sides. In the wake of the Cuban missile crisis of 1962, there emerged a growing US–Soviet awareness of their shared interests in jointly managing the problem of nuclear proliferation. Previously confrontational policies were replaced by unprecedented cooperation, aided further by impending progress towards the European détente of the 1970s. Both sides endorsed an earlier Irish resolution at the United Nations (originally made in 1958) supporting the general aims of non-proliferation. In addition, earlier US proposals concerning IAEA safeguards were now accepted by the Soviet Union, and the Partial Test Ban Treaty was concluded in July 1963. US policy in particular shifted to reflect an increasing commitment to the philosophy of controlling proliferation through norms embodied within global regimes. By the late 1960s, both superpowers had progressed sufficiently far along the policy learning curve to discover a mutual interest in constructing a global non-proliferation regime. In view of the varied and often contradictory course of policymaking that preceded it, however, the final emergence of the NPT in 1970 should more realistically be seen as the product of failure in both sides' earlier attempts to pursue unilateral approaches to the problem, than as a coherent attempt to collectively understand and conclusively *resolve* it.

Despite being the centrepiece of US–Soviet security cooperation during the Cold War, the NPT bore all the hallmarks of their pernicious domination of global security relations. First, in reflecting only the selective views and values of the dominant nuclear weapons states, subsequent policy unsurprisingly exhibited a bias towards the interests of this minority. The NPT, for example, restricts the legitimate ownership of nuclear weapons to the five declared nuclear powers. The bargain implicit within the treaty presumes that the non-nuclear weapons states will renounce the nuclear option in return for the acknowledged nuclear weapons states pursuing comprehensive nuclear disarmament. Since the treaty was signed, the nuclear powers have consistently been reproached for their failure to fulfil the provisions of Article VI. Moreover, critics of the nuclear weapons states point to the hypocrisy of those who justify nuclear weapons as vital to their security, whilst denying the same right to other states party to the treaty. This criticism has come not only from members of the NPT, but also from those states like India and Pakistan, Israel, Argentina and Brazil who have previously objected to the treaty on account of its discriminatory nature.

While it is difficult to deny the existence of a 'two-tiered' structure to the NPT, one may question to what extent concerns about discrimination are the most important factor keeping the so-called 'hold-out' states like India, Pakistan and Israel from joining the treaty. A plausible interpretation of the position taken by these states is that complaints about discrimination provide a convenient pretext for maintaining the nuclear option. India's reluctance to join the NPT, for example, not only reflects dissatisfaction with the treaty's hierarchical structure, but also demonstrates a preoccupation with its vital security interests. In other words, the key prerequisites for India joining the regime would seem to be not only elimination of the treaty's discriminatory character, but more importantly a resolution of regional tensions in South Asia.

The fundamental weakness of the NPT regime has been its neglect of such regional security problems. This continues to be a substantial flaw, given that the greatest proliferation risks since the signing of the treaty have developed out of regional conflicts in the Middle East, South Asia, Latin America and the Korean Peninsula. This inadequacy is chiefly attributable to the tendency of East–West bipolarity to marginalize the internal dynamics of regional security problems, by perceiving them in the global context of Cold War competition. Dominant thinking about proliferation has tended to thrive on oversimplified and biased images, which have often served to obscure the indigenous sources of regional insecurity and exacerbate existing tensions. By nurturing globalized perceptions of security relations in situations where a sensitivity towards more localized threats might have proved more effective, comprehensive approaches like the NPT regime have either ignored altogether the internal dynamics of 'peripheral' security concerns, or else (more typically) *globalized* their significance by emphasizing a relevance to the wider superpower security competition.

The most vivid illustration of the NPT's disregard for the real sources driving regional proliferation is to be found in Article VII of the treaty. This is the only section of the treaty in which the issue of regional security is mentioned specifically, and the possibility of incorporating alternative (i.e. sub-global) approaches to the control of proliferation acknowledged at all. It states quite simply that '[n]othing in this Treaty affects the right of any group of States to conclude regional treaties in order to assure the total absence of nuclear weapons in their respective territories'. Two features of the Article VII commitment are immediately prominent. First, as even a cursory examination of the remainder of the NPT text shows, Article VII is by far the shortest and least elaborate of the treaty's eleven articles. It is also the treaty's only substantive article that is not preceded by a preambular paragraph of its own. Both its tone and length contrast sharply with the austere manner of Article III, for example, which comprises a prolonged and detailed account of the positive restrictions incumbent upon non-nuclear weapons states in the matter of concluding adequate nuclear safeguards with the IAEA.

Second, it is interesting to note that in contrast to every other one of the NPT's 23 terms (with the single additional exception of Article IV(1) concerning the right to engage in peaceful nuclear research and energy production), the phrasing of Article VII is entirely in the passive voice. David Fischer has commented that the article is particularly striking in relation to the others, since it is 'singularly negative in its formulation' (Fischer 1993, p. 171). Rather than compelling signatories to undertake a positive commitment to the active pursuit of regional security initiatives, Article VII is limited to conceding merely that 'nothing in this Treaty affects the right of any group of States' to do so. This remains a notable departure from the style of the other articles' terms and obligations, which generally seek either to impose explicit duties on signatories through positive undertakings, or else expressly prohibit other activities through the affirmation of a negative commitment. Article VII remains unique in conferring a positive right upon the signatories by means of a commitment that is barely acknowledged through the deliberate use of a passive voice.

The understated spirit of Article VII characterizes quite neatly the standing of the conventional relationship between the formal intent of the NPT and regional approaches to thinking about and dealing with proliferation. Yet are these admittedly textual aspects of the relationship sufficient evidence to demonstrate hostility on the part of the nuclear powers towards localized security problems, or does such scrutiny of the NPT's terms amount to little more than an argument founded on semantics? The hypothesis of conscious neglect is supported by David Fischer's analysis of the minimal role accorded nuclear-weapon-free zones (NWFZ) in the treaty:

> one might have expected that the architects of the NPT would have commended the only nuclear-weapon-free zone that was in the process of formation at the time the NPT was opened for signature ... [i.e. the Latin

American NWFZ envisaged by the 1968 Treaty of Tlatelolco] ... and would
have warmly encouraged other regional groups of states to establish additional nuclear-weapon-free zones instead of merely affirming that the Treaty
would not stand in their way if they wished to do so (Fischer 1993, p. 171).

He then advances several arguments which account for the established nuclear powers' reluctance to openly endorse or legitimize these
independent initiatives (Fischer 1993, pp. 171–5). First, superpower
support for the Latin American NWFZ during the drafting of the NPT
in the 1960s was made difficult by the Tlatelolco Treaty's ambiguous
position concerning the legitimacy of peaceful nuclear explosions
(PNEs). The reluctance of the superpowers to endorse test explosions
by states interested in acquiring nuclear weapons (as both Argentina
and Brazil were then perceived to be) is understandable given their
fears that this might set a destabilizing precedent. Second, open support
for the establishment of an NWFZ in Latin America would have had
direct implications for the creation of similar zones elsewhere. While,
to the élite powers, the banning of nuclear weapons from Latin America
might have seemed an attractive prospect in itself, endorsing the general principles of the Tlatelolco Treaty would have left them in a
position of discomfort and inconsistency with regard to proposals for
similar measures elsewhere. The United States and its allies in particular were sensitive about any steps that might lead to the withdrawal of
American nuclear forces from Europe. Third, additional protocols to
the Tlatelolco Treaty (and subsequently also the 1986 Rarotonga Treaty,
which created the South Pacific nuclear-free zone), could feasibly have
limited the projection of superpower influence within the regions concerned. These protocols included various commitments limiting freedom of movement for ships and aircraft within the zone, proscribing
the manufacture, stationing and testing of nuclear devices, and the
provision of positive assurances against nuclear attack on parties to the
treaties.

It is hard to escape the conclusion that the NPT regime has proved
itself to be impotent in addressing and resolving the nuclear aspirations
of the regional 'hold-out' states. The problem is that the instruments of
the regime are exclusively focused on controlling the supply of nuclear
weapons materials, technology and expertise rather than upon remov-
ing those factors that drive the demand for them. Under Article IV of
the NPT, member states are entitled to receive access to the benefits of
civilian nuclear power with assistance from the established nuclear

states. In return, the non-nuclear weapons states agree to place their domestic nuclear facilities under IAEA safeguards, where they are subject to periodic inspections. The only formal control that the NPT regime can exercise over states outside is to require that nuclear exports be transferred only to states which have placed all their nuclear facilities under similar safeguards (these are known as 'full-scope' safeguards). However, the global dissemination of technology over the last two decades, the growth of clandestine nuclear-smuggling operations (in particular, the creation of a nuclear black market in fissile materials arising from the break-up of the Soviet Union), and the indigenous efforts of many determined proliferators suggest that, while supply-side measures are a necessary part of the battle against proliferation, they are by no means a sufficient one (Simpson 1994, pp. 50–51; Spector 1995, pp. 70–71). Ultimately, it is considerations of national security and not external strategies of technological denial that will determine whether states pursue or renounce the nuclear option.

In general terms, whereas the NPT's implicit vision of a comprehensive solution to proliferation reflected the global conception of security favoured by the superpowers, the autonomy implicit within the regional approach clearly also presented a threat to the continued dominance of this image. The evolution of independent security initiatives such as the Latin American NWFZ and South Pacific NFZ challenged mutual superpower interests, not only by endangering the exercise of their influence abroad but, more significantly, by threatening to *remove control* over patterns of thinking about security away from their primary focus on the superpower competition. Consequently, the adversarial nature of the superpower relationship ensured that neither Washington nor Moscow was willing to pursue concerted and cooperative efforts to tackle regional security conflicts. With the passing of the Cold War there exists a unique opportunity to critically assess the worth of existing policy approaches and to re-think dominant attitudes towards the problem, in an environment free from the constraining influence of bipolar security structure. The next section considers four distinct paths along which our theories and practices with regard to proliferation might proceed in the next phase of international relations.

NUCLEAR PROLIFERATION AT THE END OF THE COLD WAR

If the goal of nuclear non-proliferation was sacrificed to the exigencies of East–West conflict during the Cold War, has the collapse of the tight bipolar order increased the possibilities for the international community to control the spread of nuclear weapons capabilities, and perhaps even to roll back existing nuclear weapons programmes? If, as argued previously, the NPT regime failed to address the real sources of nuclear proliferation in the Cold War, what are the prospects for developing new approaches to proliferation at the end of the Cold War? The relaxation of previous tensions has provided a somewhat paradoxical situation with regard to the possibilities for influencing the future course of nuclear proliferation. On one hand, the decline in tensions between East and West has meant a far greater capacity for former adversaries such as the United States and Russia to act with unprecedented cohesion in seeking collectively to address tension, insecurity and nascent proliferation in problematic regions of the world. However, balanced against this opportunity is the fact that the process of superpower retrenchment from former spheres of influence has typically also meant a decline in control over the affairs of erstwhile proxy or client states. Concern over this loss of influence is particularly acute in those areas of the developing world where the removal of East–West 'overlay' has been accompanied by a resurgence of previous rivalries based on ethnic, religious, cultural or historical disputes, aggravating further the potential for nuclear proliferation (Snow 1991, pp. 16–18, 136–66). To explore the possibilities for denuclearization at the end of the Cold War we now turn to a critical assessment of four competing theories of security, which generate different analyses and policy prescriptions concerning the future role of nuclear weapons in international politics.[2]

Fatalists

Fatalists believe that there is little or nothing that the international community can do to stop the eventual spread of nuclear weapons capabilities. Not all states will have the desire to go nuclear and not all states will have the resources to finance and produce nuclear weapons, but if states are sufficiently determined they will acquire nuclear weapons. Supplier controls can significantly slow down potential proliferators, as can hostile reactions by an international community opposed to further proliferation, but the fatalist assertion is captured in the following words by Colin Gray: 'The bottom line is that a wealthy would-be proliferant cannot be denied a nuclear arsenal; it is just not possible' (Gray 1994, p. 14). Thus, fatalists agree with those critics of the NPT regime who argue that it fails to address the underlying security reasons why states choose to proliferate. However, whereas some critics of the NPT place their hopes in regional solutions to proliferation, the fatalist dismissal of the NPT extends equally to the efficacy of future regional security and arms control regimes in preventing states developing nuclear arsenals. Their claim is that global and regional arms control regimes work when they are not needed, but when they are needed to deal with rule-breakers, they will always be found wanting. Kathleen Bailey's recent analysis of Iraq's non-compliance with the NPT is grist to the fatalist mill: '[t]he key conclusion drawn from the Iraqi case is that the nuclear non-proliferation regime cannot prevent a determined proliferant, even when that nation is a participant in the regime' (Bailey 1993, p. 34).

One of the key consequences of the spread of nuclear weapons, fatalists argue, will be the erosion of the taboo against the use of nuclear weapons which has existed since 1945.[3] Colin Gray argues that the nuclear taboo will only persist for as long as it does not conflict with a state's perceived vital interests and that '[n]uclear employment is an "accident" both waiting and all but certain to happen' (Gray 1994, p. 29). He thinks that nuclear proliferation is generally undesirable, although he suggests that there are certain exceptions where it may bring some benefits to regional security.[4] However, he is adamant that a general commitment to reversing nuclear proliferation is not a vital US security interest. Only in exceptional cases where vital interests are at stake should a US president risk the costs of war in order to stop a state acquiring nuclear weapons. Offensive and defensive counter-proliferation capabilities – such as those outlined in the Clinton administration's 1993 counter-proliferation initiative – are critical if the United States is going to intervene against nuclear armed states in the future.[5] However, Gray is emphatic that these measures cannot stop proliferation, and that as a consequence, the United States is going to have to learn to live with the 'occasional nuclear war between other states' (Gray, 1994, p. 31). Although the US government has been careful not to endorse the views of the fatalists, Leonard Spector argues that there is a gradual shift in US priorities and defence expenditure towards capabilities and planning for post-proliferation contingencies (Spector 1995, pp. 66–

85). He illustrates this emerging shift in US policy by pointing to the example of the Pentagon's continuing promotion of an $8 billion ballistic missile defence system for Japan against a future nuclear-capable North Korea, despite the fact that the latter had agreed to freeze its nuclear programme in late 1994 (Spector 1995, p. 79).

Pessimism about the possibilities for controlling and reversing the spread of nuclear weapons illustrates well the fatalist conviction that there is no escape from self-help and power politics as the natural and inevitable condition of international politics. Realists like Colin Gray construct the post-Cold War nuclear security environment as a jungle where insecure and/or predator states acquire nuclear weapons as instruments of intimidation and blackmail, and where regional nuclear wars will periodically blight the global security landscape. However, not all realists share this fatalism about what Gray calls the 'second nuclear age'. Rather, there are realists who, whilst sharing with fatalists the belief that self-help is the natural condition of inter-state politics, argue that the spread of nuclear weapons could have beneficial consequences for both national and international security.

Mitigators

'Unilateral mitigators'

'Proliferation optimists'[6] such as Kenneth Waltz and John Mearsheimer are mitigators, because they believe that the spread of nuclear weapons serves to reduce the risks of conventional and nuclear war. In a similar vein, Peter Lavoy claims that nuclear weapons will prevent future wars between India and Pakistan, and Shai Feldman argues that the spread of nuclear weapons to the Middle East would stabilize the Arab–Israeli conflict (see Sagan 1994, p. 67). Most controversially, John Mearsheimer argues that European security would benefit from Germany becoming a nuclear weapons state (Mearsheimer 1990, p. 190). More recently, he has argued that Ukraine should also be allowed to possess nuclear weapons to deter any future Russian military intervention (Mearsheimer 1993, p. 51).

In making these claims, the proliferation optimists build upon Kenneth Waltz's central theme in his now seminal 1981 Adelphi Paper, that the 'measured spread of nuclear weapons is more to be welcomed than feared' (Waltz 1981, p. 30). He bases this judgement on his assessment of the effects that nuclear weapons have had in promoting cautious superpower behaviour during the Cold War. Waltz is very impressed with the war-preventing character of nuclear weapons, believing that all that is necessary for deterrence is a secure second-strike capability of a few dozen nuclear warheads. Once each side has achieved this, there is no need for either state to continue to accumulate nuclear arms. The search for nuclear superiority is an elusive quest in a world where enemies can deliver nuclear weapons against an opponent's cities. Nuclear weapons can have no other rational function than deterrence, but in this role they reduce arms race pressures and the risks of war to almost zero. Waltz does not specify how many nuclear weapons are required for nuclear sufficiency but predicts that '[n]ew nuclear states are likely to ... aim for a modest sufficiency rather than vie with each [other] for a meaningless superiority' (Waltz 1981, p. 22).

Waltz and his disciples are unilateral mitigators, because their policy prescriptions do not require the cooperation of other states or of the wider international community. Regional arms control regimes might be argued to have a role to play in stabilizing the transition from zero nuclear arsenals to secure second-strike capabilities, but Waltz does not make this a condition of a transition to a nuclear-armed world. This reflects two considerations: first, his general dismissal of the efficacy of security and arms control regimes, and second, his belief that there is little or no risk of new nuclear states launching a preventive war against states which have not yet deployed nuclear weapons, or of pre-emptive strikes against an adversary when the size of its arsenal is very small (Waltz 1981, p. 14).[7]

Unilateral mitigators stand opposed to the fatalists and to supporters of the existing non-proliferation regime, both of whom reject their optimism about the consequences of the spread of nuclear weapons. Waltz and his disciples base their pro-proliferation case on the belief that nuclear weapons induce enormous caution in all leaders and regimes that come to possess them. But critics argue that such a profound faith in state rationality is not justified. Thus, Michael Mandelbaun contends that 'the further the bomb spreads from the industrial circumference, the greater are the chances that it could find its way into the hands of persons who would not show the prudence that the guardians of existing nuclear stockpiles have so far displayed' (quoted in Hagerty 1993, p. 265). Similarly, Lewis Dunn suggests that future nuclear weapon states may not be 'coldly, calculating, cautious, and fully rational' leading them to 'take high-risk gambles to serve their causes' (quoted in Hagerty 1993, p. 265).[8]

Waltz argues that because the United States and Soviet Union avoided nuclear war during the Cold War, we should have confidence that all future nuclear weapons states will be similarly cautious. Whatever combination of luck and skill steered us through the nuclear crises of the Cold War, it is surely utopian to believe that we can rely for the foreseeable future on deterrence rationality in a world populated by an ever increasing number of nuclear-armed states. Even if it is accepted that the spread of nuclear weapons reduces the risks of nuclear war, the reduced probability of this has to be set against the terrible consequences of any nuclear wars that do occur.

Fatalists are realistic enough to reject the Waltzian 'utopianism' of the proliferation optimists, but are we condemned to accept their description of the nuclear future? The next two schools of thought think that the fatalists and the unilateral mitigators underestimate the possibilities for controlling the spread of nuclear weapons, and for reversing the proliferation which has already occurred. Where fatalists and unilateral mitigators believe that non-proliferation norms and rules have little influence on a state's decision to acquire nuclear weapons, cooperative mitigators and transcenders believe that global and regional security regimes have a crucial role to play in preventing the spread of nuclear weapons.

'Cooperative mitigators'

Whilst fatalists point to the hard cases of Iraq and North Korea's non-compliance with non-proliferation norms to illustrate their claim that the regime is 'bankrupt', cooperative mitigators retort that it has never been more successful in controlling and reversing proliferation. Here, they point to the following cases: France and China's recent accession to the non-proliferation treaty; the decision by Algeria (which was suspected of pursuing nuclear ambitions with Chinese assistance) to join the NPT in January 1995; the willingness of Brazil and Argentina to curtail any nuclear weapons ambitions by accepting IAEA full-scope safeguards and moving towards acceptance of the Treaty of Tlatelolco; and the decisions by Belarus, Kazakhstan and especially Ukraine to join the NPT and transfer Soviet nuclear weapons on their territory to Russia. In addition, South Africa took the unprecedented step in March 1993 of announcing that it would destroy its covert nuclear programme (Spector 1995, p. 69; Schneider 1994, p. 212).

Although a significant majority of the 170 NPT signatories have demonstrated their commitment to the treaty by agreeing to an indefinite extension at the 1995 Review Conference, there remains dissatisfaction from a number of non-nuclear, non-aligned and developing states. Accusations against the NPT centre on two key points: first, the *de jure* nuclear weapons states are castigated for reneging on the commitments of Article IV (which enables non-nuclear weapons states to have access to peaceful nuclear technology under IAEA safeguards); second, and most importantly, the commitment in Article VI (concerning the reduction and eventual elimination of their existing arsenals) remains unfulfilled. Despite claims by the United States and Russia that the START I and II Treaties represent significant steps towards compliance with Article VI, the NPT's discontented states point to the continuing failure of the nuclear powers to negotiate a comprehensive test ban treaty (CTBT). Indeed, the 1990 NPT Review Conference failed to reach a final consensus because of disagreements over a CTBT.

In order to strengthen the legitimacy of the treaty in the eyes of the non-nuclear, non-aligned developing states, cooperative mitigators argue that the following issues need to be addressed urgently. First, the nuclear powers must rationalize and bring consistency to their policy on providing nuclear assistance to civilian nuclear power projects in developing states. Despite two special inspections by the IAEA which discovered no evidence of diversion of civilian nuclear power to military uses, Iran (a full NPT member) is currently subject to informal export controls by the United States which is also pressurizing China and Russia not to export nuclear reactors to Tehran.[9] Whatever the loopholes in Article IV and the weaknesses of IAEA safeguards that might have been exposed in the cases of Iraq and North Korea, sanctioning a state in compliance with the treaty can only fuel criticisms that the NPT regime is a discriminatory device of the nuclear weapons élite. Second, the nuclear weapons states must make more strenuous efforts to achieve nuclear weapons reductions beyond START II, including the signing of a CTBT. Indeed, the significant pressure directed against the nuclear weapons states at the 1995 NPT Conference appears to have been successful in eliciting their commitment to a comprehensive ban on nuclear testing by the end of 1996.[10] Additionally, the nuclear weapons states have gone further than ever before in accepting a commitment to the 'complete elimination of nuclear weapons' under Article VI. This represents a significant advance upon the original language of Article VI, which called merely for 'negotiations in good faith' towards the end of 'general and complete disarmament'.[11]

The third prerequisite for strengthening the treaty is to develop the NPT regime's enforcement power in the face of states which flout its core norms and principles. Central to this is the development of a policing role for the UN Security Council which can give 'teeth' to IAEA safeguards which currently rely on the consent of sovereign governments. The new-found willingness of the UN Security Council to declare Iraq and North Korea's nuclear programmes as a threat to 'international peace and security' signals a growing readiness by the international community to strengthen non-proliferation norms. Additionally, the announcement by the nuclear weapons states before the 1995 conference that they will extend positive security guarantees to any NPT members that come under nuclear attack should serve to strengthen the regime. However, critics might question how far they would be willing in practice to intervene on behalf of any threatened non-nuclear weapons states, if this entailed the risk of nuclear attack either upon its intervening forces or against civilian and military targets in its homeland.

Cooperative mitigators see fulfilment of all the above measures as fundamental to sustaining the long-term effectiveness of the non-proliferation regime. Any future erosion of the non-proliferation norm would undermine efforts such as those conducted recently against Iraq and North Korea, and it could also prompt 'hold-outs' from the treaty like India and Pakistan to pursue more vigorously their nuclear weapons ambitions. Additionally, any future weakening of the treaty might tempt some states to take more seriously the nuclear option, fearful of the security consequences resulting from an erosion or demise of the security blanket afforded by the NPT regime. Nevertheless, it is alarmist to suggest that the only barrier to proliferation is the formal treaty itself, since the majority of states recognize that the possession of nuclear weapons would do little to enhance their security and would observe the norm of non-proliferation with or without it.

The NPT regime survived its most immediate challenge at the 1995 Review Conference, but the central problem facing it remains how to manage the proliferation challenge of the non-NPT nuclear weapons states. With the former risks of proliferation in Latin America diminishing as a result of the Argentine–Brazilian nuclear rapprochement, the principal concerns today remain Israel, India and Pakistan. The end of the Cold War has increased the prospects for the great powers to concert their efforts in promoting dialogue and confidence-building measures between the *de facto* nuclear states (Simpson 1994, pp. 50–53). The purpose of these initiatives could be twofold: at a minimal level, those whom Spector labels the 'refocused' arms controllers argue that regional nuclear proliferation is in some cases inevitable (Spector 1994,

p. 68). They therefore see the main purpose of future regional nuclear arms control as recognizing the *de facto* nuclear states as legitimate, and encouraging them to cooperate in ensuring stable mutual nuclear deterrence. This would almost certainly require these states to join the NPT regime as nuclear weapons states, and this clearly conflicts with the objectives of those cooperative mitigators who are committed to reversing nuclear proliferation through the NPT regime. The latter argue that great power cooperation should be directed at the maximalist goal of bringing hostile states into a dialogue aimed at resolving the insecurities which motivate them to acquire and develop covert nuclear capabilities.

Leonard Spector argues that since US non-proliferation policy is no longer inhibited by the constraints of the bipolar competition, there is significant potential for US-led diplomacy to control and reverse nuclear proliferation in the future (Spector 1995, p. 76). Examples here include the role played by the United States in achieving limited but significant progress on a peace treaty between Israel and the Arab states, and the concerted US–Russian diplomacy which seems to have persuaded Ukraine to join the NPT regime. Nevertheless, it would be unwise to exaggerate the ability of the great powers always to pressurize recalcitrant states into regional security regimes. Thus, it is very hard to see Israel giving up nuclear weapons without a comprehensive peace settlement, which it is currently beyond the capacity of the great powers to deliver alone. Similarly, it is unclear that the Indo–Pakistani conflict will prove susceptible to great power diplomacy, given the deep historical antagonism between New Delhi and Islamabad which is further complicated by India's perception of an extra-regional threat in the form of China.

Yet the recent progress between Brazil and Argentina in reversing their nuclear weapons programmes, and South Africa's independent decision to renounce nuclear weapons (after admitting covert deployment), suggest that great power involvement is not always a necessary condition for progress in regional denuclearization. A key factor in these recent successes seems to have been the emergence of democratic regimes whose civilian leaders have chosen to redirect resources away from costly prestige-driven nuclear programmes. The fact that Brazil and Argentina have recognized the futility of developing nuclear weapons indicates that hostile states can develop cooperative understandings that marginalize the role of nuclear weapons in their mutual relations. The difficulty with generalizing the Argentine–Brazilian case as a model for reversing nuclear proliferation relates to the fact that neither of these has formally deployed nuclear weapons. Thus, it is unclear how relevant the Latin American example is for states like India and Pakistan, both of whom are believed to be capable of deploying nuclear weapons within weeks rather than years. What the cases of Argentina, Brazil and South Africa illustrate is that there is nothing inevitable about the spread of nuclear weapons, and that the pessimism of both the fatalists and the unilateral mitigators is unjustified. However, what remains questionable is whether these examples of denuclearization represent the beginnings of a process leading towards eventual global nuclear disarmament.

'Abolitionists'

We argue that there are two distinctive and fundamentally incompatible approaches to achieving global nuclear disarmament, 'post-existential deterrence' and 'transcending'. The key difference between them is the role played by the threat of force in inter-state relations. For Jonathan Schell, the fact that nuclear knowledge cannot be disinvented means that states can have all the benefits of nuclear deterrence without possessing nuclear weapons. The deterrence value lies not in the physical presence of nuclear weapons (as is the case with existential deterrence) but in their capacity to be re-made (Schell 1984). This argument pushes the principles underlying deterrence through mutual assured destruction (MAD) to their logical conclusion, a condition which might be called 'post-existential deterrence'. Schell argues that nuclear proliferation is a terrifying prospect, but his position implies that the spread of nuclear knowledge is to be welcomed rather than feared. Thus, the striking paradox at the heart of Schell's thesis is that in offering us a vision of a nuclear-weapons-free world, his prescription relies on a post-existential version of Waltz's justification for nuclear proliferation.

Abolition through post-existential deterrence is rejected by transcenders, who argue that any disarmament agreement which bases mutual restraint solely on the threat of nuclear force is liable to collapse. This could occur as a result of suspicion and insecurity leading to a resumption of arms-racing, or through one state cheating and exploiting its coercive monopoly. Instead, transcenders argue that global nuclear abolition requires the mutual respect that derives from empathy towards the legitimate security concerns of others. Once it is accepted that the key to eliminating nuclear weapons depends upon delegitimizing the threat of force between aspiring nuclear weapons states, the challenge becomes one of constructing a patchwork of regional security communities.[12] However, one of the key impediments to achieving this is the role that extra-regional forces play in shaping the threat perceptions of parties within the region. Thus, in the case of South Asia, China continues to be a major barrier to India's willingness to renounce the nuclear option, despite the fact that Beijing has now acceded to the NPT.

How relevant are either of these competing approaches in thinking about the future possibilities for global denuclearization? In particular, does either approach shed any light on the recent decisions by Brazil, Argentina and South Africa to refrain from pursuing nuclear weapons development? The evolution of cooperation in the Argentine–Brazilian nuclear relationship seems to have developed from a growing awareness of the costs and risks of pursuing unilateral approaches to their security (Serrano 1992). We would argue that this realization reflected a growing sense of identification with the legitimate security concerns of the other, rather than appreciation of the benefits of post-existential deterrence. A series of developments since the early 1980s has improved bilateral relations, including joint security declarations, collaboration over various nuclear projects, reciprocal visits to sensitive nuclear installations and other confidence-building measures (Serrano 1992; Redick 1990). The transition to democratic rule in both these countries has perhaps been of primary importance in facilitating these steps, which have significantly marginalized the role of force in Argentine–Brazilian relations. Thus, it is not post-existential deterrence, but the emergence of a nascent security community based on shared interests and values that has made the prospect of regional nuclear abolition possible. South Africa's recent decision to renounce nuclear weapons is more pertinent to Schell's thesis, since it appears that it had deployed operational nuclear weapons. However, two reasons make the thesis of post-existential deterrence equally unconvincing in explaining Pretoria's decision to revert to non-nuclear status. First, South Africa was not in a relationship of mutual nuclear deterrence with any other states. Second, as was the case with Brazil and Argentina, it was the transition from an authoritarian regime to a more democratic political process which transformed South Africa from 'a determined proliferant into a nation that renounced nuclear weapons' (Spector 1995, p. 76).

The Brazil–Argentinean case is particularly encouraging, because it demonstrates that states can develop empathetic practices of cooperation out of hostile relationships. But is it possible to learn from this experience in any substantive way that might help other regions to evolve similar practices of security cooperation through altered perceptions of both self and other? Whilst the cases of the Middle East and the Korean Peninsula are undoubtedly pressing with regard to the long-term risks of proliferation, there are good reasons to focus on the Indo–Pakistani nuclear rivalry as the most pressing challenge for future non-proliferation policy. First, India and Pakistan are thought to be the only two states in the world locked into a regional mutual deterrent relationship which carries the real and immediate risk of nuclear war. This would not seem to be the case with Israel and its Arab neighbours, and nor is it the case with North and South Korea. Second, if we are seeking to generalize and learn from the Latin American example, there are important similarities between the conflictual history of the Argentine–Brazilian nuclear relationship over the last 40 years and the current state of Indo–Pakistani relations today.[13]

Devin T. Hagerty's analysis of Indo–Pakistani nuclear relations suggests that while each side can muster little hard evidence concerning the precise nuclear weapons capabilities of the other and the time scale that it would take to deploy weapons, deterrence nevertheless derives from the potential to weaponize (Hagerty 1993). He calls this 'existential deterrence', but the logic of his explanation of the South Asian nuclear confrontation seems closer to Schell's post-existential deterrence thesis:

> mutual calculations about the efficacy of nuclear deterrence in such a situation are based not on the details of relative nuclear capabilities, which are beyond the national technical means of each side, but on the shared notion that each side is or can soon become nuclear-weapon capable, and thus any outbreak of conflict might lead to a nuclear exchange. (Hagerty 1993, pp. 271–2)

Hagerty argues that the uncertain presence of nuclear weapons in the relationship has dampened recent tendencies towards war in South Asia. He recognizes that other factors might account for the pattern of recent restraint in Indo–Pakistani crisis behaviour such as the costs of modern conventional war and learned behaviour on the part of policymakers, but concludes: 'it is plausible that the existence of nuclear weapons is the primary cause of this new behaviour' (Hagerty 1993, p. 278). Whilst post-existential deterrence might be preferable to a full-scale nuclear arms race, we would argue that basing long-term regional security on the deterrent properties of nuclear weapons – existential or post-existential – courts the constant risk of nuclear disaster. What is notable about the Indo–Pakistani relationship is that each side hovers on the nuclear threshold, while acquiring ever more sophisticated capabilities to do damage to each other.

If we are to apply the lessons of cooperative success in Latin America to the South Asian security problem, it is clear that the first steps on the road to regional nuclear abolition lie through the growth of an Indo–Pakistani security regime. The problem here is that it remains very difficult to persuade mistrustful states to risk pursuing cooperation with those that they perceive as sworn enemies. However, the final destination of abolition – regional and global – will only be reached if enemy states identify sufficiently with each other's fears to realize that predicating their security on the threat and use of force is both dangerous and self-defeating.

CONCLUSION

No single approach to the theory and practice of managing proliferation is without its difficulties, but what is clear is that previous approaches to the problem have done little to prevent the steady dissemination of nuclear capabilities over the last 50 years. Admittedly, the prediction by President Kennedy in 1962 that there would be many additional nuclear powers by the early 1980s has proved overly pessimistic. However, this is no cause for celebration since (even with the NPT's evolution, which Kennedy could not have foreseen) the distribution of nuclear weapons has increased two-fold beyond the four states that possessed them in 1962. This comes as no surprise to the fatalists, who see it as only natural that insecure and/or predatory states will seek the most powerful weapons available to them. A shaky coexistence based on genocidal threats is the most optimistic prognosis that they can muster, but this offers little solace given their admission that nuclear deterrence is prone to occasional catastrophic breakdown. In recognizing the perils of nuclear deterrence, fatalism does not therefore succumb to what we see as the utopianism of the unilateral mitigators, whose heroic assumptions about the omnipotence of deterrence rationality conceal a potential for ultimate disaster.

We have argued that cooperative mitigation has a vital role to play in furthering global de-nuclearization. The global NPT regime in its current form has thus far only made a limited contribution to this goal, and we have argued that these deficiencies are understandable given the fundamentally adversarial context in which the first phase of nuclear non-proliferation policy evolved. Our purpose is not so much to attribute blame in this respect, as to insist that in a post-Cold War world where the constraints of bipolarity have been relaxed, it is vital that future policy seeks to correct the past limitations of the regime. Of crucial significance to the regime's long-term viability is the development of regional and global approaches that work in tandem to try to address the security concerns of the nuclear 'hold-out' states.

It is unclear how far this process might lead in terms of global nuclear disarmament, but what is certain is that without this vision we shall already have resigned ourselves to living with nuclear weapons for decades and perhaps centuries to come. The challenge is to refute both the utopianism of the Waltzian realists and the stoical fatalism of those who would condemn us to an inescapable future of periodic nuclear disaster. The most promising long-term hope for controlling and reversing nuclear proliferation lies in strengthening those processes that marginalize the role of nuclear weapons in international politics. Hedley Bull expressed precisely these sentiments when discussing the future of nuclear deterrence in the early 1980s.

> the best course is to work against all nuclear proliferation, that which has already taken place as well as that which may occur in the future ... This requires us to take every opportunity to push nuclear weapons – and the doctrines and practices of nuclear deterrence associated with them – as far into the background of international political relationships as possible. (Bull 1981, p. 16)

The end of the Cold War doubtless seemed as distant a utopia when Bull wrote these words as the vision of global nuclear disarmament appears to us today. It would have seemed utopian to predict that the 1980s, which began with superpower relations characterized by acrimony and resentment, would end with the two former adversaries peacefully managing the demise of the Cold War international system. It would be naïve to think that global nuclear disarmament is an immediate prospect, but there is nothing given about our current security practices that changing values and beliefs cannot eventually alter. This is surely the lesson to be learned from the encouraging experiences of Latin America and South Africa, which suggest that we now have more substantial grounds for believing in global nuclear disarmament than at any time since the advent of the Cold War.

NOTES

1. By the NPT regime is meant the Non-Proliferation Treaty itself, in addition to the other legal instruments, bodies, declarations and agreements that exist to collectively promote the practice of nuclear non-proliferation. This includes the global system of IAEA safeguards, regional organizations such as EURATOM and OPANAL, and supplier controls such as the Zangger Committee and the London Club.
2. The conceptualization of fatalists, mitigators and transcenders is developed in Ken Booth and Nicholas J. Wheeler, *The Security Dilemma: Anarchy, Society and Community in World Politics* (Macmillan, forthcoming 1997).
3. Gray argues that the nuclear taboo is double-edged, since rogue states might think that weapons 'uniquely worthy of a taboo on their threat and use must be weapons deemed uniquely potent, or at least awesome'. The fear is that a leader or regime might emerge which is willing to play brinkmanship with the international community's fear of nuclear war (Gray 1994, p. 20).
4. He suggests that Israel's acquisition of a nuclear capability falls into this category.
5. The Defense Counter-Proliferation Initiative was announced by Secretary of Defense Les Aspin in a speech in December 1993. The initiative covers all of the US government's anti-proliferation policies, but Spector argues that Department of Defense statements make it clear that its 'principal role concerns the application of military measures in predominantly post-proliferation missions' (Spector 1995, p. 82).
6. The term is used by Scott Sagan in his article, 'The Perils of Proliferation: Organization Theory, Deterrence Theory and the Spread of Nuclear Weapons', *International Security*, 18 (4), Spring 1994.
7. Waltz argues that pre-emption is viable only if the 'would-be attacker knows that the intended victim's warheads are few in number, knows their exact number and locations, and knows that they will not be moved or fired before they are struck. To know all of these things, and to know that you know them for sure, is exceedingly difficult' (Waltz 1981, p. 16).
8. These views are ethnocentric because they assume that Western states are the only ones capable of learning 'rational' deterrent strategies.
9. 'US draws up tough sanctions on Iran', *The Guardian*, 6 April 1995.
10. 'Chinese nuclear bomb test provokes global anger', *The Independent*, 16 May 1995.
11. 'Negotiating a nuclear-free world', *The Guardian*, 16 May 1995.
12. Writing in the late 1950s, Karl Deutsch and his co-workers developed the concept of a security community to describe situations where the threat or use of force had become an unthinkable instrument of inter-state relations. Deutsch identified NATO and relations between the Scandinavian countries as examples of security communities. See K.W. Deutsch et al., *Political Community in the North Atlantic Area* (Princeton, NJ: Princeton University Press).
13. A detailed analysis of the lessons that might be learned from the Latin American case for Indo–Pakistan security relations is the subject of an ESRC-funded doctoral thesis currently being completed by Simon Davies at the University of Wales, Aberystwyth.

8. Environmental security

Rowland T. Maddock

THE CONTEXT AND SUBSTANCE OF ENVIRONMENTAL CHANGE

Security, defined as the complete absence of threat from any source, is non-existent and, in all probability, unattainable. It is to a degree what people, communities and states wish it and make it to be, and is to that degree socially constructed. Who is to be secured, from what type of threat and from what source, is as much a social construction as it is embedded in hard reality. If, then, societies deem a degraded environment to be a security threat it must of necessity be so.

In the realist conception of the modern state system security has been construed as the conditions that make the use of force more likely, the ways the use of force affects individuals, states and societies, and the specific policies that states adopt in order to mitigate military force. Since states abrogate to themselves the legitimate use of force this conception necessarily limits security to the study of war and diplomacy within an essentially state-centric paradigm. Walt, for instance, specifically rejects expanding the conception to include *inter alia* Aids, the drug problem and ecological hazards because to do so would destroy the intellectual coherence of the current security paradigm (Walt 1991, p. 213).

But a changed and changing international context, rapid socioeconomic transformations, and an expanded policy agenda have seriously undermined the continuing validity of the realist conception. The model which limits security to relations between states draws its current legitimacy not only from an intellectual tradition which can be traced back to Thucydides and beyond, but also from the exigencies of the Cold War. That latter crisis no longer dominates world politics as even such exponents of *Realpolitik* as Henry Kissinger and Zbigniew Brzezinski acknowledge. Due to what has been described as a monumental shift in international affairs the one thing that cannot occur, in Kissinger's view, is a continuation of the *status quo* (Shuman and Harvey 1993, p. 12).

Equally destructive of the hegemony of the realist position has been the determined modern and postmodern intellectual assault on the fundamental security questions. Indeed, simple-minded concepts of security, by diverting the focus away from the real issues which create insecurity for most people, are themselves part of the problem. Evaluating the intellectual and practical utility of environmental security requires, therefore, an assessment of precisely what security is, and who it is for, as well as a view of medium- to long-term ecological dynamics. Since in the realist paradigm security focuses on inter-state war and diplomacy the state is often theorized as a black box, and what happens inside the state is not of concern. The national interest is assumed to be known and rationally and disinterestedly defended by states and their agents. The threat, by definition, must lie outside the state. This, it is argued, seriously misrepresents the real security of state and society for it rules out those challenges to the legitimacy of states posed by disaffected domestic groups and classes excluded by existing power relations. It also rules out threats to individuals, groups and classes by the state.

Indeed now that the military instrument has lost much of is utility as a tool of foreign policy, civil strife and conflict arguably raise more intractable security concerns than inter-state conflict. Internal conflict over political and economic ideology, forms of authority and social priorities are potentially more destabilizing than the stand-off typical of most bilateral disagreements. The demands of often newly emancipated populations around the globe, in developing and developed countries alike, for an equitable and growing share of the global product within an increasingly globalized economy where security of income and employment for large sections of populations cannot be guaranteed, puts severe and increasing strain on the capacity of states to mediate between conflicting demands and loyalties. Today, the threat to security lies as much within, as outside, the state (Scalapino 1994, p. 12). Political revolution in, and even the overthrow of, such apparently strong states as the Soviet Union and the Philippines shows that when they fail to meet the legitimate demands of their population, domestic clamour for revolutionary transformation can become irresistible.

Though modern developed societies with high levels of citizen emancipation are in the long run politically stable, the transition from traditional to modern is often characterized by turbulence and insecurity. Thus the state's use of its coercive power to promote or defend particular economic, social, ethnic or religious interests becomes in its own right a security problem. Real security depends on how successfully nations and their governments reconcile domestic order, equity and development, a compromise that can make the state a perpetrator of insecurity for some people, groups and communities. The forcible removal of 280 000 Chinese people to make way for the Sanmenxia Dam on the Yellow River, most of whom remain in dire poverty, has destroyed their security far more effectively than any threat by the government of a foreign state. A further staggering 1.3 million people may have to be moved to make way for the Three Gorges Dam on the Yangtze River. The same is true of the no doubt unintended but nonetheless real and catastrophic disruption to Central American communities as a consequence of rampant deforestation sanctioned by authoritarian states.

But the state also remains vital to national security. In the absence of a transcending global ethic it does defend against predation by other states or non-state actors. It is the state which maintains the legal system and protects property rights, the essential basis for political and social stability. When the distinction between presumed internal stability and international anarchy disappears and the state is perceived as both a perpetrator of insecurity as well as a defender of security, the loss of coherence which Walt warns against is very real, but is a price which must be paid for a comprehensive, multidimensional conception of security. There is, in any case, no universal definition of security for even at the national level states view and define security in their own particular interests, according to their particular geographic, historical and technological circumstances. Ambiguity rather than clarity is the essence of security. Buzan indeed argues that traditional security hierarchies deliberately foster ambiguity as a means of securing their legitimacy and status (Buzan 1991, p. 11).

However, augmenting more issues and more actors does more than add another quantitative dimension to a concept which otherwise remains unchanged. As the nature and origin of threat, its perpetrator and victim change, so does the cognitive architecture and consequently the appropriate practical responses. Comprehensive human security includes political security which has military, economic and social–humanitarian sub-components and environmental security with protection-oriented and utilization-oriented sub-components (Westing 1989, p. 129).

Both components must be simultaneously present, neither being attainable without the other. Ullman (1983, p. 133) maintains that security is undermined by threats which drastically and quickly degrade the quality of life, or narrow the range of policy choices available to governments and non-governmental entities.

The utility of fitting the environment into an expanded conception of security depends partially, therefore, on the degree to which environmental change falls into one or both of these two categories.

ENVIRONMENTAL CHANGE AND SECURITY

According to Maurice Strong, a highly respected environmental diplomat, the global community is at a critical juncture when nothing less than the survival of the planet as a sustainable home is at stake (Strong 1991, p. 287). At the core of that juncture of frightening challenge and exhilarating opportunity is mankind's proper relationship with nature. The World Watch Institute details the current outcome of that relationship thus:

> the earth's forests are shrinking, its deserts are expanding and soils eroding, all at record rates. Each year thousands of plant and animal species disappear, many before they are named and catalogued. The ozone layer in the upper atmosphere that protects us from ultra violet radiation is thinning. The very temperature of the earth appears to be rising, posing a threat of unknown dimensions to virtually all life support systems. (Finger 1991, p. 9)

If that apocalyptic vision of the ecological future is in fact true, the case for transforming the environment into a security issue, and as soon as possible, appears *prima facie* overwhelming. But not everyone believes that the vision outlined by the World Watch Institute is a valid account of the present and future state of the world's environment.

Environmental optimists insist that there is no incontrovertible evidence that pessimistic environmental predictions will in fact come to pass. Indeed quite the reverse, in that most of those which have been made in the past have already been proved wrong (Anderson and Leal 1991, p. 2). Julian Simon, a persistent critic of the environmental movement, and much derided by many of its prominent spokesmen, insists that life on earth is getting better (Simon 1990, p. 21). He, and other so-called cornucopians, mobilize much support for this view. The most convincing evidence according to Simon is the nigh universal improvement of life expectancy, which is especially dramatic in less-developed nations. Cornucopians draw their optimism not only from an empirical assessment of long-term environmental trends, but also from the theoretical analysis of the environmental efficiency of free markets. If, they argue, markets and property rights can be established in nature, and given mankind's ingenuity there is every reason to suppose this is feasible, then nature as an integrated ecosystem will not be degraded such as to create unmanageable problems of sustainability.

Though not sharing the unlimited optimism of the cornucopians, the currently dominant paradigm of sustainable development is also predicted on the assumption that, with efficient and equitable policies and careful husbandry, nature's essential bounty can at the same time be sustained and provide for mankind's needs and wants indefinitely. World Bank economists conclude that the long-term relationships between economic development and environmental outcomes is described by an inverted U-shaped function. As societies grow richer they initially degrade the environment, but after a certain level of income is reached further growth is associated with an improving environment. Grossman and Krueger (1994, p. 19) estimate the annual level of income at which the transformation occurs to be around $8000 per capita. Although they caution against assuming a necessary relationship between growth and an improving environment, their tempered optimism is widely shared in the international community. It is, for instance, the basis for the explicit recommendation contained in the declaration issued at the conclusion of the 1992 United Nations Conference on the Environment and Development (UNCED) in Rio, that sustainability requires, *inter alia*, growth and development, especially in less-developed countries. In neither of these paradigms need the environment become a security issue. Such theoretical analyses and empirical investigations must be treated with respect, but nonetheless there are grounds for believing that this view of environmental futures is overly optimistic.

Economists have long questioned the presumption that markets are necessary and sufficient to guarantee long-term ecological sustainability. Many who are convinced by the general case accept the fact of such market failures as external costs and benefits and public goods, which are especially prevalent in environmental media. Although the free market economists may be confident that man's ingenuity will eventually lead to well defined and enforceable property rights in atmospheric, oceanic and biological resources, these are in fact conspicuous by their absence and most economists remain unconvinced. Moreover markets are just not capable of determining the proper scale of macroeconomic output. They have been technically effective in periods of resource abundance when the primary social aspiration was to realize nature's potential, but now that the proper objective in an environmentally constrained ecosystem is conservation, failure to determine proper scale is profoundly debilitating.

At an empirical level statistical studies which show an eventually converging trend between growth and environmental outcomes are limited both in the number of countries in the sample and the data available for measurement. Grossman and Kreuger are careful to point out the paucity of environmental data on which their study is based and insist that income levels beyond $8000 per capita do not of themselves guarantee an improving environment. This depends on deliberate and effective policies by societies and their governments. In fact, of course, most of the world's countries with large populations are currently far below the per capita $8000 figure. In just the eight most populous less-developed nations, with a combined population of over three billion, average per capita income is less than $2500, and in many instances well below that. If these, still growing, as well as the other Third World countries, are to achieve the $8000 target figure, the demand on global environmental resources cannot but increase phenomenally. If China and India alone increase their emissions of carbon dioxide (CO_2) to average industrial levels, world emissions will more than treble. Although it may statistically be true that income and environmental trends converge after a certain level, it is also the case that most of the world's environmental resources are consumed by rich people and rich societies. Nations which between them account for 20 per cent or so of the world's population produce 91 per cent of the world's industrial waste, 95 per cent of its hazardous waste, 87 per cent of the world's emissions of chlorofluorocarbon (CFC) gases and 74 per cent of its CO_2 gas emissions. In the United States the richest 10 per cent consume 12 tons of CO_2 per person whereas the poorest 20 per cent consume 1.2 tons per person. In the United Kingdom the poorest 20 per cent consume per person the average for Chad, and in Malaysia the richest 10 per cent consume the European average (Harrison 1993, p. 258). In the absence of heroic assumptions about enabling technology and social preferences it is overly sanguine to believe that further growth in income and output will not harm the environment.

In the past critical shortages appeared singly and slowly and were therefore capable of reasonably easy resolution by governments and societies. Today local, regional and global ecosystems are facing multiple and often interconnected scarcities that exhibit complex negative and positive feedbacks that can, with little warning, approach critical thresholds. Deforestation, biodiversity loss, thinning of the ozone layer, overfishing, soil erosion and pollution of air, land and water resources all offer multiple but interrelated challenges to societies which often lack the institutional capacity to respond in a carefully calibrated manner. The sheer momentum of global environmental change due to modernization and population growth so greatly exceeds the historical norm that social and economic institutions which coped when ecological demands were reasonably modest might easily collapse under the current weight of change.

Markets are not mechanistic organisms existing in a social void. They are, when effective, embedded within stable and supportive social and political systems. But environmental degradation on the scale which is currently being witnessed, especially in less-developed countries, is itself a source of political instability which can undermine the very political framework necessary for markets to work. In the interdependent ecosystem ecological collapse, if and when it occurs, will be rapid, sudden, unpredictable and uncontrollable. Surprise and unanticipated events may, paradoxically, have to be assumed to become the norm. Traditional security practice is predicted on worst case assumptions. It is no more than a sensible precaution to make the same assumption with regard to the world's environment where an ultimately unwarranted optimism could have incalculable consequences.

But even a belief in the acuity of crisis is not enough, according to Deudney, to transform the environment into a security issue, for there is, he argues, only a weak analytic link between environmental degradation and national security (Deudney 1990). Although the prosecution of, and the preparation for, war have ecological consequences, environmental degradation is not in essence an episodic and exceptional abnormality, but is embedded in the normal daily processes of production and consumption.

THE ENVIRONMENT AS A SECURITY ISSUE

Essential to the traditional conception is the assumption that a threat to national security requires intent, the deliberate mobilizing and targeting of resources on well identified and predetermined objectives. Other than the use of environmental instruments in war such as agent orange in the Vietnam War, or deliberate depletion of scarce water resources by upstream riparian states, intent is not normally a feature of transboundary environmental invasion. Resources to target or combat environmental threats cannot easily be mobilized. Victims and sources are usually large in number and geographically diffuse. Often the sources of decay are simultaneously domestic and foreign, making it difficult to apportion blame. Because of the diffuse nature of both source and victim the normal response to threats to the security of the state, namely nationalism, is not in this instance appropriate. War and the threat of war are not real Norwegian options to induce the United Kingdom to reduce its acid rain deposits on Norwegian rivers and lakes, even though the Norwegian Foreign Ministry has indicated that Norway regards this issue as being as important to its security as a trade dispute.

Security in the realist discourse has strong zero-sum characteristics, whereas ecological outcomes are almost always either positive or negative-sum: the attainment of an improving environment in one country cannot be achieved without the active cooperation of, and benefit to, another. This necessarily alters the mutual perception of antagonists and their incentive to cooperate to achieve collectively beneficial outcomes. Finally, there is a real possibility that if the environment does become a security issue it will simply be appropriated into the existing intellectual and institutional security framework which may be entirely inappropriate to ameliorate the real problem of environmental decay.

Despite the merits of the above arguments they are not convincing even in their own narrow terms. Intent is not important to the victim, nor is it true that victims do not know the source of transboundary pollution. Japan, for instance, knows that 65 per cent of depositions of sulphur dioxide (SO_2), one of the two acid rain gases, have their origin in China and South Korea: 50 per cent from China and 15 per cent from South Korea. The Netherlands also knows that pollution of the Rhine and the other rivers that flow to the sea through its territory derives from industrial and agricultural activities in Switzerland, France and Germany. Since international law recognizes states as juridical entities redress is technically feasible.

Although environmental decay has not so far caused inter-state war, Homer-Dixon, for one, believes this will change as the demands on regional and global resources become unsustainable. In his view environmental scarcities are already leading to violent confrontations and there are unmistakable early signs of increasing conflict in the coming decade, either induced or aggravated by ecological scarcities (Homer-Dixon 1994, p. 6). Although military security has not vanished as a key element of national security, 'it has certainly declined relative to the issues of economic energy and environmental security' (Romm 1993, p. 1). The environment in short 'is very much on the security agenda' (Buzan 1991, p. 258). If, after all, the functioning integrity of the earth is jeopardized, the search for other securities becomes futile. The security of man cannot be achieved if the security of the earth is destroyed. But how is this best attained?

Prins argues (Prins 1993) that security must be wholly reconceptualized to make it compatible with ecological rationality. Rationality has two components: the processes of choice that employ the intellectual faculty, as well as the actual choices themselves. The primary fact or presumption of ecological rationality is interdependence: everything is connected to everything else. Thus the essential referent for ecology is the ecosystem as a collective interconnected entity. The dimensions and complexity of interdependence demand a holistic perspective which values diversity and equality of status between all species, including our own, and not the hierarchy which exists in human society. Ecological principles are contingent and mutually supportive, not based on 'power over' and dominance. These are the principles and norms which societies living in constrained ecological circumstances must cultivate if they are to avoid domestic and inter-state conflict. Ecological rationality emphasizes mutual dependence and therefore the realization that threats do not lie outside, but are rather within us, indicative of our failure to appreciate our organic interconnectedness to others.

Security based on the sovereignty of states and on the system of states, and therefore on exclusion, cannot be sustainable because an interconnected planetary biosphere cannot be protected or rationally managed within a fragmented and uncoordinated social order. Juridical sovereignty, and the pursuit of narrow self-interest in its name, is incompatible with global ecological interdependence. The competitive state system is in fact the primary cause of insecurity. The modern world political structure and economic practices have been, and are, increasingly out of step with nature, but the conclusion of the Cold War offers an apposite moment in world history to begin the fundamental reconceptualization of transnational relations. Not only is a global perspective vital for real personal and national security, but ecology, if given its proper place, will be a means to bring about that necessary transformation in perspectives and priorities. It is, in the current jargon, a win–win outcome.

States and the system of states are deficient in three respects:

1. the state system as a whole is dysfunctional;
2. many states cannot provide the necessary domestic order which will allow them to tackle ecological decay effectively;
3. because of, *inter alia*, ecological degradation the normative appeal of the state as the guarantor of security has diminished.

The state system has been characterized by institutional poverty in its response to the ecological crisis. There are strong structural and political reasons why the environment has been marginalized in domestic and international politics, but the exigencies of ecological congestion are forcing nations to face up to the futility of claiming sovereignty over resources which, though nominally theirs, are in practice non-excludable. Despite the validity of its juridical claim to sovereignty Swedish air space is in fact partly a British resource, a sink for unwanted waste products. Nations have willingly conceded sovereignty over ecological resources by joining international agreements to limit environmental damage, a process which the UNCED system is gradually institutionalizing, thereby providing a permanent mechanism for environmental regulation and monitoring.

Following the 1992 UNCED conference in Rio annual meetings have been sanctioned to reach international agreement on global warming, the first of which was held in Berlin in April 1995. The UNCED system has also legitimized non-governmental actors, environmental groups and organizations which push often reluctant governments in the direction of compliance with international norms. But despite some progress international environmental coordination has in fact been modest. With a few notable exceptions, such as the Montreal Protocol to limit emissions of gases harmful to the ozone layer, many ecological regimes reflect the least ambitious programme (LAP) principle, their structures and processes determined by the least committed important negotiator, and since there is almost always a good rationale for at least one state not to cooperate, the principle of the LAP is a powerful conservative force. Although sovereignty is severely constrained in practice, it remains of paramount concern to nations.

Inter-state compliance with international environmental obligations requires a domestic capacity to push through often unpopular policies which in many, especially so-called weak countries (but not exclusively so), is lacking. Indeed in many instances ecological decay is in large measure due to policies sanctioned by national governments. Powerful national and international commercial interests have to be accommodated. Military interests degrade local environments in the pursuit of an, often illusory, national security (Goldenberg and Durham 1992, p. 29). Local environments are mediated through local, domestic, regional and international political economy such as local land practices, distribution of income and wealth, ethnic and religious antagonisms and the predation of transnational corporations. Environmental issues are in reality economic, social and political issues, and in societies where those forces are inimical to environmental values the statist response is weak and unavailing.

Finally, and partly a consequence of the above, states have lost much of their normative appeal. They are simultaneously too small and too large. They are too small to deal with global issues such as the destruction of global sinks and the articulation of a planetary ethic, but are too distant from, and often dismissive of, local conditions which lead to environmental decay such as the transformation of marginal arid areas into deserts. Nevertheless there is little evidence of serious erosion of loyalty to the state, especially in Third World countries rightly concerned to defend their newly won political independence, however compromised by economic interdependence.

UNDERSTANDING AND MANAGING ENVIRONMENTAL THREATS

Despite, therefore, the theoretical validity of much critical thinking about the role of the state 'there is no reason to believe that an alternative to the state system will be better at achieving ecological sustainability' (Hurrel 1994, p. 165). States remain the dominant actors in international environmental politics, and environmental security requires therefore a pragmatic and limited internationalism to reflect this reality. Since there can be no such thing as total security, societies must seek that which is feasible. What is appropriate at this stage is not a wholesale redefinition of security but a better understanding of the nature of real contemporary threats to security. Environmental security, like other securities, is contextual, depending on the particular circumstances of countries and their neighbours. It depends on the fact, the intensity and the pace of environmental change and also on the capacity of particular states, either singly or collectively, to manage that change.

Thus not all environmental change can usefully be categorized as a security issue. Determining what is, and is not, a threat is therefore judgemental, but since one criticism of much of the current debate is its failure to locate insecurity in the particular circumstances of time and place, a rough and ready empiricism is not without merit. Rule of thumb criteria suggest that environmental change becomes a security issue if:

1. it is extensive, rapid and sustained;
2. there is a high degree of real incompatibility between the attainment of ecological and other important values;
3. the real and monetary costs of attaining an acceptable trade-off between the conflicting objectives are large and/or increasing;
4. it interacts in a negative way with other structural or political weaknesses within states which lead to social turbulence.

Intensity of threat and the means to deal with that threat therefore vary. Environmental insecurity may usefully be assessed at three different levels of analysis:

- global
- regional/bilateral
- unilateral.

At the global level the potentially most threatening environmental outcomes stem from changes to the global climate and the consequences thereof. The fact and consequences of global warming remain uncertain but there is a scientific and by now growing political consensus that human activity is changing the global climate. Projections of climate change are no more than that, but the influential intergovernmental Panel on Climate Change predicts that on a business-as-usual assumption, global mean temperature will increase about 1 degree Celsius above the present value by the year 2025, and 3 degrees Celsius by the end of the next century. Sea levels are predicted to increase in the same period by 20cm. Land surfaces warm more rapidly than the oceans, and polar latitudes more than tropical and equatorial latitudes. If correct, climate zones will shift polewards, the circulation of ocean currents may change and the variability and intensity of extreme weather will increase. The security consequences of climate change derive from a chain of multiple interconnections.

Climate → Ecology
Ecology → Economy
Economy → Politics
Politics → Security

These relations reflect themselves in a number of ways, but climate change is more likely to exacerbate than relieve current and near-term issues (Meyer-Abich 1993, p. 73). Low-lying islands, such as the Maldives and Tuvalu, and land along major river estuaries may simply disappear. Populous deltas in Egypt, Bangladesh, Indonesia and elsewhere are threatened by only a modest increase in water levels. Some of China's largest cities, including Shanghai and Guandong, could be inundated. An increase in one metre would put 12 per cent to 15 per cent of Egypt's and 14 per cent of Bangladesh's arable land below sea level. If such areas were to suffer permanent flooding food supplies would be reduced and migration would increase, almost inevitably aggravating civil strife.

Agricultural output would be affected by pollution of freshwater sources and by an increase in the incidence of storms, flooding and drought. Food supplies depend on a number of biological and human factors, so the consequences of a permanent change in climate depend not only on the degree of climate change but also on geology, and the ability of communities and societies to manage change. Changes in the global climate could reduce overall food supplies, increasing the incidence of chronic malnutrition and episodic famine, perhaps transforming food into a diplomatic weapon of real menace. Since 1970 food production per capita has increased in every geographical region other than sub-Saharan Africa, and much of the all-too-distressing incidence of famine and hunger is social in origin, the consequence of war or unequal access to entitlements. But higher outputs have been obtained at the expense of soil erosion, and poisoning of land and water systems jeopardizes long-term sustainability.

If dislocation caused by climate change is imposed upon agricultural practices and social norms which already leave an estimated 200 million people suffering from malnutrition, the consequences could be catastrophic. Vegetation zones could shift polewards by perhaps hundreds of miles in the next 50 years or so, the consequence of which will depend as much on the pace as on the dimension of change. Climate change could even impinge on access to some strategic resources such as oil and gas. Arctic regions contain between 21 per cent and 37 per cent of the oil and gas reserves of the United States and Russia, but at the present time costs are high, up to 60 times higher than in Saudi Arabia. Thawing of the Arctic permafrost as a consequence of global warming could alter the strategic balance of world reserves (Glieck 1989, p. 318).

The costs of global warming are likely to vary across regions in that not all countries will be affected to the same degree. Indeed it is possible that some countries may actually benefit, and even if eventually they do not they may respond to the political and security implications of global warming on the assumption that they will. Policy proposals predicted on the belief that global warming is a pure public bad, that is, everyone suffers and it is in everyone's interest to prevent this, may underestimate the difficulty of crafting a global strategy. Beneficiaries are likely to be northern regions of the United States, Canada, China, Japan and Russia. In the latter country 60 per cent of grain-growing areas suffer from inadequate moisture, and greater precipitation, as a consequence of climate change, which could transform marginal to secure agricultural regions. In Japan the rice harvest could double. The most vulnerable populations are almost certainly in developing countries, living in low-lying islands or estuarine areas, or in semi-arid grasslands already prone to drought. Agriculturally the two major losers almost inevitably will be the semi-arid regions in the Sahel and elsewhere, and humid tropical and equatorial regions in Southeast Asia and Central America (Meyer-Abich 1993, p. 79).

The security consequences of environmental change are also most acute at the regional and bilateral levels. Transboundary intrusion of national ecological space is, in language perfectly consistent with the conventional security discourse, 'not only a kind of modern invasion but also a special form of violence' (Breitmeier and Wolf 1993, p. 349). The sovereignty of states is compromised if they cannot guarantee the integrity of their own ecological space as Japan, Norway and The Netherlands know to their cost. Transboundary environmental decay is usually the consequence of external costs, those which the consumer, the producer or the nation can effectively ignore but which, nonetheless, impinge upon the welfare and eventually the security of the host. The structure of transboundary externalities is quite complex as the following taxonomy makes clear (the arrows shows the direction of the externality):

1. $A \rightarrow B$
2. $A \rightarrow BC$

3. AB → C
4. AB → CD
5. AB ↔ CD

Although the structural characteristics appear indentical the political implication and the probability of successful solution depend on the number of countries involved and on the intensity of the spillovers. It is easy to come up with serious infractions of ecological sovereignty for each of the above:

1. Vietnam is concerned that Thailand is withdrawing too much water from the Mekong River especially in the dry season.
2. Russian nuclear waste disposal in the Sea of Japan pollutes Japanese and Korean coastal waters.
3. France, Germany and Switzerland pollute Holland's waterways.
4. Developed countries export hazardous wastes to less-developed countries.
5. Mutual pollution of environmental resources which are non-excludable, for example, pollution in the Baltic or the Mediterranean Sea.

One of the most acute regional security issues is the irregular and uneven distribution of freshwater resources. The United Nations Secretary-General, Boutros Ghali, surveying the imbalance between supply and demand for freshwater in the Middle East, predicted that 'the next war in our region will be over water' (Thomas 1992, p. 139). Water is, and has at different times been, an instrument, a target of, and a reason for, inter-state conflict. Of the world's major river basins over 200 are shared by two or more countries and on them around 40 per cent of the world's population depends. Not all these create security problems, though in the early 1980s the American government identified ten nations with a high propensity to go to war over water, and predicted that by the beginning of the next century demand for water could more than double. The degree to which freshwater resources become security concerns depends on

1. the level of shortfall
2. the extent to which the resource is shared
3. the distribution of relative power in the river basin, whether for instance the dominant nation lies upstream or downstream

4.   the ease with which alternative supplies can be made available (Glieck 1993, pp. 83–4).

Areas of greatest vulnerability, and therefore of potential conflict, can be identified according to different criteria. One is where demand is more than 30 per cent in excess of sustainable supply. Twenty-one countries fit this category, the most vulnerable being Libya where current withdrawals exceed the sustainable demand by over 370 per cent. Moreover, where rapid population growth coincides with modernization of industry and agriculture, societies where demand and supply are currently in rough balance can within a very short time collide against real limits. Another critical criterion is the degree to which one nation's water resources are shared with others. In 31 nations more than 33 per cent of supplies are shared, the most vulnerable according to this criterion being Egypt where the ratio is 97 per cent. Nations which are dependent on hydroelectric power can also be vulnerable if the river systems are shared.

Shortages are provocative enough in themselves but when they impinge upon other disagreements among riparian states the security implications are made more acute. Turkey, which controls the upper reaches of the Euphrates, has been in conflict with Syria and Iraq over their policies towards the Kurdish peoples who straddle the borders of the three nations. In the Middle East disagreement between Israel, on the one hand, and her Arab neighbours who share the Jordan and the Litani Rivers as well as a number of aquifers, is particularly acute. Over 40 per cent of Israel's groundwaters rise in the occupied territories with few alternative supplies. The war between Israel and the Arab nations in 1967 was in part occasioned by the attempt of the Arab League to divert the headwaters of the Jordan away from Israel (Cooley 1984, p. 3).

SOURCES AND CONSEQUENCES OF ENVIRONMENTAL SCARCITY

At the national level a central preoccupation of the modern state is how stability and development can be simultaneously attained. Homer-Dixon has identified three avenues of potential stress (Homer-Dixon 1994). Human-induced environmental degradation reduces the quantity and quality of ecological resources available for sustainable consumption. Rising

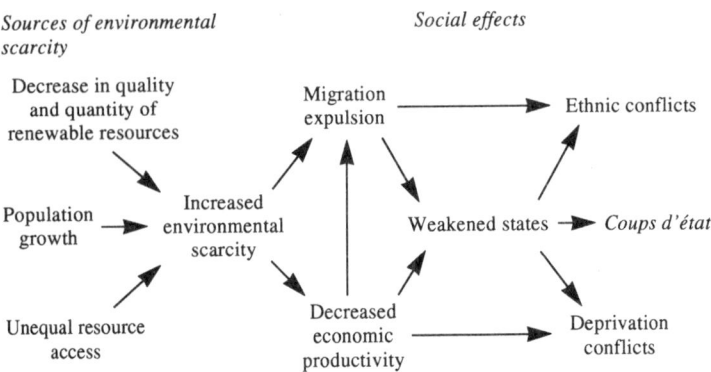

Source: Homer-Dixon (1994), 'Environmental Scarcities and Violent Conflict', *International Security*, 19 (1), p. 31.

Figure 8.1   Sources and consequences of environmental scarcity

populations have a similar impact. Unequal access concentrates the resource(s) in the hands of relatively few people, subjecting the majority to greater scarcity. Reducing the quantity and/or the quality of a resource shrinks the environmental pie, population growth divides the pie into smaller slices while unequal access means that some groups get disproportionately large slices. Shortage is most likely to spill over into conflict when all three are simultaneously present, as shown in Figure 8.1.

This combination is more likely to be present in less-developed countries. Traditionally population growth has been associated with poverty, and though some countries have in recent years managed to break that historic link, countries with a high population growth remain amongst the poorest in the world as measured by per capita income. This is particularly true of sub-Saharan Africa where in some countries population growth of over 3 per cent coincides with per capita incomes of less than $1000 per annum.

It is also the case that access to environmental and other natural resources is particularly unevenly distributed in the Third World. In Brazil the lowest 40 per cent of households share just 8 per cent of the nation's income, and in Central America on average 4 per cent of the population own 73 per cent of the land, and 77 per cent of the population own only 7 per cent of the land. Dr Bukar Shaib, a member of the World Commission on the Environment, argues that Africa's drought, famine, desertification, refugee and poverty crises are essentially environmental in origin: 'Africa is dying because her environment has been plundered, over-exploited and neglected' (Akpan 1990, p. 18). In East Asia over 60 per cent of rural communities live in rain-fed watershed areas where ecological degradation has transformed their relationship with nature from one of harmony to one of war with the land (Burnett 1992, p. 166). And in Central America rebellion and guerrilla activity have been traced to ecological roots (Karliner 1989, p. 798).

The destruction of nature, population growth and unequal access force peoples and communities to leave their homeland to seek more sustainable livelihoods elsewhere. Migration from the land to towns and cities has always been part of the modernization process and is not always, and in itself, necessarily destructive. But if the host region cannot sustainably absorb more people, or local populations are unwelcoming due to religious, ethnic or social reasons economic migrants may be transformed into environmental refugees. In South Asia and in Africa in particular, people have been forced to flee because of soil erosion, desertification, deforestation and pollution of water systems, often brought about or aggravated by population movements and patterns of land tenure and resource use. Tickell estimates the number of environmental refugees to be around 10 million (Tickell 1993, p. 21).

Yet the precise relationship between movement of peoples and environmental stress is not at all clear. Some migration experts see the environment as a contextual variable that influences the economic, social and risk calculation of individuals and communities but is only one in a cluster of causes. Others give to the environment a more decisive role in population movements. Legally refugees are people who are forced to live outside their country of origin for reasons of persecution due to race, religion, nationality or membership of a particular social group or political opinion (Suhrke 1994, p. 478). Persons who are internally displaced or who move other than for the above reasons are not legally classified as refugees. The modern concept of environmental refugee is rooted in sociology rather than international law, reflecting the commonsense view that anyone who is forced to flee involuntarily, leaving them vulnerable and powerless, should be considered a refugee and not a migrant. The number of environmental refugees is clearly related to how widely or narrowly the concept is defined and all data must therefore be handled with great care.

Concern about the security consequences of a degraded environment has not been reflected in practical policies at the institutional level. The

1977 Environmental Modification Convention, negotiated under the auspices of the United Nations, states that each party to the convention undertakes not to engage in military or any other hostile use of environmental modification techniques having long-lasting or severe effects. In 1982 the United Nations General Assembly promulgated the World Charter for Nature which *inter alia* seeks to prevent military action damaging to nature. At the forty-second session of the United Nations in 1988 a group of East European nations introduced the concept of environmental security which they defined as 'a state of affairs in international relations within which a system of norm setting, organisational and material measures adopted within a framework of broad cooperation on the basis of international law will safeguard preservation of the environment in its quality with a view to creating appropriate conditions for life worthy of human beings and securing sustainable and safe development for all states' (Schrijver 1989, p. 115).

Innovative transformations of some of the United Nations' institutions have been tentatively mooted. The Security Council has the primary responsibility for maintaining international peace and security, and although these are generally understood to be compromised when one state seeks to change the *status quo*, they have, on occasion, been more widely interpreted. If the community of nations were so inclined, ecological security could be consolidated into the prevailing consensus and thus be included in the mandate of the Security Council. A second possibility is to change the function of the Trusteeship Council now there are so few trust nations to administer. More radical is the suggestion for an environmental security council. Eduard Shevardnadze, when he was Soviet foreign minister, proposed a discussion on how to transform the existing United Nationals Environment Programme (UNEP) into an environmental council capable of taking effective decisions to ensure ecological security. At that time both he and Mikhail Gorbachev insisted that the possibility of regional and global ecological collapse was as great a threat to international security as was the nuclear arms race. A final proposal is the establishment of a so-called green UN police force or green cross which might for instance have the task of preventing illegal dumping at sea or monitoring compliance with international obligations (Schrijver 1989). Progress has also been at best modest outside the United Nations. In the Nordic Convention citizens of one member state have been given rights in the legal system of the others to pursue ecological objectives that have cross-border implications.

A different response to regional ecological security is embodied in programmes to create cross-border 'peace parks' which are deemed to contribute to common security by inducing nations to seek security in cooperation with, and not against, other countries. The collaboration of nations on transborder issues has in itself the potential for reducing international tension and adding to regional security. The basis of such initiatives is the presumed fact of eco-regions, land areas which are ecologically compact, whose natural boundaries do not coincide with political boundaries and where therefore there are good reasons to organize international space in accordance with ecological as opposed to political principles. Peace parks exist in Eastern Europe but are especially fruitful in Central America, a region where ecological exploitation and decay are so debilitating as to be described as 'another war' (Karliner 1989, p. 789). Many of the military, economic and social conflicts which ravage the region are linked in some way to its ecology. At the moment there are five peace parks in different stages of planning, involving in some capacity all seven of the region's nations, as well as, in some instances, Mexico. Because of ecological and economic interdependence in a relatively small land mass, the region is characterized by high levels of ecological spillovers. The parks are rich in ecological resources and, given population growth, debt and development objectives, there are strong pressures for the exploitation of nature to relieve the poverty brought about by the unequal access to land and political rights.

Successful management of potentially conflictual resources may thus be seen both as symbol and effective manifestation of regional cooperation. The willing suspension of sovereignty over ecological space at the state level, though necessary, is not in itself sufficient; it must be supplemented by the participation of the people who live in, and on the edge of, the protected areas. Peace parks may not only be important for ecological sustainability but many believe them to be a positive step towards regional conflict resolution where ecology is forcing nations to cooperate and where the habit of cooperation will spill over into other contentious areas. They become the forcing ground of new norms, an integral part of the creation of comprehensive security, and have therefore a great potential to serve as the centrepiece of a regional peace process, a new and innovative regional approach to the joint problems of conflict resolution and ecological sustainability (Weed 1994, p. 182).

The reality is that the environment remains on the fringes of the modern security discourse. This in part reflects the dominant interests of the international arena where politics, economics and more traditional security concerns carry more weight. It is also a reflection of the peculiar characteristic of environmental security which Prins (1993) describes as 'threats without enemies', which is by its very nature difficult to visualize and therefore to mobilize against. Environmental security requires, moreover, non-marginal changes in conceptions of well-being, in national and international organizations as well as in status, which strike at core Western, modernist values and which conservative forces, be they of the political left or the political right, are bound to resist. Environmental security is not a state of affairs which is for most people of the world a reality in the here and now. It is something rather to be sought for, and if unsuccessful the era of the Cold War could soon be replaced by the era of environmental conflict (Glieck 1989, p. 21).

9.   The security dilemma

Alan Collins

The purpose of this chapter is to explain what the security dilemma is and how states fall victim to its effects. The chapter is divided into two parts. The first is concerned with how the security dilemma has been used in the literature and whether it is actually a dilemma; the second demonstrates how the security dilemma operates to the detriment of those states affected by it and how its effects might be mitigated.

DEFINING THE SECURITY DILEMMA

What does Dilemma mean?

The term is of Greek origin and literally interpreted means two or double (*di*) assumptions or propositions (*lemma*). A dilemma is thus where there are two propositions, which implies ambiguity or uncertainty exists over which proposition is the best (Partridge 1990, p. 156).[1] There appears to be widespread agreement that these propositions are incompatible. Hence Walter Skeat writes that a dilemma is 'an argument in which one is caught between two difficulties' (Skeat 1946, p. 169). These propositions, or difficulties, are further interpreted to be equally unfavourable. Hence Dr Ernest Klein defines a dilemma as 'a choice between two unpleasant alternatives' (Klein 1966, p. 449) and Dr C.T. Onions as 'a choice between two equally unfavourable alternatives' (Onions 1966, p. 268). The *Chambers Twentieth Century Dictionary* summarizes the term's development by defining dilemma, 'as a form of argument in which the maintainer of a certain proposition is committed to accept one of two propositions each of which contradicts his original contention: a position where each of two alternative courses (or of all feasible courses) is eminently undesirable' (*Chambers Dictionary* 1972, p. 361).

The term dilemma is thus particularly interesting because its usage suggests that the problem encountered has no satisfactory solutions since all the choices available appear undesirable. The following chess example can be used to explain how a dilemma can occur.

In a game of chess if player A can challenge a bishop and a rook of player B with one piece (a knight for example), which is itself invulnerable to attack, player B is faced with a dilemma. Since player B is unable to prevent player A from taking one of his pieces, player B is faced with the undesirable choice of saving either his bishop or his rook. In other words player B cannot choose a satisfactory solution; the only solution available to the player is an unsatisfactory one. Thus all possible moves by player B are undesirable and hence no satisfactory solutions are possible: player B faces a dilemma.[2]

A security dilemma would seem to be where the policy pursued by a state to achieve security proves to be an unsatisfactory one. By definition, if the achievement is unsatisfactory, then the policy the state chose failed to realize all that state's security concerns or created new concerns. The state must therefore still be insecure. The state is in a paradox, by falling foul of the security dilemma any solution the state chooses is unsatisfactory and is thus not a solution at all. The result of the security dilemma is that security cannot be realized. This is what led Wheeler and Booth to assert that '[i]n an ordinary sense, a security dilemma would seem simply to refer to situations which present governments, on matters affecting their security, with a choice between two equal and undesirable alternatives' (Wheeler and Booth 1992, pp. 29–30). However, when the concept has been used by writers on international relations this has not always been the meaning they have attributed to the security dilemma. It was this that led Wheeler and Booth to assert, '[i]n the literature on international politics ... the term has come to have a special meaning' (Wheeler and Booth 1992, p. 30).

How has the Security Dilemma been Defined?

The definitions of the security dilemma and the references to this concept by writers on the subject have been quite diverse. This has not only created a large degree of ambiguity as to what a security dilemma is, but has also raised the question of whether the situation they are referring to is actually a dilemma. The references to the concept can be broadly categorized into four features: reducing the security of others; reducing the security for all; uncertainty of intention; no appropriate policies. These features relate to one another and form a coherent explanation of a traditional security dilemma. The ambiguity of the dilemma is compounded when the same author interchanges these categories when referring to the concept.

Reducing the security of others

In defining the security dilemma some writers tend to explain what the concept manifests. Hence Charles Glaser has written, 'the US faces a "security dilemma" [when] it cannot increase its security without reducing Soviet security' (Glaser 1990, p. 72). Glaser explains how this occurs elsewhere in his writings when he defines the security dilemma as 'a situation in which the military forces required by a state to protect itself threaten the forces other states need to protect themselves; in that situation states seeking security cannot avoid threatening each other's military capabilities' (Glaser 1992, pp. 506–7).

Robert Jervis has also defined the security dilemma in this manner. He has written that a security dilemma occurs when 'most of the ways in which a country seeks to increase its security have the unintended effect of decreasing the security of others' (Jervis 1988, p. 317), and elsewhere he confirms this by noting: 'many of the policies that are designed to increase a state's security automatically and inadvertently decrease the security of others' (Jervis 1982, p. 358). Barry Buzan likewise comments on explaining what the concept refers to: 'In seeking power and security for themselves, states can easily threaten the power and security aspirations of other states' (Buzan 1991, pp. 295 and 324 n.1).[3]

The emphasis of these definitions is on how the state inadvertently reduces the security of its neighbours by the actions it takes (Snyder 1985, pp. 153–79).[4] This is an extremely important feature of the security dilemma since the unintentional effect of reducing the security of others does not indicate that the state has malign intent towards others; it just appears that it does. Thus although other states may regard the action as aggressive this is actually a misperception of a benign intent. This first feature of the security dilemma therefore highlights that benign intent lies at the core of the security dilemma and hence the incompatibility which states perceive is illusory.

These references, though, do not relate to the definitions of dilemma given earlier, and thus, although this is an important feature of the concept, it is not on its own a sufficient description of the security dilemma. The security dilemma is more than just the reduction in others' security.

Reducing the security for all

References to the security dilemma that fall within this category also tend to explain what the concept manifests. In this instance they centre on the self-defeating nature of the security dilemma. Thus Robert Lieber notes that by increasing their power, states 'do not necessarily increase their own security, because their neighbours and rivals also resort to the same means. Indeed, this arming tends to make all states less secure, since it increases the level of potential threat to which all are exposed' (Lieber 1991, pp. 5–6).

In other words, in Lieber's definition, the emphasis is on the reciprocity inherent within the security dilemma. Emphasizing this element is common. Charles Reynolds has referred to the security dilemma as 'the existence of a number of sovereign states each providing for [their] own defence and in so doing [they] creat[e] a general and permanent condition of insecurity for all' (Reynolds 1981, p. 24). Barry Posen also notes this self-defeating aspect when he defines the security dilemma as a situation in which 'what one does to enhance one's own security causes reactions that, in the end, can make one less secure' (Posen 1993, p. 28). Bruce Blair has also made reference to this aspect of the security dilemma by arguing: 'One state's gain in security achieved through growth in its armaments is another state's loss. The second state is compelled to fortify its strength, which then redounds to the first state's disadvantage. That spurs another round of arms expansion. The cycle repeats itself endlessly, leaving all sides worse off than they were at the start' (Blair 1993, p. 28).

The failure to achieve security by these policies was the aspect of the security dilemma that Jervis was referring to when he wrote that it is the 'unintended and undesired *consequences* of actions meant to be defensive [that] constitutes the "security dilemma" (emphasis added)' (Jervis 1976, p. 66). The point of this second feature is that victims of the security dilemma actually make their situation worse through the policies they are pursuing. In other words, the decisionmakers appear unable to empathize with each other and although they may recognize a decrease in security, they fail to appreciate that it is because of, rather than despite, their policies. Since these references centre on the feature of self-contradictory policies, rather than having to make a choice between undesirable alternatives, the situation would seem to resemble a paradox rather than a dilemma. Consequently, as with the first category, while this is an important feature of the security dilemma there appears to be some doubt that on its own it is describing a dilemma.[5]

Uncertainty of intention
Those authors who focus on the role of uncertainty are seeking to explain why states fall victim to the security dilemma. That is, the focus of attention moves away from why these policies make matters worse to explaining why the reciprocal nature of the security dilemma, or the tit-for-tat action, occurs. Hence Butterfield wrote: '[Y]ou know that you yourself mean him no harm, and that you want nothing from him save guarantees for your own safety; [yet] it is never possible for you to realise or remember properly that since he cannot see the inside of your mind, he can never have the same assurance of your intentions that you have' (Butterfield 1951, p. 21). In other words the focus of attention moves to why states perceive hostility and why statesmen fail to appreciate that their benign actions may appear threatening to others. Concern therefore centres upon the interaction between states. According to Wheeler and Booth: 'A security dilemma exists when the military preparations of one state create an *unresolvable uncertainty* [emphasis added] in the mind of another as to whether they are for "defensive" purposes only (to enhance its security in an uncertain world) or whether they are for offensive purposes (to change the status quo to its advantage)' (Wheeler and Booth 1992, p. 30).

'Unresolvable uncertainty' is thus an extremely important feature of the security dilemma since, as will be shown later in a hypothetical example, it explains why states fall victim to the concept. Indeed it is such an important feature that Wheeler and Booth consider it to be the defining characteristic of the security dilemma: the dilemma's special meaning. This is a contentious claim since although 'unresolvable uncertainty' is vital in understanding the security dilemma, to consider it as the defining characteristic would require a challenge to those definitions of dilemma noted earlier. After all, is not 'special' a euphemism for 'different'? The contention here is that unresolvable uncertainty, rather than the defining characteristic of a security dilemma, is a necessary condition. To fully understand the security dilemma also requires the fourth feature: no appropriate policies.

No appropriate policies
As the heading suggests this definition is much closer to the dictionary definitions of dilemma than the other three categories. Here emphasis is placed on the hopelessness of the state's situation. It is this feature of the security dilemma that Richard Smoke refers to when he writes:

'The idea of the "security dilemma" holds, in essence, that one nation will feel insecure if it makes no effort to protect its security, but that any effort to do so must threaten the security of one or more nations ... Thus the first nation faces a dilemma: it will be insecure if it doesn't act and insecure if it does' (Smoke 1991, p. 76). Geoffrey Wiseman made a similar reference to the security dilemma when he wrote: 'This process where states constantly arm themselves in an upward spiral against adversaries arming on worst-case assumptions creates a dilemma for decision makers who are required to choose between two equally unfavourable alternatives: to become locked into the cycle of arms accumulation or to reject it and expose the country to the dangers of military inferiority' (Wiseman 1989, p. 1).

The emphasis therefore is on the perception that no matter what option is chosen an unsatisfactory solution is the only result. Therefore it is a perceived lack of desirable outcomes that makes this situation a dilemma. It is important to note that it is not necessary for the state to be aware that its position is hopeless for this to be a dilemma.[6] Indeed, unless the decisionmakers are sensitive to the security dilemma it is unlikely that continuing to accumulate arms will appear inappropriate. While it is likely that an arms race which exacerbates a deteriorating relationship will be considered undesirable, it may still be considered the only means of guaranteeing security. This is an important feature of the security dilemma since it reveals why states continue to pursue what, to a third party, are clearly inappropriate policies.

This feature can be seen in the comments made by the United States president Theodor Roosevelt in 1904 regarding Britain and Germany. Roosevelt noted that the Kaiser

> sincerely believes that the English are planning to attack him and smash his fleet, and perhaps join with France in a war to the death against him. As a matter of fact, the English harbour no such intentions, but are themselves in a condition of panic terror lest the Kaiser secretly intend to form an alliance against them with France or Russia, or both, to destroy their fleet and blot out the British Empire from the map! It is as funny a case as I have ever seen of mutual distrust and fear bringing two peoples to the verge of war. (Jervis 1976, p. 74)

So, despite the inappropriateness of the policies Britain and Germany were pursuing, they were perceived as appropriate. This fourth feature therefore becomes more complex than the Smoke and Wiseman comments suggest. After all, if the policies Britain and Germany were pursuing were the cause of their problem, then logically if they both altered policy they could overcome this difficulty. In this case, instead of a lack of appropriate policies, the option of rejecting arms becomes the means of escaping the spiral of decreasing security and heightening distrust. Since there exists an appropriate option can this situation really be termed a dilemma?

The answer lies in understanding the participants' perception of the situation. It can be termed a dilemma because the means of escape will be considered extremely risky by the participants since the other state is perceived as aggressive. As the other state has benign intent a third party will see this option as appropriate, but because each participant cannot be certain that the other state has benign intent, it cannot know that this is appropriate. Consequently the objectively appropriate option appears just as unfavourable and thus, to all intents and purposes, the participants are faced with a dilemma. It is evident that to fully understand the dynamics of the security dilemma it is necessary to consider the four features as a whole.

Therefore, while it is certainly true that the literature on the security dilemma creates much ambiguity by focusing on different aspects of the concept (indeed in some instances the term 'paradox' appears to be a more accurate description), all these differing interpretations do 'connect' to form a situation that can accurately be regarded as a dilemma. How they do this will be illustrated by using a hypothetical example in which states A and B will fall victim to a security dilemma. This example will also help to explain how, arguably, the security dilemma can be mitigated.

THE SECURITY DILEMMA IN OPERATION

The first time that the two states encounter one another they have no reason to assume that their security is endangered; instead they can only infer each other's intention from the actions that are taken. As Alexander Wendt remarks, '[s]ocial threats are constructed, [they are] not natural' (Wendt 1992, p. 405). The question is, therefore, what actions would the states be expected to take? Wendt uses the hypothetical case of aliens visiting earth to suggest what might happen in the first encounter. What is interesting is that even in the non-threatening scenario the expected human response is to place military forces on alert. In other words, while determining the intent of the other it is prudent to prepare for the worst.[7] Of course such preparations can send the wrong signal and be regarded as a threatening move, though this does not necessarily have to occur. If both (states A and B/humans and aliens) do not mean harm to one another, then how these first moves are interpreted will determine whether they become victims of a security dilemma. As Wendt acknowledges; 'The first social act creates expectations on both sides about each other's future behaviour: potentially mistaken and certainly tentative, but expectations nonetheless' (Wendt 1992, p. 405). Wendt is thus correct to note that '[w]e do not begin our relationship with the aliens in a security dilemma' (Wendt 1992, p. 407).[8]

Let us assume that in the first contact between states A and B, state B places its military forces on alert and state A observes this increase in military activity. This military activity may be the result of state B warning the newcomer that its military forces are properly trained to defend its territory. Although a reasonable explanation, it might not be true. State B's increase in military activity might be because it is preparing a force to invade state A. In other words, the uncertainty regarding the intent behind state B's military manoeuvres has led to uncertainty regarding state B's foreign policy intentions. The situation that may arise (security dilemma) is thus a result of uncertainty regarding these two aspects of statecraft. This is acknowledged by Wheeler and Booth: 'Security dilemmas arise from a perennial problem in interstate relations, namely the inherent ambiguity of some military postures and some foreign policy intentions' (Wheeler and Booth 1992, p. 30). In fact both explanations for state B's actions are plausible; state A cannot be certain as to state B's intentions. How will state A react?

Since state A has done nothing to provoke this increase in military activity by state B, state A is likely to conclude that state B is deploying its forces for hostile reasons. This is a crucial point in understanding the dynamics of the security dilemma. State A has been unable to accurately determine State B's intentions and has assumed the worst. There are many reasons why state A may have reached this pessimistic conclusion. It may have been that the states were once enemies and state B's military activity might be the first move in the resumption of hostilities. For instance after the First World War the French were aware that Germany might seek to reverse the verdict of 1918. It was this fear of Germany that led France to seek such a punitive peace at Versailles, a system of alliances that encircled Germany and the erection of the Maginot line. Such actions indicated a French suspicion of Germany's long-term intentions. Even if the states had not been enemies it might be that state B can only feel secure if it expands its territory. Many commentators consider the oil resources in Kuwait to be the prime reason behind Iraq's invasion of that country in 1990. In this case not only had these states not been enemies, but Kuwait was an Arab country that had provided Iraq with financial assistance during its lengthy war with Iran (Stein 1992, pp. 150, 155–9). Another reason for state A's pessimistic conclusion could be that it thought itself safe from danger and as such would be quicker to assume hostility on the part of state B. Arnold Wolfers made this point when he wrote: 'nations tend to be more sensitive to threats that have either experienced attacks in the recent past or, having passed through a prolonged period of an exceptionally high degree of security, suddenly find themselves thrust into a situation of danger' (Wolfers 1962, p. 151).[9]

However, the real intentions of state B need not be aggressive for state A to assume hostility. State A will automatically be insecure because state B now has the military capability to do harm. Of course just because it can do harm does not mean that it will, but there are a number of cognitive barriers which make this distinction hazy. If state A is ideologically opposed to state B, or if it adopts worst-case analysis, or zero-sum thinking, or strategic reductionism, or indeed any number of what Wheeler and Booth refer to as 'permanent aggravating factors', then accurate threat perception is severely impaired. The distinction between capability and intent is not quite so definite. Even if state B did not intend to do harm now, there is no guarantee that this will remain the case. It is this concern about long-term intentions that has led many European states to remain suspicious of Russian actions. More Chechnya-type operations, especially if they involve other republics of the Commonwealth of Independent States (CIS) and indicate a growing nationalistic furore, could indicate a resurgent Russia seeking to reassert its influence over its near abroad. Therefore, due to the lack of any protector in international society, state A, having assumed hostility, is likely to respond to state B's action by increasing its own military capabilities. The likelihood of this pessimistic outcome is supported by Barry Posen who notes that even if statesmen are sensitive to the security dilemma, a rare event, '[t]he nature of their situation compels them to take the steps they do' (Posen 1993, p. 28).[10]

State A, by choosing this action, can be said to be 'playing safe'. If state B were seeking to invade, then state A's action might deter state B. If this deterrence fails, then state A by increasing its military capabilities may still be able to defend itself successfully. If, on the other hand, state B were conducting military exercises and had no intention of attacking state A, then state A, by playing safe, would perceive itself as being no worse off by raising its own military profile. State A, by playing safe, believes it has chosen an appropriate option and gained a satisfactory solution to this security threat. However, the success of playing safe can only be ascertained by knowing the reaction of state B to state A's increase in military activity.

At this point let us assume that state B did not intend to attack, and the increase in military activity which state A observed was simply a military exercise. State A has assumed hostility even though none was intended by state B. How does state B react? State B is in exactly the same situation as state A had been in earlier. State B cannot be certain of state A's intention. State B will therefore also play safe, that is, raise its military profile; it is the logical and prudent action to take. References to the security dilemma at this stage fall within the category of reducing the security of others. State A did not intend to create concern in state B for its own security. State B's understandable concern is thus an inadvertent and unintentional consequence of state A's action. In other words, the unintentional effect of state A's action (perceived reduction in security by state B) is the result of B's uncertainty regarding state A's intention. Thus while it is understandable that European states may be concerned about Russian intentions, Western actions to safeguard other states' security could have the undesired effect of generating Russian insecurity. Such an outcome is given evidence by Russia's Defence Minister, Pavel Grachev, warning that too rapid a NATO expansion eastward could result in Russia 'tearing up' the Conventional Forces in Europe agreement. The insecurity such an expansion would generate has also been noted by Vladimir Lukin, a former Russian ambassador to Washington: 'It will be very difficult to explain to people in Russia that we should continue to disarm when there is a chance the biggest military machine in the world will move closer to our borders'.[11]

This little exchange between states A and B will have quite a profound impact on their relationship. As they cannot be sure of the other's intentions they have played safe and assumed the worst. The result of playing safe is that they will become suspicious and mistrustful of each other. For instance, this second increase in military capabilities by state B is more likely to convince state A that state B has aggressive designs. If state B did not intend to attack, why increase its military capabilities again? This inability by state A to appreciate the position state B is in, and vice versa, is fundamental to understanding the security dilemma. Since they did not know the other's intention they embarked upon understandable, but inappropriate, policies. References to the security dilemma that emphasize the states' inability to accurately determine the intent of each other fall within the category of uncertainty of intention. Since this crucial ingredient explained why state A felt threatened by state B, and vice versa, it is not surprising that certain authors consider uncertainty to be of paramount importance. Thus Wheeler and Booth claim quite emphatically:

> If the threat posed by one state to another, be it inadvertent or deliberate, is accurately perceived by the potential or actual target state, then the situation cannot be classified as a security 'dilemma'. It is simply a security 'problem', albeit perhaps a difficult one. Whatever the actual intentions of the state engaging in the military preparations, it is the unresolvable uncertainty in the mind of the potential or actual target state about the meaning of the other's intentions and capabilities which creates the 'dilemma'. (Wheeler and Booth 1992, p. 31)

Whether Wheeler and Booth are right to place such importance on uncertainty that it becomes the defining characteristic of a dilemma is contentious. At this stage, however, it is clear that the states' unresolvable uncertainty was a necessary condition for their choice of an inappropriate policy.

As their relationship deteriorates, war may result. Since both states are suspicious of each other's motives, and therefore regard the actions by the other as possibly threatening, both will believe they need to show resolve in their relations with each other. By doing this they hope to deter one another from initiating hostilities. In the field of defence this will mean displaying the ability and willingness to wage war. Jervis notes that even '[i]ssues of little intrinsic value become highly significant as indices of resolve' (Jervis 1976, p. 58). Therefore, although it was a change in military activity that set in motion this chain of events, a further deterioration of relations could be a result of something far less threatening and obscure. An example of this is the dismissal of General Glubb by Jordan's King Hussein on 1 March 1956. This was regarded by Eden as a deliberate affront to Britain contrived by the Egyptian leader Nasser. The dismissal in itself is a minor event, yet its timing is seen as one of the factors that caused a deterioration in Anglo–Egyptian relations that would culminate in the Suez crisis (Eden 1960, pp. 347–50).[12] The more states A and B increase their military capabilities and seek to gain the upper hand, the more insecure they feel and the greater the feelings of mistrust and suspicion. By playing safe they perceive that they are gaining security, whereas they are really fuelling their insecurity. Those references to the security dilemma which emphasize this aspect fall within the category of reducing the security for all. John Herz captured this when he defined the security dilemma as 'a condition, a feeling of insecurity, deriving from mutual suspicion and mutual fear, [which] compels these units to compete for ever more power in order to find security, an effort which proves self-defeating because complete security remains ultimately unobtainable' (Herz 1966, p. 231).

It is quite possible that the insecurity spiral which the two have created will lead to the outbreak of hostilities. Jervis writes 'statesmen … rarely … consider seriously the possibility that such a policy will increase the danger of war instead of lessening it' (Jervis 1982, p. 360). States A and B have become enemies, even though they may never have intended any harm to each other. As Herz comments, 'it is one of the tragic implications of the security dilemma that mutual fear of what initially may never have existed may subsequently bring about exactly that which is feared the most' (Herz 1966, p. 241). In the hypothetical example this could be an outbreak of hostilities leading to the defeat of state A, or B, or even both. The reason for this outcome, Butterfield claims, is that each side is only 'conscious of its own rectitude, so [it becomes] enraged with the other for leaving it without any alternative to war' (Butterfield 1951, p. 21). In the case of post-Cold War Europe Glaser captures the tragedy of the security dilemma by noting:

> If Western policies for guaranteeing Central European security appear threatening to Russia, then these policies could pressure the Russians to pursue the very actions they were designed to prevent. Extending the West's military sphere of influence into the East could raise Russian concerns about Western intentions, increasing the value it sees in controlling additional territory. (Glaser 1993, p. 14)

The hypothetical example is the classic security dilemma at work and it highlights the different features, or stages, to which writers on the subject refer when defining the term. This not only helps to explain why there are different references to the concept, but also reveals the connection between the categories and hence why the scenario can be termed a dilemma. The crux of the connection is Wheeler and Booth's special meaning – unresolvable uncertainty.

It becomes evident from this scenario that if states were able either accurately to determine each other's intent, or provide for their own defence without creating fear in each other, the circle of the security dilemma could be broken. Herein lie two means which might mitigate a security dilemma. If either state had been able to deploy its forces in a non-provocative manner then neither would have inadvertently created insecurity in the other. The dynamics of the security dilemma would have been negated. Unfortunately in the hypothetical example neither state was able to exhibit such defensiveness even though providing for their defence was their only goal. The second method of mitigation centres not on the force postures states adopt but rather on their misperception of one another's intent. If the uncertainty they have about each other's intention could be reduced so that they became more confident about determining each other's intent, then choosing an appropriate policy option becomes much easier. In the hypothetical example this would mean both states believing that the other had benign intent; unfortunately accurately determining intent is extremely difficult. There are, however, indications that in post-Cold War Europe such measures are being embarked upon. First there is an awareness among Western states that their actions, while benign, may indicate a malign intent towards Russia and so create Russian insecurity. This is one of the reasons behind NATO's unwillingness to expand its membership eastward. Instead NATO has adopted a process of 'extending the hand of friendship' by the twin functions of dialogue and consultation. With the establishment of the North Atlantic Cooperation Council (NACC) and the Partnership for Peace (PFP) programme the Western alliance is able to create transparency (reduce uncertainty) between the old Eastern and Western blocs while also satisfying Russian security interests. A second trend concerns the relationship among Central and East European states. The Hungarian–Romanian relationship provides an interesting case study. The Trianon Peace Treaty of 1920 placed over 3 million ethnic Hungarians under foreign rule (2 million live in Romania) and there is widespread acknowledgement that they are discriminated against (Valki 1992, pp. 7–9). Despite this potential source of conflict the Hungarians and Romanians are embarking upon measures that could mitigate a security dilemma's effects should it arise: in November 1994 the two states agreed to a fifteen-point cooperation package which included 'the closer cooperation of the two armies in the fields of training and exercises'.[13]

The security dilemma operates where states are *status quo* powers but believe that one or more of their neighbours harbour malign intent.

Their unresolvable uncertainty leads them to 'play safe' by pursuing policies that have the unintended effect of lessening others' security; these policies, while intended as purely defensive, indicate an aggressive ambition. A likely outcome, as states seek to acquire security in what they perceive as a hostile environment, is an arms race; the policies they pursue to gain security paradoxically generate insecurity. With the end of the Cold War the security dilemma continues to exist, ready to exacerbate and inflame nationalistic hatreds generated by historical rivalries or economic deprivation. It is difficult not to surmise, even without the Cold War, that the state system shows little sign of retreating from what has long been one of its most resilient, not to say endemic, characteristics.

NOTES

1. Eric Partridge claims that logically a dilemma is an ambiguous proposition. See Partridge (1990).
2. It could of course be argued that since a rook has a higher value than a bishop player B will save the rook. Although this might be true the resulting loss of the bishop is not a desirable or satisfactory outcome for player B. It could be argued that player B will resort to a counter-attack in order to save both pieces; indeed there are many manoeuvres player B might be able to perform to save both pieces and ultimately gain a satisfactory outcome. However, in this simplistic example such actions are not available to player B.
3. Buzan prefers the term power–security dilemma. See Buzan (1991).
4. A similar definition has been used by Jack Snyder but it contains a crucial difference. Snyder refers to the security dilemma arising where states believe their security requires the insecurity of others. In other words there is nothing inadvertent about the other state's reduction in security. Snyder's definition is very different from the accepted understanding of the concept. See Snyder (1985).
5. At this point the term 'dilemma' may appear to be a misnomer and the concept under discussion is really a paradox. While this may seem correct, I intend to explain how these different definitions relate to one another and thus show that 'dilemma' is the correct term. As such I will continue to refer to the concept as a security dilemma rather than a security paradox.
6. A useful analogy in explaining this can be made with the game of chess. Player B knew that he would lose one piece regardless of what he did. If player B had been unaware of his predicament then he would still have lost one piece and been in a dilemma. The only difference is that player B would only have been aware of the dilemma after he had lost either his rook or bishop. This also works in reverse, since if player A were unaware of his advantageous position then player B would have a good chance of saving both pieces. However B would not realize this and perceive that he was in a dilemma. Thus the thought that went into his next move would be built upon this premise. Player B for all intents and purposes is in a dilemma.
7. In keeping with the aliens theme a useful analogy can be made with what could be called the Star Trek phenomenon. The mission of the crew, among other things,

was to discover and contact alien life forms in a peaceful fashion. Yet the vessel chosen for this peaceful mission was the latest battleship armed with an array of sophisticated weapons systems. In other words, when encountering something for the first time it is considered prudent to carry a big stick.

8. Wendt refers to the security dilemma in category one terms, that is, the state reduces the security of others as it seeks security. Wendt is thus arguing that when the first social contact takes place neither participant has yet undertaken an action which can be considered dangerous – a security dilemma is not in operation. However, if the criterion of uncertainty is used to define dilemma then Wendt is wrong, since the participants even before the first action are uncertain of each other's intention. Wendt's comment is thus contentious; however it is the contention in this argument that unresolvable uncertainty is not the defining characteristic and thus I agree with Wendt's assertion that states do not begin their relationship in a security dilemma.

9. Wolfers (1961) suggested that the United States fitted this pattern after 1945.

10. Posen (1993, p. 28). 'Compel' may be too deterministic, but the implication that most statesmen sensitive to the security dilemma may be unable to avoid it is probably correct. To mitigate or avoid the security dilemma requires a special type of statesman, aided by favourable conditions.

11. 'Russia and the West: Nag, nag', *The Economist*, 8 April 1995.

12. For Eden's view of the dismissal see Eden (1960).

13. For more details see 'Hungarian–Romanian ministerial talks', *Newsletter Hungarian Office of NATO/WEU Information*, no. 3, February 1995.

10. 'Travel without maps': thinking about security after the Cold War

Richard Wyn Jones*

> I think we may now be living, this year and for many years ahead, through episodes as significant as any known in the human record ... There would not be decades of détente, as the glaciers slowly melt. There would be very rapid and unpredictable changes; nations would become unglued from their alliances; there would be sharp conflicts within nations; there would be successive risks. We could roll up the map of the Cold War, and travel without maps for a while.
>
> E.P. Thompson (1982)[1]

Fred Kaplan's magisterial account of the evolution of US nuclear strategy, *The Wizards of Armageddon* (Kaplan 1984), is prefaced by a vignette depicting Bernard Brodie's reaction to the news of Hiroshima's destruction by an atomic bomb on 6 August 1945. By the end of the Second World War, Brodie had established himself as a respected naval strategist. However, upon reading a newspaper account of the destruction wreaked on the Japanese city and its inhabitants by a single bomb, known to its creators by the incongruous diminutive 'Little Boy', Brodie turned to his wife and said, 'Everything that I have written is obsolete' (Kaplan 1984, p. 10). As is well known, Brodie's longer-term response to the dawning of the 'nuclear age' was to pioneer the nuclear deterrence theory which became 'the jewel in the crown' of strategic studies (Booth 1987, p. 254).[2]

It is contended here that the end of the Cold War, a development perhaps best symbolized by events in Berlin on 9 November 1989, is of similar epoch-making import as the tragedies which befell the cities of Hiroshima and Nagasaki 44 years earlier. Since the populace of divided Berlin breached the infamous wall – a wall which had not only sepa-

*The author wishes to acknowledge the invaluable assistance of Ken Booth, Susan L. Carruthers, Guto Thomas and Nicholas J. Wheeler who all made detailed comments on earlier drafts of this chapter.

rated them, but had come to symbolize the division of the developed world, and much of the so-called 'Third World', into two armed camps – international politics has entered a new era. As E.P. Thompson had correctly surmised, this has proven an era characterized by unpredictable change, uncertainty, and conflict.[3] This chapter will contend that Thompson was also correct to argue that we are travelling into this new era 'without maps'. That is, the concepts and theories which were the dominant source of orientation and direction during the Cold War have lost whatever limited relevance they once enjoyed. Thus it is only through realizing, as Brodie did half a century ago, the obsolescence of much of what has previously passed muster as timeless wisdom, and engaging in a fundamental reconsideration of the ways in which we *think* about security, that we can hope to draw up new maps for understanding the post-Cold War world. Such maps must not only enable us to understand how we have reached our present position, but also signpost possible routes by which this present position may be transcended. In other words, attempts at rethinking security should take place in the context of a renewed commitment to emancipatory change (Smith 1992).

The chapter is divided into four sections. The first criticizes the inadequacy of the traditional approach to thinking about security, and in particular the state-centrism and scientific objectivism which underlies the orthodox discourse. The next two sections focus in turn on the key axes of the contemporary debate about how security should be conceptualized: the debate over *broadening* the security agenda to incorporate other, non-military issues, and over *extending* the agenda away from a state-centric view of what constitutes the correct 'referent object' for security discourse. Specifically, the second section discusses attempts from within the traditional approach to *broaden* our conceptualization of security to include various issues which lie beyond the purview of the Cold War era focus on military force. In particular, it focuses on Barry Buzan's call in his seminal work *People, States and Fear* (1991 [1983]), for the incorporation of political, economic, environmental, societal, as well as, of course, military issues, on to the security agenda. While in broad agreement with these attempts to broaden our understanding of security, the third section argues that we must also reject the state-centric approach which still underlies Buzan's work and, rather, *extend* our concept of security. It is argued that any attempt to rethink security in the post-Cold War era must move beyond the traditional focus on the state as the referent object for security discourse. Consideration is then given to suggestions by more radical scholars for alternative referents for security, including individuals, society, identity and community.

The fourth section argues that new thinking about security must root itself in the emancipatory project of critical theory. Given the increasingly untenable nature of the scientific objectivist position which characterizes the traditional approach, it is argued that it is only critical theory that can supply the necessary methodological sophistication and normative direction for attempts at rethinking security in this new era. It is on this foundation that a new critical security studies can be developed in place of the traditional approach to security.

THE INADEQUACY OF THE TRADITIONAL APPROACH

There are obvious difficulties and potential pitfalls awaiting anyone bold enough to attempt to generalize about any major body of thought, let alone a body of work as vast as the one which constitutes postwar strategic studies – what this writer terms the traditional approach to security. Perhaps the main danger lies in oversimplification. It appears almost inevitable that any attempt to distil a set of arguments to their 'essence' – a necessary operation if we are to make generalizations – will lead one to disregard nuance, richness and diversity in favour of simplistic caricature. Nevertheless, and while bearing this warning in mind, it is plausible to argue that despite the often hotly contested differences that have divided, and continue to divide, strategic studies (or security studies)[4] into rival camps, almost all the participants in these debates appear to share broadly similar ontological and epistemological assumptions (Williams 1992; Reus-Smit 1992; Krause and Williams 1995). That is, all have a similar view of the world with which they are trying to engage, and all share a similar conception of what constitutes knowledge about that world. In the former case, those who have adopted the traditional approach to the study of security have viewed the world from a *state-centric* perspective. In the latter case, all the arguments have been premised on a *scientific objectivist* understanding of knowledge (Reus-Smit 1992, p. 2). Therefore, the differences between various groups of strategists are actually based, whether the protagonists are aware of it or not, on a broad measure of agreement on the nature of the enterprise on which they are engaged. This section will briefly explain, and criticize, the ontological and epistemological foundations of this agreement.

The state centrism of the traditional approach to security is a product of the fact that the whole approach is itself based on the foundations of a realist understanding of world politics. As John Garnett (1987) argues in his chapter on 'Strategic Studies and its Assumptions': 'Perhaps the most pervasive assumptions underlying contemporary strategy are those associated with the theory of political behaviour known as realism' (p. 9). State-centrism is one of the central tenets – if not indeed, *the* central tenet – of realism. For realists, justification for placing states centre-stage arises from two distinct, although interrelated sources, one empirical and the second normative.

Empirically, realists regard state-centrism as being justified, indeed necessary, as this reflects the reality of international relations: states are placed centre-stage quite simply because they are at the centre of the international stage, particularly so where security issues are concerned. Indeed for realists, international relations is defined in terms of the interaction of states. Thus one arrives at the tautological argument that states are at the centre of the study of international relations because international relations is about the interrelationship of states. But even leaving aside any qualms about the logical status of such an argument, we are left with a far more fundamental question. How realistic is the realists' state-centrism?

While very few would want to doubt the importance of states in world politics, no matter what theoretical perspective is being adopted, state-centrism, even empirically speaking, does appear to be highly problematic. One of the major consequences of what one might describe as this fetishization of the state is the construction and reification of the so-called inside–outside dichotomy based around the concept of sovereignty. This dichotomy resonates throughout the realist view of international politics (see Walker 1993). Analytically, one of the implications of this binary is a rather rigid differentiation between the sub-state and the supra-state 'level of analysis'. While the latter is seen as the preserve of international relations specialists, 'our field', as it were, the former is seen as falling within the purview of other disciplines, and largely irrelevant to the concerns of international relations. Although domestic politics within a state may be interesting in itself, one does not need to know anything about it in order to understand that state's international political behaviour. This is because realists argue that a state (any state) will behave in certain state-like ways no matter what its internal composition because of the constraining influence of international anarchy (Waltz 1979). Thus Colin Gray can confidently proclaim that 'The strategic theorist does not know, cannot know, who will be in office, who will be aligned with whom .... But the theorist does know how statesmen behave and why they behave as they do' (Gray 1992, p. 627).

Although no one can doubt the elegant simplicity of this position, the crucial question remains: is the realist's state-centrism analytically useful? Can we ignore the internal politics of the state and simply concentrate on the determining influence of the international 'realm of necessity'? The experience of the end of the Cold War, undoubtedly the greatest change in the international security environment for decades, suggests not.

The failure of any international relations specialist working within the realist paradigm to foresee the end of the Cold War and the remarkably peaceful disintegration of the Soviet Union has been much commented upon.[5] According to Gray, 'The fact that most realists or neo-realists did not predict the fall of the House of Lenin in the 1980s was a failure in prescience, not of paradigm. The ending of the Cold war has occurred for reasons fully explicable without strain by realist argument' (Gray 1992, p. 629). Many realist writers have indeed tried to provide *ex post-facto* explanations for the end of the Cold War working from realist precepts and arguing that the Gorbachev reforms were, in the words of Waltz, 'an externally imposed necessity' (Lebow 1994, p. 266). However, these arguments are not persuasive. The reforms instituted in the Soviet Union in the years after 1985 went far beyond what was necessary if Gorbachev and his colleagues were simply concerned with adjusting to relative economic decline. As Lebow trenchantly observes,

> None of ... [the realists] insisted that the Soviet Union's relative decline demanded a leader who would introduce Western-style democratic reforms, hold relatively free elections, acknowledge the legal right of republics to secede from the Soviet Union, encourage anti communist revolutions in Eastern Europe, agree to dissolve the Warsaw Pact, withdraw Soviet forces from the territories of its former members, accept the reunification of Germany within NATO, ...[etc.] Such recommendations, let alone a prediction that all this would soon come to pass, would have been greeted derisively as the height of *un*realism. (Lebow 1994, p. 264)

Quite simply, to understand the end of the Cold War, one cannot simply concentrate on state–system interaction. Rather, the focus must also embrace analysis of events within the state, and of transnational, but non-state, interaction. For example, the Western European peace movement, the Eastern European dissidents, and their interaction; the influence of Western alternative security thinking on the Soviet leadership; the rise of nationalism amongst subservient nationalities in Eastern Europe; the collapse of confidence in the shibboleths of Marxism–Leninism; and many other factors not amenable to interrogation within the traditional realist framework are crucial to any understanding of events after 1985 (Risse-Kappen 1994; Wyn Jones 1995a). As Lebow observes, 'Soviet foreign policy under Gorbachev is outside the Realist paradigm. To explain it, the analyst must go outside the paradigm and look at the determining influence of domestic politics, belief systems, and learning' (Lebow 1994, p. 268).

In a comment apparently aimed at recent critics of the traditional approach to security, Gray has stated, 'People who have not functioned competently as strategic thinkers on the old agenda, are simply going to perpetuate familiar means–ends errors as they transition to exciting new topics on a new agenda' (Gray 1992, p. 626). Given the complete failure of exponents of the very traditional approach championed by Gray to anticipate, let alone satisfactorily understand or explain, the most significant transformation in the security environment for many years, one may be forgiven for regarding this charge as having a somewhat double-edged quality. If the traditional approach's statism means that it is so conceptually fragile in the face of such a massive, tectonic shift as the end of the Cold War, it seems highly unlikely that scholars and analysts who persist in holding to these views have anything of significance to contribute to any new agenda.

A less familiar corollary to these empirical claims regarding state-centrism is the realist assumption that states have normative value in themselves. This assumption is often left implicit by authors working within this tradition, yet, as Reus-Smit convincingly demonstrates, the realists' proclivity to view the so-called nation-state as an 'idealised political community' plays a vitally important simplifying role in their world-view (Reus-Smit 1992). It is important to stress that Reus-Smit is not claiming that realists view the state in a way analogous to that adopted by romantic nationalist philosophers in the nineteenth century, that is, as some kind of organic entity to whose interests all individuals, and all other forms of community, should become instrumental and subservient. This may have been the view of Treitschke and Meinichke, but it is not one shared by contemporary strategists.

Rather, the argument is that the ideal of the state as a unified and relatively homogenous (nationally, ethnically and ideologically), coherent and peaceful community 'is fundamental to the logical structure and coherence' (Reus-Smit 1992, p. 14) of the traditional approach to security. For proponents of this view, the nation-state is a sovereignty-bounded realm within which order, justice, liberty and prosperity (the good life) are possible. In the words of Osgood and Tucker, the state is the 'indispensable condition of value' (Osgood and Tucker 1967, p. 284). The profound implications of this claim for security discourse are summarized by Reus-Smit:

> Once the nation-state is seen as a unified political community, it is assumed that there exists such a homogeneity of interests and identification within that community that security can be reduced to a minimal conception of state survival which is seen as synonymous with aggregate individual security ... Political action ... is thus explained in terms of a unity of purpose among citizens coalescing around a common desire to limit threats by maximising military capabilities. (Reus-Smit 1992, p. 17)

Here we see the important simplifying effects of the assumption of an 'idealised political community'. If it is assumed that there is an essential harmony of interests between individuals and their state, then analysts working within the traditional paradigm can claim that their state-centrism is justified because state security is a precondition for individual well-being within that state. In other words, here we have a normative justification for privileging the state as the referent object of security discourse based on the claim that states are the agents which provide citizens with security at the domestic level. The main threat to their security is seen as emanating from other states who are perceived, in purportedly Hobbesian fashion, as viewing their neighbours rapaciously, ready to pounce at the slightest sign of weakness.

But again, once this idealized view of the state is measured against the empirical evidence, the state-centrism of the traditional approach to security appears highly problematic. Far from fostering an atmosphere within which stability can be attained and prosperity created, in much of the world, states are one of the main sources of insecurity for their citizens. As Tickner points out, 'In an international system which, in parts of the South, amounts to domestic disorder and stability of international borders, often upheld by the interventions and interests of great powers, the realist assumptions about boundaries between anarchy and order is turned on its head' (Tickner 1995, p. 181). Even if we apply a very narrow, military understanding of security we find that it is not only in the disadvantaged South that the arms purchased, and powers accrued, by governments in the name of 'national' security are far more potent threats to the liberty and physical safety of their citizens than any putative foreign threat. When we apply a broader definition of security (see below), we find that many states are deeply implicated in the creation of other forms of insecurity for their own populations, for example, in issues of food security, environmental security and so on.

Viewed empirically, apparently aberrant 'gangster states' like Mobuto's Zaire are closer to the norm of state behaviour than the Eurocentric notion of the state central to the traditional approach to security would suggest (Wheeler forthcoming). Furthermore, radical understandings of global politics suggest that those few developed states which do indeed provide their citizens with a good deal of security (however defined) can only do so because of their dominant, privileged position within the global economy. However, the very structure of this global economy creates and reinforces the gross disparities of wealth, the environmental degradation, and the class, ethnic and gender inequalities which are the source of insecurity in the South. In other words, the relative security of the inhabitants of the North is purchased at the price of chronic insecurity for the vast majority of the world population. Indeed, radical critics also suggest that the ideological function of the traditional approach's state-centrism is actually to discipline those *within* the state who deign to challenge the *status quo*.[6] For example, dissident voices on both sides of the 'Iron Curtain' argued that 'the principle [*sic*] axis of the Cold War conflict lay, not between the superpowers, but between states and civil society' (Reus-Smit 1992, p. 22). So, far from being a necessary condition for the good life, states appear to be one of the main sources of insecurity: part of the problem rather than the solution.

So we find that the empirical justifications for this state-centric ontology are highly dubious, and furthermore, it appears that one of the main functions of the statist discourse of the traditional approach to security is to provide an ideological justification for the political and economic *status quo*. The latter point is particularly striking when contrasted with the epistemological position upheld by those who champion the traditional approach to security. For this epistemology is one that aims to describe the world 'as it is'; that claims to distinguish sharply between fact and value and between subject and object, and seeks objective knowledge of the world, untainted by the analyst's own standpoint and predilections (Williams 1992, pp. 69–73). Unsurprisingly, therefore, the charge that a particular (pro *status quo*) bias is smuggled into, or even embedded in, traditional analysis, is anathema to its proponents.

Historically, there have been varying degrees of epistemological self-consciousness among traditional security specialists. However, in line with developments in the study of international relations in general, recent years have witnessed a growing awareness among analysts of the theoretical issues at stake. This increased awareness has been prompted both by attempts among mainstream scholars to develop more sophisticated theoretical underpinnings for their work (e.g. Waltz 1979), and by trenchant criticism from those beyond that mainstream (for examples, see Smith, Booth and Zalewski forthcoming). The net result of these developments for strategic-security studies has been an increasingly self-conscious embrace of the 'scientific' epistemology particularly associated with neorealism.[7] This 'scientific' method is seen by Stephen M. Walt as the foundation stone for the study of security, and it is worth quoting him a some length:

> security studies seeks *cumulative knowledge* about the role of military force. To obtain it, the field must follow the standard canons of scientific research: careful and consistent use of terms, unbiased measurement of critical concepts, and public documentation of theoretical and empirical claims …. The increased sophistication of the security studies field and its growing prominence within the scholarly community is due in large part to the endorsement of these principles by most members of the field. (Walt 1991, p. 222)

As Krause and Williams point out, proponents of this view seek to work within the 'strictures of a particular conception of science and knowledge: the search for timeless, objective, causal laws that govern human phenomena' (Krause and Williams 1995, p. 6). The particular 'conception of science' is based on the Newtonian understanding of the physical world. The Newtonian paradigm also posits a rigid distinction between subject and object, between observer and observed, and regards the physical world as governed by cast-iron laws, which, even if not presently understood, are potentially discoverable.

It is particularly ironic that strategic-security studies, a field which has at its heart the study of the implications of nuclear weapons, has adopted this particular view of the natural sciences as a model for emulation. For the very scientific discoveries that made the development of nuclear weapons possible formed part of a paradigm shift away from this Newtonian understanding of the physical world towards the Einsteinian paradigm (Wyn Jones 1995b). The new quantum physics rejected the Newtonian view that there is a world 'out there' existing independently of our observations. Rather, following Heisenberg's Uncertainty Principle, physicists realized that the very act of observation influences the behaviour of the object being observed. At one fell swoop this discovery undermines the rigid distinction between subject and object, and hence fact and value, that forms the epistemological foundations of the traditional approach to security. The implications of this breakdown in the rigid separation between fact and value will be expanded on later in this chapter.

Our discussion thus far has revealed serious weaknesses in the theoretical underpinnings of the traditional approach to security. The state-centric ontology of strategic-security studies not only appears to be empirically unhelpful, but also to act as an ideological justification for the prevailing *status quo*. Furthermore, the scientific objectivist conception of knowledge adopted by the field appears to have been undermined by the very scientific discoveries that acted as the catalyst for its development.

BROADENING THE AGENDA: BOTH GUNS AND BUTTER

Barry Buzan's *People, States and Fear* (1991 [1983]) can, in a sense, be viewed as the high point of this traditional approach to the study of security.[8] While remaining grounded in a scientific objectivist epistemology and, ultimately, in a state-centric ontology, Buzan has produced a rich, suggestive and sophisticated discussion of the concept of security. In this section we shall examine Buzan's case for broadening our understanding of 'security' beyond the traditional concern with military threats.[9] In particular, we shall examine some of the criticisms that have been made of this attempt to view other problems through the lens of 'security'. It will be suggested that these criticisms are either unwarranted or misplaced, and that, in this respect at least, Buzan's project deserves support.

The argument advanced in *People, States and Fear* for moving beyond a purely military focus for the security agenda is inextricably bound up with Buzan's wider attempt to delineate and define the scope of (international) security studies and strategic studies (see also Buzan 1987). For Buzan, strategic studies should be concerned with the study of the military aspect of the security agenda, and specifically with the impact of military technology on international relations. What he terms international security studies, on the other hand, should concern itself with more broadly defined threats to the 'security of human collectivities' (Buzan 1991, p. 19). Buzan identifies these threats as emanating from five main sectors: political, societal, economic, environmental, as well as military.

Buzan's original call for a broader security agenda was made in less than propitious circumstances. The first edition of *People, States and Fear* was published in 1983, the year in which Ronald Reagan made his infamous 'evil empire' speech, and in which the Soviets appeared to attempt to live up to the sobriquet by shooting down a South Korean Boeing 747 over Soviet air space, killing all 269 people on board. The second Cold War was at its zenith. Reflecting on his own reaction to the first edition, Steve Smith comments that, although he was impressed by the intellectual argument for a broader agenda, Buzan's concerns seemed somewhat 'utopian and removed from the world that was the subject of my teaching and analysis. But', he goes on, 'Buzan was right, as the events since the publication of the first edition have proved' (Smith 1991, p. 325). Certainly there can be no doubt that, as Smith recognizes, the end of the Cold War has added legitimacy and credibility to demands for a broader security agenda: the collapse of the Soviet bloc, and the numerous problems that have emerged since its demise, have highlighted the inadequacy of adopting a narrowly military conceptualization of security. So whereas in the past calls for a broader conception had been confined to (marginalized) peace researchers, World Society thinkers, and a few more iconoclastic international relations scholars such as Buzan (1991) and Ullman (1983), they have now become commonplace in the mainstream of security studies (e.g. Crawford 1991; Matthews 1989).

At least rhetorically, most analysts are now willing to admit non-military issues on to the security agenda. Indicative of this change is the introduction to a reader put together by the editors of the most prominent and prestigious journal in the field of security studies, *International Security*. Sean M. Lynn-Jones and David E. Miller argue that the end of the East–West confrontation has

> Revealed in its wake ... a different set of dangers, not really new but previously overshadowed by Cold War preoccupations .... No longer will

the field of international security be overwhelmingly fixated on how to deter the Soviet Union or how to reduce the risk of nuclear war between the superpowers. The newly revealed agenda is broader in its focus, giving much greater attention to previously neglected sources of conflict. (Lynn-Jones and Miller 1995, p. 4)

The 'previously neglected sources of conflict' focused on in the text are environmental threats, threats arising from international migration, and threats emanating from resurgent nationalism.

Of course, attempts to interlink issues of peace and war with wider questions of economic and social equity and justice are hardly novel. Indeed they are a recurring feature in the statements of various international organizations. Article 55 of the United Nations Charter, for example, links the creation of 'friendly and peaceful relations among nations' with the resolution of 'economic, social, health, and related problems', as well as respect for human rights. However, two sets of critics have objected to current attempts to broaden the concept of security traditionally utilized in the field of security studies. On the one hand, traditionalists have argued that such a move will lead to a loss of focus, while on the other, some commentators have pointed to the dangers of viewing problems such as those associated with environmental degradation as security issues.

The traditionalist argument has been put forward forcefully by Walt (1991). In his programmatic essay confidently entitled 'The renaissance of security studies', Walt criticizes Buzan on the grounds that introducing non-military issues on to the security agenda undermines the field's 'intellectual coherence'. However, as Booth points out, there appears to be a major inconsistency in Walt's argument. While wishing to uphold a restrictive conception of security, Walt's own proposed research agenda includes such issues as the role of domestic politics, the power of ideas, and the influence of economic issues. The serious consideration of any of these issues would wholly undermine the traditional, parsimonious approach favoured by Walt (Booth and Herring 1994, pp. 126–7). One might argue that Walt is inevitably forced into such a contradictory position by the inherent limitations of his conception of security. Quite simply, if one were to adopt the narrowly military focus advocated, but not apparently practised, by Walt, one would have no analytical handle on many of those factors that create and accentuate conflict situations. For example, one cannot hope to understand the dynamics of the (military) security situation in former Yugoslavia without reference to the processes of identity formation and disintegration occurring in the region. Quite simply, if we continue to conceive security in such a restrictive manner, then from Sarajevo to Berlin, and from Kigali to Pyongyang, we shall continue to miss much of what is most relevant to the global security agenda. As Booth argues, 'when studying any human phenomenon it is preferable to have open intellectual boundaries (which risk only irrelevance) rather than rigid ones (which risk ignorance)' (Booth 1994, p. 20). Ultimately, it is vital that we bear in mind that all disciplinary boundaries are merely a convenience: perhaps necessary for both intellectual and administrative orientation and organization, but for no more than that. When these boundaries become reified, even fetishized, they can become a hindrance to the very understanding which they were intended to promote. Given that, as Theodor Adorno argues, 'all reification is a forgetting', it is surely right that we worry more about what lies beyond security studies' artificial borders – that which has been 'forgotten' – than about any loss of focus or 'intellectual coherence'.

A second, and perhaps more serious, challenge to those seeking to broaden our understanding of security has arisen from some of those who object to the 'securitization' of problems such as those relating to the environment and migration (e.g. Deudney 1990; Huysmans forthcoming). For these critics, there is a real danger involved in the process of 'hyphenating security', that is the attachment of different appellations, such as economic and identity, to the term security. This danger lies in the militarization and confrontation-oriented attitude conjured up by the traditional conception of security as 'national security'. For example, Deudney argues that environmental problems cannot be solved by the 'national security' mind-set; indeed that this very 'mind-set' is inimical to the development of 'environmental awareness and action' (Deudney 1990, p. 461).

There are at least two possible responses to these criticisms. Ole Wæver, himself a close collaborator with Buzan, has argued in response to Huysmans that the intention in broadening the concept of security to encompass non-traditional issues is not to trigger a traditional security-type response to them (Wæver 1994, p. 19). Rather, it is to focus on the way in which security discourse is used to identify some threats as being 'existential' – part of the 'drama of survival'. Thus, 'Issues [become] phrased as "no way back": after we have lost our sovereignty/identity/the sustainability of the eco-system, it will be too late; therefore it is legitimate that we take extraordinary measures' (Wæver 1994, p. 10f). Wæver wishes to interrogate the status of 'security' as a 'speech act' whereby the attachment of the label to a particular problem serves to give that problem special status, and legitimates 'extraordinary measures' by state representatives to deal with it (Wæver 1994, p. 6. See also Buzan 1991 [1983] p. 17). Here Wæver's argument seems to be that analysts are justified in broadening their conception of security beyond traditional concerns, precisely because politicians already utilize the term in relation to 'non-traditional' problems. In other words, if practitioners have a broader understanding of what constitutes a security issue, then it is high time that theorists caught up with them!

Wæver's arguments, at least on this point, are premised on a definite, if unorthodox, state-centrism (but see Wæver et al. 1993, pp. 17–40). However, elements of his argument may still be utilized by those who reject such a perspective. In particular, Wæver's insightful comments on the status of 'security' as a 'speech act' certainly have wider resonance. It is not only 'state representatives' who use security discourse to identify particular threats, and to mobilize and legitimate particular responses to them. All kinds of social groups, at both sub and suprastate levels, 'securitize' many different types of issue in this manner, often with far-reaching sociocultural, political and economic implications. Thus, once again, it appears that the adoption of a broader conception of security by analysts is justified in the light of the empirical praxis of individuals, social groups and movements.

Those who reject a state-centric ontology may point to further evidence to support their efforts to broaden the concept of security. When one begins to focus on security referents other than the state, it becomes apparent that 'existential' threats to those referents – be they individuals, nations and so on – are far broader than those posed by military force. For most of the world's population, such 'marginal' and 'esoteric' concerns as environmental security and food security, to give only two examples, are far more real and immediate threats to existence than inter-state war. Of course, according to critics like Deudney, while this may indeed be the case, posing these issues as 'security' issues will lead to their militarization rather than their resolution. However, those who reject state-centrism as a foundation for thinking about security also, as a corollary, embrace some notion of common security (see Independent Commission on Disarmament and Security Issues 1982). Common security is based on the notion that there can be no long-term resolution of threats through unilateral, militarized, zero-sum action. Rather it is only a holistic and empathetic theory and practice of security that can hope to mitigate threats. Indeed one might argue that the alternative perspective on security is wholly consistent with the type of globalist strategies that environmentalists, for example, are advocating. This is a point which Deudney himself accepts (Deudney 1990, pp. 468–9). However, he counters by implying that the term' security' is so tainted by militarized statism that advocates of 'common security' are in effect deluded in their hope that the concept can somehow be 're-visioned' (Tickner 1995, pp. 175–97). But, given the important role of 'security' as a speech act, it is vital to dispute the terrain of 'security' rather than abandon it to traditional notions. Indeed, as has already been mentioned, the experience of the end of the Cold War demonstrates that alternative understandings of security can become influential. Therefore, *contra* Deudney, conducting a 'war of position' around the concept, for example through broadening it to include non-traditional issues, is a valuable if not vital exercise (Wyn Jones 1995a).

EXTENDING THE AGENDA: FROM A STATE-CENTRED TO A PEOPLE-CENTRED CONCEPT OF SECURITY

People, States and Fear is an arresting title; it is also a somewhat misleading one. 'States and fear' is a more accurate representation of Buzan's ultimate focus. To be sure, he does pay attention to the security of individuals, as well as security at the supra-state levels of particular regions and of the international system itself. However, in the final analysis, his interest in these other levels centres on their impact upon states. As the Buzan-endorsed 'hourglass' model of security devised by Ole Wæver demonstrates (Figure 10.1), the conceptual focus of this view of security remains at the state level.

Buzan has two main justifications for adopting this state-centric perspective. Empirically, his case is that the security dynamics at the international and sub-state levels are all mediated through the state: 'It is the job of government, indeed almost the definition of its function, to find ways of reconciling these two sets of forces. The fact that no other agency exists for this task is what justifies the primacy of national [i.e. state] security.' So, once again, the argument is that states should be the 'conceptual focus of security' because it is states that 'have to cope with the whole security problem' (1991 [1983], p. 329). Allied to this argument is Buzan's contention that states can in fact provide individuals with security. Buzan is, of course, aware that states are often a

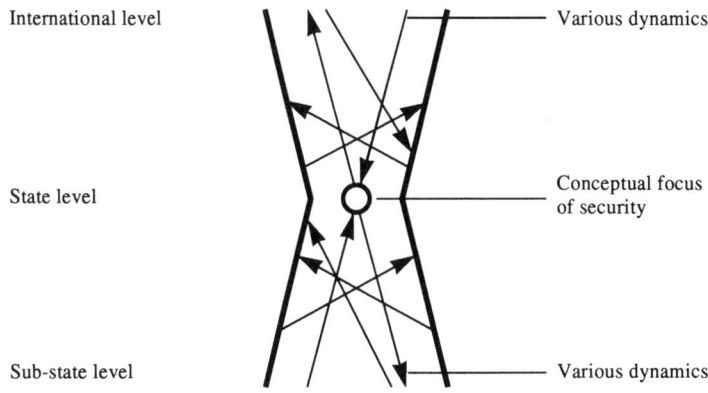

International level — Various dynamics

State level — Conceptual focus of security

Sub-state level — Various dynamics

Source: Buzan (1991 [1983], p. 328).

Figure 10.1   Conceptual focus of security

mortal danger to their own citizens; however he holds that the problem is not states themselves (that is, states *qua* states) but rather particular kinds of state. Individual security can be obtained when there are 'strong states' (states with a high degree of internal stability and cohesion) coexisting in a 'mature anarchy' (a developed international society).

As these arguments are sophisticated variants of those discussed and criticized in the first section of this chapter, we need not rehearse the counter-arguments to them here. Suffice it to say that since its publication, Buzan himself appears to have distanced himself somewhat from the state-centrism of *People, States and Fear*. In particular, his work on European security which led to the collaborative volume *Identity, Migration and the New Security Agenda in Europe* (Wæver et al. 1993), attempts to develop the concept of 'societal security' as a 'distinctive referent object alongside' state security. Certainly, Buzan's state-centrism has been subjected to strong criticism by those who argue that the state should not be the privileged reference object of security discourse. These critics have sought to *extend* the security agenda by shifting the focus away from states and on to other levels of analysis.

A number of alternative 'referent objects' for security have been proposed with suggestions emanating both from scholars working from an alternative defence perspective, and those engaged in the praxis of social movements. Some have argued that the conceptual focus should be placed on 'individuals' (Booth 1991b; Smith 1991). Others have suggested that the correct focus is on society, and particularly on some notion of 'civil society' (Shaw 1994; Reus-Smit 1992). Yet others have proposed that ethno-national and religious identities are crucial referents for conceptualizing security (Wæver et al. 1993). Another suggestion is that there should not be one 'referent object' for security, but rather that the appropriate approach is to focus on different referents at different times, in different locations, and in relation to different issue areas (Booth and Vale forthcoming).

One of the most prominent advocates of making individuals the conceptual focal point of security is Ken Booth. In his 'Security and Emancipation' (1991b) he argues against privileging the state as the referent object of security on the grounds that to do so is to confuse means with ends. States are, or at least can be, a means of providing security, but ultimately, it is only with reference to individuals that the notion of security has any meaning: 'It is illogical therefore to privilege the security of the means as opposed to the security of ends' (Booth 1991b, p. 320). Rather, Booth argues, 'following the World Society School, buttressed on this point by Hedley Bull, ... individual humans are the ultimate referent' (p. 319).

Booth's argument is certainly an important corrective to the state-centrism of Buzan and the traditional approach in general. However, at least as it is framed in 'Security and Emancipation', the argument is also somewhat reductive and hence, limiting. Some threats *are* perhaps best viewed in light of their effects, or potential effects, on individual human beings. Specifically, these threats include those relating to so-called basic human needs, that is to the basic *material* prerequisites for life. Here one might follow Booth in arguing that any form of human collectivity is ultimately a means, and that the ultimate referent object should be individual human beings. But there is another category of threats where it seems singularly unhelpful to place individuals at the conceptual core of our thinking about security. These threats may be broadly defined as those relating to identity.

Identity is a central aspect of the human experience. Even when conceived of in traditional terms, it is clear that questions relating to the formation, the expression, and the disintegration of different forms of identity – of which 'national identity' is only one of the most prominent – should be of vital concern to those interested in security issues. When our conceptualization of security is broadened and extended, identity is even more self-evidently important. However, questions relating to identity cannot simply be reduced to the level of individuals. Identities are by definition collective phenomena. One creates, negotiates or receives one's identity through interaction with others. As a result, to reduce questions relating to identity to individuals or aggregations of individuals is, at best, misleading. Where identity is concerned, the whole is more than the sum of the parts. Therefore, in relation to questions of identity – one of the key variables in any discussion of security – Booth's focus on individuals appears both problematic and limiting.

Other analysts have attempted to overcome the liberal individualism implicit in the view of humanity adopted by thinkers like Booth, by proffering other social groups as referent objects for security discourse. Wæver, for example, focuses in particular on ethno-national groupings (Wæver et al. 1993; Wæver 1994). Implicit in Samuel Huntington's argument concerning 'The Clash of Civilizations?' is the rather grandiose notion that civilizations should become the conceptual focus of security (Huntington 1993a). But as Keith Krause and Michael Williams point out, there are dangers involved in redirecting attention to social groups: 'The risk is that a shift ... to a prima facie focus on structures of exclusionary group-identity will merely replicate the inside/outside structure of anarchy in a different form' (Krause and Williams 1995, p. 22). This certainly appears to be the case with the clash of civilizations argument, and it is also a charge that has been laid against Ole Wæver (Shaw 1994, pp. 100–3).

Although the danger highlighted does indeed appear to be real, it is not insurmountable. Without wishing to stray too far into deep philosophical waters, it should be recognized that inside–outside, self–other dichotomies – however they have been constituted – do have a certain 'reality'. These dichotomies cannot simply be wished away, or deconceptualized out of existence: ultimately they can only be overcome or transcended through praxis, of which theories and theorizing forms a part, but only a part. This highlights the need for an analytical framework which is sensitive to difference and diversity but, simultaneously, avoids their reification. Such a framework also needs to be able to accommodate the fact that identities very rarely occur in the singular, but are overlapping. For example, each person has a number of different identities, all (potentially) in flux, and all of which come into play at different times and in different situations.

Obviously, once identity begins to be conceived of in this manner, a very complex picture emerges. Some will bemoan this complexity;

indeed Krause and Williams complain that a focus on group identity 'hardly provides us with a clear capacity for thinking about security' (Krause and Williams 1995, p. 22). Certainly, when viewed in the abstract, 'group identity' may seem too opaque and amorphous to be regarded as a referent object for security. However, once we move from the abstract to the particular, this becomes less problematic. When we historicize our analysis by looking at specific issues in specific areas, it becomes apparent that the appropriate referent object for analysis varies considerably. In some areas, in regard to certain issues, the appropriate referent may well be 'national identity' or 'civil society'. However, in other circumstances, these categories may be irrelevant or meaningless. Then smaller, more localized communal identities, or individual human beings, may be the appropriate referent object. In other words, the problem of what to privilege as the conceptual focus of security discourse can only be resolved through concrete analysis (e.g. Booth and Vale forthcoming).

To extend the concept of security in the manner advocated in this section is to initiate a radical rupture with the state-centric perspective adopted by Buzan in *People, States and Fear*. Rather than accept the idealized, not to say ideological, view of world politics which characterizes the traditional approach to security, my argument is that we must centre our attentions on 'real people in real places' (Booth 1995a, p. 123). Although the picture (or pictures) that will emerge from such an approach will undoubtedly be complex, understanding this complexity is a prerequisite for bringing about comprehensive security.

FROM TRADITIONAL SECURITY STUDIES TO CRITICAL SECURITY STUDIES

Apart from its state-centrism, another feature which anchors *People, States and Fear* firmly to the traditional approach to thinking about security is its scientific objectivist epistemology. Buzan's approach is premised on a claim that we are able to differentiate between subject and object, fact and value, description and prescription. These delineations form part of an explicitly neorealist outlook.[10] Summing up his approach to security, Buzan comments: 'Some might even see International Security Studies as a liberal reformulation of Realism, emphasising the structural and security-oriented approach of Neorealism, and applying it across a broader agenda. I would support such a view' (1991 [1983], p. 373).

objectivism. It aligns itself to the praxis of critical social movements rather than that of governments. It attempts to denaturalize and question 'commonsense' assumptions rather than accepting a reified, ahistorical account of the present. Thus although the international relations community may be travelling without maps into the post-Cold War era, this does not mean that all of us are journeying without a sense of direction. That sense is being shaped by the developing theory and praxis, understandings and axioms of critical security studies.

NOTES

1. E.P. Thompson in *Beyond the Cold War*, (London: Merlin, 1982, pp. 1, 34). Cited by Reus-Smit (1992, p. 27).
2. Given the present, seemingly all-pervasive confusion concerning the nomenclature of this particular subject area, it is perhaps as well to make my own usage explicit from the outset. I regard strategy as concerned with the military dimension of security, and security itself as a sub-field of the study of world politics. See Booth and Herring (1994, p. 132).
3. This should not be read as an endorsement of the current vogue of hankering after the certainties of the Cold War, e.g. Mearsheimer (1990). For a valuable corrective to such views see Mueller (1995, pp. 7–25).
4. Once again the nomenclature is a potential source of confusion. In recent years, many erstwhile strategists in the United States and Britain have adopted the moniker 'security studies' as a replacement for 'national security studies' (US) and 'strategic studies' (mainly Britain) as a label for their endeavours. However, this rebaptism appears to have been a typically 1990s piece of repackaging: although the name change is intended to signify a sensitivity to the changed security environment after the collapse of the Soviet bloc, the substance of the enterprise remains very much the same (Krause and Williams 1995). Some of the main arguments in the debate over the nature and scope of strategic/security studies are conveniently summarized in Booth and Herring (1994, pp. 120–31).
5. See, for example, the essays by Wohlforth, Waltz and Mearsheimer, collected in Brown, Lynn-Jones and Miller (1995), and the symposium on the end of the Cold War and theories of international relations in *International Organization*, **48** (2), 1994, pp. 155–277.
6. Some of these arguments are summarized in Reus-Smit (1992, pp. 18–25).
7. According to Gray, 'Strategists may be termed and should acknowledge that they are, without apologies, neo-realists' (1982, p. 188).
8. For a useful critical summary of *People, States and Fear* see Smith (1991).
9. Confusion can arise here because Buzan uses the term 'broadening' to refer to both what has been described here as the 'broadening' and 'extending' of the security agenda. (Despite their myriad differences, the same is also true for Walker, e.g. 1990, p. 4.) That is, Buzan regards his call for an increased awareness of the international, regional, individual, as well as state levels of security, as part of his wider attempt to 'broaden' the security agenda (1991, pp. 363–74). However, as will be argued below, for Buzan, the state still remains 'ontologically prior' to these other levels (Smith 1991, p. 334). Fundamentally, he is only interested in them in as much as these levels affect the state which still remains, in the final

analysis, the referent object for security discourse: in other words, Buzan wants to 'broaden' the security debate around the central pole of the state. However, by differentiating between 'broadening' and 'extending', the aim here is to suggest that another 'level of analysis', or indeed other levels, could claim to be regarded as the referent object of security.

10. Although it is beyond the purview of this chapter, it should be noted that Buzan's modifications to neorealism are such as to lead some commentators to question whether the label has any meaning in relation to his work. See Wheeler (1993).

11. Among the work that has contributed to the development of critical security studies are those (already cited) by Booth, Krause and Williams, Walker and Wyn Jones. See, especially, Krause and Williams (forthcoming).

Bibliography

Abir, M. (1993), *Saudi Arabia: Government, Society and the Gulf Crisis*, London: Routledge.

Acharya, A. (1993), 'A New Regional Order in Southeast Asia: ASEAN in the Post-Cold War Era', *Adelphi Paper*, 279, London: International Institute for Strategic Studies.

Adomeit, H. (1995), 'Russia as a "Great Power" in World Affairs: Images and Reality', *International Affairs* (London), **71** (1).

Ajami, F. (1993), 'The Summoning', *Foreign Affairs*, **72** (4), September–October.

Akpan, F. (1990), 'Environment and Development', *APRI Newsletter*, **5** (5), September–October.

Anderson, T. and Leal, D. (1991), *Free Market Environmentalism*, Boulder, Colorado: Westview Press.

Avruch, K. and Black, P. (1987), 'A Generic Theory of Conflict Resolution: A Critique', *Negotiation Journal*, **3** (1), January.

Avruch, K. and Black, P. (1991), 'The Culture Question and Conflict Resolution', *Peace and Change*, **16** (1) January.

Bailey, K.C. (1993), *Strengthening Nuclear Non-Proliferation*, Boulder, Colorado: Westview Press.

Bartley, R. (1993), 'The Case for Optimism: The West Should Believe in itself', *Foreign Affairs*, **72** (4), September–October.

Baylis, J. and Rengger, N. (eds) (1992), *Dilemmas in World Politics*, Oxford; Oxford University Press.

Bell, C. (1994), 'Why an Expanded NATO must Include Russia', *Journal of Strategic Studies*, **17** (4), December.

Berger, P. and Luckmann, T. (1966), *The Social Construction of Reality*, New York: Anchor Books.

Binnendijk, H. and Simon, J. (1994), 'Preventing a Sixth Twentieth-Century Balkan War', *Strategic Forum*, no. 9, October.

Binyan, L. (1993), 'Civilization Grafting: No Culture is an Island', *Foreign Affairs*, **72** (4), September–October.

Blair, B.G. (1993), *The Logic of Accidental Nuclear War*, Washington: The Brookings Institution.

Blumberg, D. (1991), 'Islam and Democracy' in Piscatori, J. (ed.), *Islamic Fundamentalisms and the Gulf Crisis*, Chicago: American Academy of Arts and Sciences.

Bluth, C. (1993), 'American–Russian Strategic Relations: From Confrontation to Cooperation?', *The World Today*, **49** (3).

Bonthus, J.-M. (1994), 'Understanding Intelligence Across Cultures', *International Journal of Intelligence and Counterintelligence*, **7** (3), Fall.

Booth, K. (1987), 'Nuclear Deterrence and "World War III": How Will History Judge?' in Kolkowicz, R. (ed.), *The Logic of Nuclear Terror*, Winchester, Mass.: Allen and Unwin.

Booth, K. (1990), 'The Concept of Strategic Culture Affirmed' in Jacobsen, C. (ed), *Strategic Power: USA–USSR*, Basingstoke: Macmillan.

Booth, K. (ed.) (1991a), *New Thinking about Strategy and International Security*, London: HarperCollins.

Booth, K. (1991b), 'Security and Emancipation', *Review of International Studies*, **17** (4).

Booth, K. (1995a), 'Human Wrongs and International Relations', *International Affairs*, **71** (1), pp. 103–26.

Booth, K. (1995b), 'Dare not to Know: International Relations Theory versus the Future' in Booth, K. and Smith, S. (eds), *International Relations Theory Today*, Cambridge: Polity Press.

Booth, K. and Smith, S. (eds) (1995), *International Relations Theory Today*, Cambridge: Polity Press.

Booth, K. and Herring, E. (1994), *Keyguide to Information in Strategic Studies*, London: Mansell.

Booth, K. and Macmillan, A. (1994a), 'Strategic Culture: Framework for Analysis', paper prepared for a conference on 'Strategic Culture and Conflict Resolution in the Asia–Pacific Region', Langkawi Island, Malaysia, August 1994.

Booth, K. and Macmillan, A. (1994b), 'Strategic Culture: Concept and Development', paper prepared for a conference on 'Strategic Culture and Conflict Resolution in the Asia–Pacific Region', Langkawi Island, Malaysia, August 1994.

Booth, K. and Vale, P. (forthcoming), 'Critical Security Studies and Regional Insecurity: the case of South Africa' in Krause, K. and Williams, M. (eds), *Critical Security Studies*, University of Minnesota Press.

Booth, K. and Wheeler, N. (1992), 'Beyond Nuclearism', in Cowen-Karp, R. (ed.), *Security Without Nuclear Weapons? Different Perspectives on Non-Nuclear Security*, Oxford: Oxford University Press for SIPRI.

Breitmeirer, H. and Wolf, K. (1993), 'Analysing Regime Consequences' in Rittenberger, V. (ed.), *Regime Theory and International Relations*, Oxford: Clarendon Press.

Brown, C. (1995), 'International Political Theory and the Idea of World Community; in Booth, K. and Smith, S. (eds), *International Relations Theory Today*, Cambridge: Polity Press.

Brown, M.E., Lynn-Jones, S.M. and Miller, S.E. (eds) (1995), *The Perils of Anarchy: Contemporary Realism and International Security*, Cambridge, Mass.: MIT Press.

Brzezinski, Z. (1994), 'The Premature Partnership', *Foreign Affairs*, **71** (1), March–April.

Buchan, A. (1963), 'The Age of Insecurity', *Encounter*, **20** (6), June.

Bull, H. (1981), 'Future Conditions of Strategic Deterrence' in Bertram, C. (ed.), *The Future of Strategic Deterrence*, London: International Institute for Strategic Studies.

Burnett, A. (1992), *The Western Pacific: Challenge of Sustainable Growth*, Aldershot: Edward Elgar.

Buszynski, L. (1993), 'Russia and Japan: The Unmaking of a Territorial Settlement', *The World Today*, **49** (3).

Butterfield, H. (1951), *History and Human Relations*, London: Collins.

Buzan, B. (1987), *An Introduction to Strategic Studies: Military Technology and International Relations*, London: Macmillan.

Buzan, B. (1991), *People, States and Fear: An Agenda for International Security Studies in the Post-Cold War Era*, second edition, first edition published in 1983, London and Boulder, Colorado: Harvester Wheatsheaf and Lynne Rienner Publishers.

Buzan, B. (1994), 'The Interdependence of Security and Economic Issues in the "New World Order"' in Stubbs, R. and Underhill, G.R.D. (eds), *Political Economy and the Changing Global Order*, London: Macmillan.

Caldwell, J.A. (1974), *American Economic Aid to Thailand*, Lexington, Mass.: D.C. Heath.

Chambers Twentieth Century Dictionary, (1972), Edinburgh: W. & R. Chambers Ltd.

Chaney, D. (1994), *The Cultural Turn: Scene-setting Essays on Contemporary Cultural History*, London and New York: Routledge.

Chay, J. (ed.) (1990), *Culture and International Relations*, New York, Westport, Connecticut and London: Praeger.

Chubin, S. and Tripp, C. (1993), 'Domestic Politics and Territorial Disputes in the Persian Gulf and Arabian Peninsula', *Survival*, **35** (4), Winter.

Clarke, J.G. (1994), 'Beckoning Quagmires: NATO in Eastern Europe', *Journal of Strategic Studies*, **17** (4), December.

Claude, I.L. Jr (1962) (1965), *Power and International Relations*, New York: Random House.

Claude, I.L. Jr (1984), *Swords into Plowshares: The Problems and Progress of International Organisations*, Fourth edition, New York: McGraw-Hill.

Clausen, P.A. (1993), *Nonproliferation and the National Interest: America's Response to the Spread of Nuclear Weapons*, New York: HarperCollins College Publishers.

Cobden, R. (1862), *The Three Panics: An Historical Episode*, third edition, London: Ward.

Cohen, R. (1990), *Culture and Conflict in Egyptian–Israeli Relations: A Dialogue of the Deaf*, Bloomington, Indianapolis: Indiana University Press.

Collett, N. (1994), 'Kuwait's Real Enemy – the Budget Deficit', *Middle East International*, no. 488.

Cooley, J. (1984), 'The War Over Water', *Foreign Policy*, **54**, Spring.

Cordesman, A. (1993), 'Saudi Military Forces in the 1990s: The Strategic Challenge of Continued Modernization', Washington: Smithsonian Institute, Woodrow Wilson Centre: unpublished paper, August.

Cox, R.W. (1981), 'Social Forces, States and World Orders: Beyond International Relations Theory', *Millennium: Journal of International Studies*, **10** (2).

Crawford, N.C. (1991), 'Once and Future Security Studies', *Security Studies*, **1** (2).

Deegan, H. (1993), *The Middle East and Problems of Democracy*, Buckingham: Open University Press.

de Madariaga, S. (1936), 'Current Problems and Progress in Disarmament' in Bourquin, M. (ed.), *Collective Security*, Paris: International Institute of Intellectual Cooperation.

de Nevers, R. (1994), 'Russia's Strategic Renovation', *Adelphi Paper*, no. 289, London: International Institute for Strategic Studies.

Denoon, D.H. (1987), 'Defence Spending in ASEAN: An Overview' in

Chin Kin Wah (ed.), *Defence Spending in Southeast Asia*, Singapore: Institute of Southeast Asian Studies.

Deudney, D. (1990), 'The Case Against Linking Environmental Degradation and National Security', *Millennium: Journal of International Studies*, **19** (3).

Deutsch, K.W. et al. (1957), *Political Community and the North Atlantic Area*, Princeton, NJ: Princeton University Press.

Doyle, M. (1983), 'Kant, Liberal Legacies and Foreign Affairs (Parts I & II): *Philosophy and Public Affairs*, **12** (3 & 4), Summer and Fall.

Duffey, T. (1994), 'A Theoretical Examination of the Role of Culture in Conflict Resolution with Special Reference to Japan: Implication for Practice and Training', paper prepared for the conference on Conflict Resolution in the Asia–Pacific Region: Culture, Problem Solving and Peacemaking, Penang, Malaysia.

Dunn, D. (1991), 'Peace Research versus Strategic Studies' in Booth, K. (ed.), *New Thinking About Strategy and International Security*, London: HarperCollins.

Economist Intelligence Unit (1968), *The Economic Effects of the Vietnam War in East and Southeast Asia*, QER Special no. 3, November, London: Economist Intelligence Unit.

Eden, A. (1960), *The Memoirs of Sir Anthony Eden: Full Circle*, London: Cassell.

El-Doufani, M.M. (1993), 'Yeltsin's Foreign Policy – A Third World Critique', *The World Today*, **49** (6).

Esposito, J. (1992), *The Islamic Threat: Myth or Reality?* New York and Oxford: Oxford University Press.

Faksh, M.A. and Faris, R.F. (1993), 'The Saudi Conundrum: Squaring the Security–Stability Circle', *Third World Quarterly*, **14** (2).

Faour, M. (1993), *The Arab World After Desert Storm*, Washington DC: United States Institute of Peace Press.

Faure, G. and Rubin, J. (eds) (1993), *Culture and Negotiation: The Resolution of Water Disputes*, London: Sage.

Finger, M. (1991), 'New Horizons for Peace Research: the Global Environment' in Kakonen, J. (ed.), *Perspectives on Environmental Conflict and International Politics*, London: Pinter.

Fischer, D. (1992), *Stopping the Spread of Nuclear Weapons: The Past and the Prospects*, London: Routledge.

Fischer, D. (1993), *Towards 1995: The Prospects for Ending the Proliferation of Nuclear Weapons*, Dartmouth: Dartmouth Publishing.

Fischer, G. (1971), *The Non-Proliferation of Nuclear Weapons*, London: Europa Publications.

Franck, T. and Rodley, N. (1973), 'After Bangladesh: The Law of Humanitarian Intervention by Force', *American Journal of International Law*, **67**.

Freedman, L. (1993), 'War and Peace: European Conflict Prevention', *Challiot Papers*, no. 11, October.

Fukuyama, F. (1989), 'The End of History?', *The National Interest*, **16**, Summer.

Gardner, G.T. (1994), *Nuclear Non-Proliferation: A Primer*, London: Lynne Rienner Publishers.

Garnett, J.C. (ed.) (1970), *Theories of Peace and Security*, London: Macmillan.

Garnett, J.C. (1987), 'Strategic Studies and its Assumptions' in Baylis, J., Booth, K., Garnett, J.C. and Williams, P., *Contemporary Strategy, Vol. 1: Theories and Concepts*, London: Croom Helm.

Garnham, D. (1994), 'The Future of NATO', *Journal of Strategic Studies*, **17** (4), December.

Gasteyger, C. (1991–92), '"European Security and the New Arc of Crisis, II", in New Dimensions in International Security', *Adelphi Paper*, no. 265, London: International Institute for Strategic Studies, Winter.

Giddens, A. (1979), *Central Problems in Social Theory*, London: Macmillan.

Girling, J.L.S. (1981), *Thailand: Society and Politics*, Ithaca: Cornell University Press.

Glaser, C.L. (1990), *Analyzing Strategic Nuclear Policy*, Princeton: Princeton University Press.

Glaser, C.L. (1992), 'Political Consequences of Military Strategy', *World Politics*, **44** (4), July.

Glaser, C.L. (1993), 'Why NATO is Still Best', *International Security*, **18** (1), Summer.

Glieck, P. (1989), 'The Implications of Global Climatic Changes for International Security', *Climate Change*, **15**.

Glieck, P. (1991), 'Environment and Security: The Clear Connection', *Bulletin of the Atomic Scientists*, **47** (3), April.

Glieck, P. (1993), 'Water and Conflict: Freshwater Resources and International Security', *International Security*, **18** (1), Summer.

Goldenberg, J. and Durham, E. (1992), 'Amazonia and National Sovereignty', *International Environmental Affairs*, **4** (4), Winter.

Goldstein, J.S. (1994), *International Relations*, New York: HarperCollins.

Goodrich, L. and Hambro, E. (1949), *Charter of the United Nations: Commentary and Documents*, second edition, London: Stevens and Sons.

Gray, C.S. (1982), *Strategic Studies and Public Policy: The American Experience*, Lexington: The University Press of Kentucky.

Gray, C.S. (1986), *Nuclear Strategy and National Style*, Lanham, MD: Hamilton Press.

Gray, C.S. (1992), 'New Directions for Strategic Studies? How Can Theory Help Practice?', *Security Studies*, **1** (4), Summer.

Gray, C.S. (1994), 'The Second Nuclear Age: Insecurity, Proliferation and the Control of Arms', University of Hull, unpublished paper.

Griffiths, F. (1994), 'From Situations of Weakness: Foreign Policy of the New Russia', *International Journal*, **49** (4).

Grossman, G. and Krueger, A. (1994), *Economic Growth and the Environment*, NBER Working Paper no. 4634, Washington, DC: National Bureau of Economic Research.

Hagerty, D.T. (1993), 'The Power of Suggestion: Opaque Proliferation, Existential Deterrence and the South Asian Nuclear Arms Competition', *Security Studies*, **2** (3–4), Spring–Summer.

Harris, D. (1991), *Cases and Materials on International Law*, fourth edition, London: Sweet and Maxwell.

Harris, J. (1987), 'The Determinants of Defence Expenditure in the ASEAN Region' in Chin Kin Wah (ed.), *Defence Spending in Southeast Asia*, Singapore: Institute of Southeast Asian Studies.

Harrison, P. (1993), *The Third Revolution: Population, Environment and a Sustainable World*, London: Penguin Books.

Hassner, P. (1993), '"An Overview of the Problem", in War and Peace: European Conflict Prevention', *Chaillot Papers*, no. 11, October.

Held, D. (1980), *Introduction to Critical Theory: Horkheimer and Habermas*, Cambridge: Polity Press.

Herz, J. (1966), *International Politics in the Atomic Age*, New York: Columbia University Press.

Higgins, R. (1963), *The Development of International Law Through the Organs of the United Nations*, London: Oxford University Press.

Hilderbrand, R. (1990), *Dumbarton Oaks: The Origins of the United Nations and the Search for Peace*, Chapel House: University of North Carolina Press.

Homer-Dixon, T.F. (1991), 'On the Threshold: Environmental Change as Causes of Acute Conflict', *International Security*, **16** (2), Fall.

Homer-Dixon T. (1994), 'Environmental Scarcities and Violent Conflict', *International Security*, **19** (1), Summer.

Horowitz, D.L. (1985), *Ethnic Groups in Conflict*, Berkeley, Los Angeles and London: University of California Press.

Howard, M. (1990), 'The Springtime of Nations', *Foreign Affairs*, **69** (1).

Hughes, R. (1994), *The Culture of Complaint: The Fraying of America*, revised edition, London: HarperCollins.

Huntington, S. (1993a), 'The Clash of Civilizations?', *Foreign Affairs*, **72** (3), Summer.

Huntington, S. (1993b), 'Response: If not Civilizations What? – Paradigms of the Post-Cold War World', *Foreign Affairs*, **72** (5), November–December.

Hurd, D. (1993), Speech at Chatham House, London, 27 January.

Hurrell, A. (1994), 'The Crisis of Ecological Viability: Global Governmental Change and the Nation State', *Political Studies*, **143**, Special Issue.

Huysmans, J. (forthcoming), 'Migrants as a Security Problem: Dangers of "Securitizing Societal Issues"' in Miles, R. and Thanhardt, D. (eds), *Migration and European Integration: the Dynamics of Inclusion and Exclusion*, London: Pinter.

Independent Commission on Disarmament and Security Issues (1982), *Common Security: A Programme for Disarmament*, London: Pan.

Institute of Southeast Asian Studies (1994), *Regional Outlook: Southeast Asia, 1994–95*, Singapore: Institute of Southeast Asian Studies.

Jackson, R. (1990), *Quasi-states: Sovereignty, International Relations and the Third World*, Cambridge: Cambridge University Press.

Jackson, R. (1995), 'The Political Theory of International Society' in Booth, K. and Smith, S. (eds), *International Relations Theory Today*, Cambridge: Polity Press.

Jacobsen, C. (ed.) (1990), *Strategic Power: USA–USSR*, Basingstoke: Macmillan.

Japanese Economic Institute, *JEI Reports*, various dates.

Jarrah, N. (1995), 'Dissidents Banished' *Middle East International*, no. 492, January.

Jarrah, N. (1995), 'Round One to Doha', *Middle East International*, no. 495, March.

Jervis, R. (1976), *Perceptions and Misperceptions in International Politics*, New York: Princeton University Press.

Jervis, R. (1982), 'Security Regime', *International Organization*, **36** (2), Spring.

Jervis, R. (1988), 'Realism, Game Theory, and Cooperation', *World Politics*, **40** (3), April.

Jervis, R., Lebow, R.N. and Stein, J.G. (eds) (1985), *Psychology and Deterrence*, Baltimore: The Johns Hopkins University Press.

Joffe, G. (1991–92), '"European Security and the New Arc of Crisis, 1", in New Dimensions in International Security', *Adelphi Paper*, no. 265, London: International Institute for Strategic Studies, Winter.

Joffe, J. (1992), 'Collective Security and the Future of Europe', *Survival*, **34** (1), Spring, pp. 36–50.

Joffe, J. (1994), 'A Clash Between Civilizations – or Within Them?', *Atlas: World Press Review*, **41** (2), February.

Kakonen, J. (1992), *Perspectives on Environmental Conflict and International Politics*, London: Pinter.

Kaplan, F. (1984), *The Wizards of Armageddon*, New York: Simon and Schuster.

Karliner, J. (1989), 'Central America's Other War: The Environment Under Siege', *World Policy Journal*, **6** (4), Fall.

Keegan, J. (1994), *A History of Warfare*, London: Pimlico.

Kellner, D. (1989), *Critical Theory, Marxism and Modernity*, Cambridge: Polity Press.

Kennan, G. (1967), *Memoirs 1925–1950*, New York: Pantheon Books.

Keohane, R.O. and Nye, J.S. (1977), *Power and Interdependence: World Politics in Transition*, Boston: Little, Brown & Co.

Kirkpatrick, J. et al. (1993), 'The Modernizing Imperative: Tradition and Change', *Foreign Affairs*, **72** (4), September–October.

Klein, E. (1946), *A Comprehensive Etymological Dictionary of the English Language*, Amsterdam: Elseiner Publishing Company.

Krause, K. and Williams, M.C. (1995), 'From Strategy to Security: Foundations of Critical Security Studies', paper presented at the International Studies Association annual conference, Chicago, USA, unpublished.

Kritsiotis, D. (ed.), *Studies in Law. Self-Determination: Cases of Crisis*, Hull: Hull University Press.

Kuiper, M.A. (1993), 'Keeping the Peace: Reflections on the Rules of the Game for International Intervention in the 1990s', *The Journal of Slavic Military Studies*, **6** (4).

Kupchan, C.A. and C.A. (1991), 'Concerts, Collective Security and the Future of Europe', *International Security*, **16** (1), Summer.

Kuper, L. (1981), *Genocide: Its Political Use in the Twentieth Century*, New Haven and London: Yale University Press.

Larrabee, F.S. (1990–91), 'Long Memories and Short Fuses: Change and Instability in the Balkans', *International Security*, **15** (3), Winter.

Lawson, S. (1995), 'The Politics of Culture: Critical Issues for Comparative and International Studies', paper presented to the 36th Annual Convention of the International Studies Association, Chicago, February 1995.

Lebow, R.N. (1994), 'The Long Peace, the End of the Cold War, and the Failure of Realism', *International Organization*, **48** (2), Spring.

Lepingwell, J.W.R. (1994), 'The Russian Military and Security Policy in the "Near Abroad"', *Survival*, **36** (3).

Lieber, R. (1991), *No Common Power*, New York: HarperCollins.

Lippman, W. (1943), *U.S. Foreign Policy: Shield of the Republic*, Boston: Little, Brown & Co.

Luard, E. (1982), *A History of the United Nations. Volume 1: The Years of Western Domination, 1945–1955*, London: Macmillan.

Lynn-Jones, S.M. and Miller, D.E. (1995), *Global Dangers: Changing Dimensions of International Security*, Cambridge, Mass.: MIT Press.

McNamara, R.S. (1968), *The Essence of Security*, London: Hodder & Stoughton.

Mahbubani, K. (1993), 'The Dangers of Decadence: What the Rest Can Teach the West', *Foreign Affairs*, **72** (4), September–October.

Mahncke, D. (1993), 'Parameters of European Security', *Chaillot Paper*, no. 10, September.

Marantz, P. (1994), 'Neither Adversaries nor Partners: Russia and the West Search for a New Relationship', *International Journal*, **49** (4).

Marr, P. (1993), 'The Persian Gulf After the Storm' in Marr, P. and Lewis, W. (eds), *Riding the Tiger: The Middle East After the Gulf War*, Boulder, Colorado: Westview Press.

Marr, P. and Lewis, W. (eds) (1993), *Riding the Tiger: The Middle East After the Gulf War*, Boulder, Colorado: Westview Press.

Matthews, J.T. (1989), 'Redefining Security', *Foreign Affairs*, **68** (2).

Mattar, P. (1994), 'The PLO and the Gulf Crisis', *Middle East Journal*, **48** (1), Winter.

Mearsheimer, J.J. (1990), 'Back to the Future: Instability in Europe After the Cold War', *International Security*, **15** (1), Summer.

Mearsheimer, J.J. (1993), 'The Case for a Ukrainian Nuclear Deterrent', *Foreign Affairs*, **72** (3), Summer.

Melissen, J. (1993), *The Struggle for Nuclear Partnership: Britain, the*

United States and the Making of an Ambiguous Alliance 1952–1959, Groningen: Styx Publications.

Melvin, N. (1994), 'Forging the New Russian Nation', *Discussion Paper No. 50*, London: The Royal Institute of International Affairs.

Meyer-Abich, K. (1993), 'Winners and Losers in Climate Change' in Sachs, W. (ed.), *Global Ecology: A New Arena of Political Conflict*, London and New Jersey: Zed Books.

Millennium (1993), Special Issue: Culture in International Relations, *Millennium: Journal of International Studies*, **22** (3), Winter.

Milne, R.S. (1993), 'Singapore's Growth Triangle', *The Round Table*, **327**.

Morgan, P. (1992), 'Safeguarding Security Studies', *Arms Control*, **13** (3), December.

Morgenthau, H. and Thompson, K. (1985), *Politics Among Nations: The Struggle for Power and Peace*, sixth edition, New York: Knopf.

Morley, J.W. (ed.) (1993), *Driven by Growth: Political Change in the Asia–Pacific Region*, Armonk, New York: M.E. Sharpe.

Morris, J. (1991), 'The Concept of Humanitarian Intervention in International Relations', unpublished MA dissertation, University of Hull.

Morris, J. (1994), 'Haiti: State Sovereignty, Self-Interest and the New World Order' in Kritsiotis, D. (ed.), *Studies in Law. Self-Determination: Cases of Crisis*, Hull: Hull University Press.

Morrison, J. (1993), 'Pereyaslav and After: The Russian–Ukrainian Relationship', *International Affairs* (London), **69** (4).

Morrison, J. (ed.) (1994), 'Vladimir Zhirinovskiy: An Assessment of a Russian Ultra-Nationalist', Washington: National Defense University, *McNair Paper*, no. 30, April.

Mortimer, E. (1992), 'European Security After the Cold War', *Adelphi Paper*, no. 271, London: International Institute for Strategic Studies, Summer.

Mueller, J. (1995), *Quiet Cataclysm: Reflections on the Recent Transformation of World Politics*, New York: HarperCollins College.

Muscat, R.J. (1990), *Thailand and the United States: Development, Security and Foreign Aid*, New York: Columbia University Press.

Muzaffar, C. (1994), 'The West's Hidden Agenda', *Atlas: World Press Review*, **41** (2), February.

Nagara, B. and Balakrishnan, K.S. (eds) (1994), *The Making of a Security Community in the Asia–Pacific*, Proceedings of the Seventh Asia–Pacific Roundtable, Kuala Lumpur: ISIS Malaysia.

Nelson, D. (1994), 'The Future of NATO', *Journal of Strategic Studies*, **17** (4), December.

Norton, A.R. (1993), 'The Future of Civil Society in the Middle East', *Middle East Journal*, **47** (2), Spring.

Norton, A.R. and Wright, R. (1994), 'The Post-Peace Crisis in the Middle East', *Survival*, **36** (4), Winter.

Nuechterlein, D.E. (1967), 'Thailand: Another Vietnam?', *Asian Survey*, **7**, February.

Nye, J.S. (1988), 'US–Soviet Cooperation in a Nonproliferation Regime', in George, A., Farley, P. and Dallin, A. (eds), *US–Soviet Security Cooperation: Achievements, Failures, Lessons*. Oxford: Oxford University Press.

O'Hagan, J. (1995), 'Civilizational Conflict? Looking for Cultural Enemies', *Third World Quarterly*, **16** (1), March.

Onions, C.T. (1966), *The Oxford Dictionary of English Etymology*, Oxford: Clarendon Press.

Osgood, R.E. and Tucker, R.W. (1967), *Force, Order, and Justice*, Baltimore: The Johns Hopkins Press.

Pacifica Review (1994), Special Issue: Culture and Conflict Management in Asia Pacific, *Pacifica Review: Peace, Security and Global Change*, **6** (2), twice-yearly.

Page, S. (1994), 'The Creation of a Sphere of Influence: Russia and Central Asia', *International Journal*, **49** (4).

Partridge, E. (1990), *Origins*, London: Routledge.

Piscatori, J. (ed.) (1991), *Islamic Fundamentalisms and the Gulf Crisis*, Chicago: American Academy of Arts and Sciences.

Piscatori, J. (1991), 'Religion and Real Politik: Islamic Responses to the Gulf War' in Piscatori, J. (ed.), *Islamic Fundamentalisms and the Gulf Crisis*, Chicago: American Academy of Arts and Sciences.

Piscatori, J. (1992), 'Islam in World Politics' in Baylis, J. and Rengger, N. (eds), *Dilemmas of World Politics*, Oxford: Clarendon Press.

Posen, B. (1993), 'The Security Dilemma and Ethnic Conflict', *Survival*, **35** (1), Spring.

Powell, C.L. (1992), 'The American Commitment to European Security', *Survival*, **34** (2), Summer.

Prins, G. (1993), *Threats Without Enemies: Facing Environmental Insecurity*, London: Earthscan.

Rathmell, A. (1995), 'Letter from Muscat', *Middle East International*, no. 495. See also 'Yemen and Oman: Troubles Contained?', *Royal United Services Institute Briefing Paper*, 19 October 1994.

Redick, J.R. (1990), 'Argentina and Brazil: An Evolving Nuclear Relationship', *Programme for Promoting Nuclear Non-Proliferation Occasional Paper*, no. 7, Southampton: PPNN.

Rengger, N. (1992), 'Culture, Society and Order in World Politics' in Baylis, J. and Rengger, N. (eds), *Dilemmas of World Politics: International Issues in a Changing World*, Oxford: Oxford University Press.

Reus-Smit, C. (1992), 'Realist and Resistance Utopias: Community, Security and Political Action in the New Europe', *Millennium: Journal of International Studies*, **21** (1).

Reynolds, C. (1981), *Modes of Imperialism*, Oxford: Martin Robertson.

Richmond, A. (1994), *Global Apartheid: Refugees, Racism and the New World Order*, Oxford, Toronto and New York: Oxford University Press.

Rifkind, M. (1993), Speech at the Royal Institute for International Affairs, London, 16 December.

Risse-Kappen, T. (1994), 'Ideas Do Not Float Freely: Transnational Coalitions, Domestic Structures, and the End of the Cold War', *International Organization*, **48** (2), Spring.

Rittenberger, V. (ed.), *Regime Theory and International Relations*, Oxford: Clarendon Press.

Robertson, R. (1992), *Globalization: Social Theory and Global Culture*, London: Sage.

Romm, J. (1993), *Defining National Security: The Non-Military Aspects*, New York: Council on Foreign Relations Press.

Rosenbaum, H.J. and Tyler, W.G. (1975), 'South–South Relations: the Economic and Political Content of Interactions among Developing Countries', *International Organization*, **29** (1).

Ross, A.L. (1989), 'The International Arms Trade, Arms Imports, and Local Defence Production in ASEAN' in Jeshurun, C. (ed.), *Arms and Defence in Southeast Asia*, Singapore: Institute of Southeast Asian Studies.

Ross, M. (1993), *The Culture of Conflict: Interpretations and Interests in Comparative Perspective*, New Haven and London: Yale University Press.

Rouleau, E. (1994), 'Le Peuple Irakien Première Victime de L'Ordre Américain' (The Iraqi People: the Main Victims of the American Order), *Le Monde Diplomatique*, no. 48, November.

Rubenstein, R. and Crocker, J. (1994), 'Challenging Huntington', *Foreign Policy*, **96**, Fall.

Sagan, S. (1994), 'The Perils of Proliferation: Organization Theory, Deterrence Theory and the Spread of Nuclear Weapons', *International Security*, **18** (4), Spring.

Scalapino, R.A. (1993), 'A Framework for Regional Security in Asia', *The Korean Journal of Defence Analysis*, **5** (3), Winter.

Scalapino, R.A. (1994), 'Challenges to the Sovereignty of the Modern State' in Nagara, B. and Balakrishnan, K.S. (eds), Proceedings of the Seventh Asia–Pacific Roundtable, *The Making of a Security Community in the Asia Pacific*, Kuala Lumpur: ISIS Malaysia.

Schell, J. (1984), *The Abolition*, London: Picador.

Schneider, B.R. (1994), 'Nuclear Proliferation and Counter-Proliferation: Policy Issues and Debates', *Mershon International Studies Review*, **38**.

Scholte, J. (1993), *International Relations of Social Change*, Buckingham: Open University Press.

Schrijver, N. (1989), 'International Organizations for Environmental Security', *Bulletin of Peace Proposals*, **20** (2), Spring.

Schwarz, B.C. (1994), 'The Future of NATO', *Journal of Strategic Studies*, **17** (4), December.

Serrano, M. (1992), 'Common Security in Latin America: The 1967 Treaty of Tlatelolco', University of London: *Institute of Latin American Studies Research Paper*, no. 30.

Shashenkov, M. (1994), 'Russian Peacekeeping in the "Near Abroad"', *Survival*, **36** (3).

Shaw, M. (1994), *Global Society and International Relations: Sociological Concepts and Political Perspectives*, Cambridge: Polity Press.

Shehadi, K.S. (1993), 'Ethnic Self-Determination and the Break-up of States', *Adelphi Paper*, no. 283, London: International Institute for Strategic Studies, December.

Shuman, M. and Harvey, H. (1993), *Security Without War*, Boulder, Colorado: Westview Press.

Simpson, J. (1994), "Nuclear Non-Proliferation in the Post-Cold War Era', *International Affairs*, **70** (1), January.

Simon, J. (1990), *Population Matters: People, Resources, Environment and Migration*, New Brunswick, Transactions Publishers.

Simon, J. (1993), 'Does Eastern Europe Belong to NATO?', *Orbis*, **37** (1), Winter.

Skeat, W.W. (1946), *An Etymological Dictionary of the English Language*, Oxford: Clarendon Press.

Smith, S. (1991), 'Mature Anarchy, Strong States and Security', *Arms Control*, **12** (2).

Smith, S. (1992), 'The Forty Years Detour: The Resurgence of Normative Theory in International Relations', *Millennium: Journal of International Studies*, **21** (3).

Smith, S., Booth, K. and Zalewski, M. (forthcoming), *Theory and International Relations: Positivism and Beyond*, Cambridge: Cambridge University Press.

Smoke, R. (1991), 'A Theory of Mutual Security' in Smoke, R. and Kortunov, A. (eds), *Mutual Security*, London: Macmillan.

Snider, D.M. (1992–93), 'U.S. Military Forces in Europe', *Survival*, **34** (4), Winter.

Snow, D. (1991), *Distant Thunder: Third World Conflict and the New International Order*, New York: Plenum Press.

Snyder, J. (1977), *The Soviet Strategic Culture: Implications for Limited Nuclear Operations*, Santa Monica: RAND Report R-2154-AF.

Snyder, J. (1990), 'The Concept of Strategic Culture: Caveat Emptor' in Jacobson, C. (ed.), *Strategic Power: USA–USSR*, Basingstoke: Macmillan.

Snyder, J.L. (1985), 'Perceptions of the Security Dilemma' in Jervis, R., Lebow, R.N. and Stein, J.G. (eds), *Psychology and Deterrence*, Baltimore: The Johns Hopkins University Press.

Soesastro, H. (1994), 'Economic Integration in the Asia Pacific: Implications for Security', paper presented at the Eighth Asia Pacific Roundtable, Kuala Lumpur, June.

Sokov, N. (1994), 'A New Cold War? Reflections of a Russian Diplomat', *International Journal*, **49** (4).

Sorensen, G. (1992), 'The Ideas of Kant and Processes of Democratization', Paper delivered at the European Consortium for Political Research, Inaugural Pan-European Conference, Heidelberg, Germany.

Spector, L. (1995), 'Neo-Nonproliferation', *Survival*, **37** (1), Spring.

Spencer, C. (1993), 'The Maghreb in the 1990s', *Adelphi Paper*, no. 274, London: International Institute for Strategic Studies, February.

Stein, J.G. (1992), 'Deterrence and Compellance in the Gulf', *International Security*, **17** (2), Fall.

Stern, J.E. (1994), 'Moscow Meltdown: Can Russia Survive?', *International Security*, **18** (4).

Strong, M. (1991), 'Eco 92: Critical Challenges and Global Solutions', *Journal of International Affairs*, **44** (2), Winter.

Stubbs, R. (1989), *Hearts and Minds in Guerrilla Warfare: The Malayan Emergency 1948–1960*, Singapore: Oxford University Press.

Stubbs, R. (1989), 'Geopolitics and the Political Economy of Southeast Asia', *International Journal*, **44**, Summer.

Stubbs, R. (1994), 'The Political Economy of the Asia–Pacific Region' in Stubbs, R. and Underhill, G.R.D. (eds), *Political Economy and the Changing Global Order*, London: Macmillan.

Stubbs, R. and Underhill, G.R.D. (eds) (1994), *Political Economy and the Changing Global Order*, London: Macmillan.

Suhrke, A. (1994), 'Environmental Degradation and Population Flows', *Journal of International Affairs*, **47** (2), Winter.

Szajkowski, B. (1993), 'Will Russia Disintegrate into Bantustans?', *The World Today*, **49** (8).

Tarock, A. (1995), 'Civilisational conflict? Fighting the Enemy Under a New Banner', *Third World Quarterly*, **16** (1) March.

Thomas, C. (1985), *New States, Sovereignty and Intervention*, Aldershot: Gower.

Thomas, C. (1987), *In Search of Security: The Third World in International Relations*, Hemel Hempstead and Boulder, Colorado: Harvester Wheatsheaf and Lynne Rienner.

Thomas, C. (1992), *The Environment in International Relations*, London: Royal Institute of International Affairs.

Thompson, K. (1953), 'Collective Security Reexamined', *American Political Science Review*, **27** (3).

Tickell, C. (1993), 'The Inevitability of Environmental Insecurity' in Prins, G. (ed.), *Threats Without Enemies: Facing Environmental Insecurity*, London: Earthscan.

Tickner, J.A. (1995), 'Re-visioning Security' in Booth, K. and Smith, S. (eds), *International Relations Theory Today*, Cambridge: Polity Press.

Toynbee, A. with Caplan, J. (1972), *A Study of History*, London: Oxford University Press (new, revised and abridged edition).

Ullman, R. (1983), 'Redefining Security', *International Security*, **8** (1), Summer.

Umozurike, U.O. (1979), 'The Domestic Jurisdiction Clause in the OAU Charter', *African Affairs*, **78**.

Valki, L. (1992), 'Security Concerns in Central Europe', *European Security*, **1** (4), Winter.

van Evera, S. (1990–91), 'Primed for Peace: Europe After the Cold War', *International Security*, **15** (3), Winter.

van Ham, P. (1994), 'Ukraine, Russia and European Security: Implications for Western Policy', *Challiot Papers*, no. 13, February.

Vaziri, H. (1994), 'Iran and Saudi Arabia in the 1990s: From Hostility to Regional Cooperation?', *US–Iranian Review*, 2 (4), April–May.

Wæver, O., Buzan, B., Kelstrup, M. and Lemaitre, P. (1993), *Identity, Migration and the New Security Agenda in Europe*, London: Pinter.

Wæver, O. (1994), 'Insecurity and Identity Unlimited', *Working Paper 14*, Centre for Peace and Conflict Research, Copenhagen.

Wah, Chin Kin (ed.) (1987), *Defence Spending in Southeast Asia,* Singapore: Institute of Southeast Asian Studies.

Walcott, J. (1993), 'Beware the Clash of Civilizations', *US News and World Report*, 28 June.

Walker, R.B.J. (ed.) (1984), *Culture, Ideology and World Order*, Boulder, Colorado and London: Westview Press.

Walker, R.B.J. (1990), 'The Concept of Culture in the Theory of International Relations' in Chay, J. (ed.) *Culture and International Relations*, New York, Westport, Connecticut and London: Praeger.

Walker, R.B.J. (1990), 'Security, Sovereignty, and the Challenge of World Politics', *Alternatives*, 15 (1).

Walker, R.B.J. (1993), *Inside/outside: International Relations as Political Theory*, Cambridge: Cambridge University Press.

Wallerstein, I. (1991), *Geopolitics and Geoculture: Essays on the Changing World-system*, Cambridge: Cambridge University Press.

Walt, S.M. (1991), 'The Renaissance of Security Studies', *International Studies Quarterly*, 35 (2).

Waltz, K.N. (1959), *Man the State and War: A Theoretical Analysis*, New York: Columbia University Press.

Waltz, K.N. (1979), *Theory of International Politics*, London: McGraw Hill.

Waltz, K.N. (1981), 'The Spread of Nuclear Weapons: More May Be Better', *Adelphi Paper*, no. 171, London: International Institute for Strategic Studies.

Waltz, K.N. (1990), 'Nuclear Myths and Political Realities', *American Political Science Review*, 84 (3), September.

Weed, T. (1994), 'Central American Peace Parks and Regional Conflict Resolution', *International Environmental Affairs*, 6 (2), Spring.

Weede, E. (1984), 'Democracy and War Involvement', *Journal of Conflict Resolution*, 28 (4), December.

Wellens, K. (ed.) (1993), *Resolutions and Statements of the United*

Nations Security Council – A Thematic Guide, Dordrecht: Martinus Nijhoff.

Wendt, A. (1992), 'Anarchy is What States Make of it: the social construction of power politics', *International Organization*, **46** (2), Spring.

Westing, A. (1989), The Environmental Component of Comprehensive Security', *Bulletin of Peace Proposals*, **20** (2), Spring.

Whautaker, B. (1995), 'Crisis Over the Border', *Middle East International*, no. 492, January.

Wheeler, N.J. and Booth, K. (1992), 'The Security Dilemma' in Baylis, J. and Rengger, N.J. (eds), *Dilemmas of World Politics*, Oxford: Clarendon Press.

Wheeler, N.J. (1993), Book review of Buzan, B., Jones, C. and Little, R., *The Logic of Anarchy: Neorealism to Structural Realism* in *International Affairs*, **69** (4).

Wheeler, N.J. and Morris, J. (forthcoming 1996), 'Humanitarian Intervention and State Practice at the End of the Cold War' in Larkins, J. and Fawn, R. (eds), *International Society After the Cold War: Anarchy and Order Reconsidered*, London: Macmillan.

Wheeler, N.J. (forthcoming), 'Guardian Angel or Global Gangster: A Review of the Ethical Claims of International Society', *Political Studies*.

White, N.D. (1993), *Keeping the Peace. The United Nations and the Maintenance of International Peace and Security*, Manchester and New York: Manchester University Press.

Whitley, A. (1993), 'Minorities and the Stateless in Persian Gulf Politics', *Survival*, **35** (4), Winter.

Williams, M.C. (1992), 'Rethinking the "Logic" of Deterrence', *Alternatives*, **17** (1).

Wiseman, G. (1989), *Common Security and Non-Provocative Defence*, Canberra: Australian National University.

Wolfers, A. (1962), *Discord and Collaboration: Essays on International Politics*, Baltimore: The Johns Hopkins University Press.

World Bank Policy Research Report (1993), *The East Asian Miracle: Economic Growth and Public Policy*, Oxford: Oxford University Press.

Wyn Jones, R. (1995a), '"Message in a Bottle"?: Theory and Praxis in Critical Security Studies', paper presented at the International Studies Association annual conferences, Chicago, USA, unpublished.

Wyn Jones, R. (1995b), 'The Nuclear Revolution' in Danchev, A. (ed.),

Fin de Siècle: The Meaning of the Twentieth Century, London: I.B. Tauris.

Zaldivar, C. (1993), '"The Conditions for Peace", in War and Peace: European Conflict Prevention', *Challiot Papers*, no. 11, October.

Zalewski, M. and Enloe, C. (1995), 'Questions About Identity in International Relations' in Booth, K. and Smith, S. (eds), *International Relations Theory Today*, Cambridge: Polity Press.

Zartman, W. (1993), 'A Skeptic's View' in Faure, G. and Rubin, J. (eds), *Culture and Negotiation: The Resolution of Water Disputes*, London: Sage.

Zelikow, P. (1992), 'The New Concert of Europe', *Survival*, **34** (2), Summer.

Zielonka, J. (1992), 'Security in Central Europe', *Adelphi Paper*, no. 272, London: International Institute for Strategic Studies, Autumn.

Index